Discourse Analysis
for Language Te

CAMBRIDGE LANGUAGE TEACHING LIBRARY

A series of authoritative books on subjects of central importance for all language teachers.

This title was prepared with Michael Swan as editor.

Discourse Analysis
for Language Teachers

Michael McCarthy

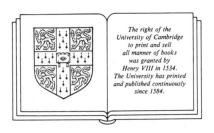

The right of the
University of Cambridge
to print and sell
all manner of books
was granted by
Henry VIII in 1534.
The University has printed
and published continuously
since 1584.

Cambridge University Press
Cambridge
New York   Port Chester
Melbourne   Sydney

Published by the Press Syndicate of the University of Cambridge
The Pitt Building, Trumpington Street, Cambridge CB2 1RP
40 West 20th Street, New York, NY 10011–4211, USA
10 Stamford Road, Oakleigh, Victoria 3166, Australia

© Cambridge University Press 1991

First published 1991
Second printing 1991

Printed in Great Britain by Bell and Bain Ltd, Glasgow

Library of Congress catalogue card number: 90-20850

British Library cataloguing in publication data
McCarthy, Michael 1947–
    Discourse analysis for language teachers. — (Cambridge language teaching library).
    1. Language. Discourse. Analysis
    I. Title
    415

ISBN 0 521 36541 4 hard covers
ISBN 0 521 36746 8 paperback

ᗷ ᴏᴏ366965ᴜ

CE

Contents

Contents

Chapter 4   Discourse analysis and phonology

Chapter 5   Spoken language

Chapter 6 Written language

Acknowledgements

Thanks are due to Jim Lawley, of Ávila, Spain, for permission to use conversational data reproduced in Chapter 5, to Roger Smith, Gill Meldrum and Hilary Bool of CELE, University of Nottingham, for assistance with the gathering of written data, and to the late Michael Griffiths, Senior Prison Officer at HM Prison, Cardiff, for permission to use an interview with him, part of which is transcribed in Chapter 4.

The author and publishers are grateful to the authors, publishers and others who have given permission for the use of copyright material. It has not been possible to trace the sources of all the material used and in such cases the publishers would welcome information from copyright owners.

Edward Arnold for the extract from M. A. K. Halliday (1985) *An Introduction to Functional Grammar* on pp. 47, 58; *The Birmingham Post* for the article on p. 27; British Nuclear Forum for the advertisement on p. 49; *Cambridge/Newmarket Town Crier* for the article on p. 170; Cambridge University Press for the extract from Brown and Yule (1983) *Discourse Analysis* on pp. 102–4; *Cambridge Weekly News* for the article on pp. 75, 85, 159; Collins ELT for the extracts from the *Collins COBUILD English Language Dictionary* on p. 84; the Consumers' Association for the extracts from *Which?* on pp. 25, 26, 37, 86, 160; Elida Gibbs for the advertisement on p. 56; A. Firth for the extract on p. 50; Ford Motor Company for the advertisement on p. 32; Headway Publications for the article from *Moneycare* on p. 158; Hunting Specialised Products (UK) Ltd for the advertisement on p. 72; Imperial Chemical Industries plc and Cogents for the advertisement for Lawnsman Mosskiller on p. 83; International Certificate Conference and Pädagogische Arbeitsstelle des DVV for the extracts on pp. 124, 125, 126, 140–1, 150–1; D. Johnson for the article from *The Guardian* on p. 41; Longman Group UK Ltd for the extract from D. Crystal and D. Davy (1975) *Advanced Conversational English* on p. 69; *New Statesman & Society* for the extracts from *New Society* on pp. 77, 80, 81 and 82; Newsweek International for the extracts from *Newsweek* on pp. 37, 41–2; *The Observer* for the extracts on pp. 28, 30, 40, 57, 77, 79; Oxford University Press for the extract from J. McH. Sinclair and R. M. Coulthard (1975) *Towards an Analysis of Discourse* on p. 13; J. Svartvik for the extract from Svartvik and Quirk (1980) *A Corpus of English Conversation* on pp. 70–1; the University of Birmingham on behalf of the copyright holders for the extracts from the *Birmingham Collection of English Text* on pp. 10, 17; World Press Network for the extracts from *New Scientist* on pp. 37, 57.

Preface

Any language teacher who tries to keep abreast with developments in Descriptive and Applied Linguistics faces a very difficult task, for books and journals in the field have grown in number at a bewildering rate over the last twenty years. At the same time, with the pressures created by the drive towards professionalisation in fields such as ELT, it has become more and more important that language teachers *do* keep up-to-date with developments within, and relevant to, their field.

One such area is discourse analysis. Arising out of a variety of disciplines, including linguistics, sociology, psychology, and anthropology, discourse analysis has built a significant foundation for itself in Descriptive, and latterly, Applied, Linguistics. The various disciplines that feed into discourse analysis have shared a common interest in language in use, in how real people use real language, as opposed to studying artificially created sentences. Discourse analysis is therefore of immediate interest to language teachers because we too have long had the question of how people *use* language uppermost in our minds when we design teaching materials, or when we engage learners in exercises and activities aimed at making them proficient users of their target language, or when we evaluate a piece of commercially published material before deciding to use it.

Experienced language teachers, in general, have sound instincts as to what is natural and authentic in language teaching and what is artificial or goes counter to all sensible intuition of how language is used. They also know that artificiality can be useful at times, in order to simplify complex language for initial teaching purposes. But they cannot hope to have an instinctive possession of the vast amount of detailed insight that years of close observation by numerous investigators has produced: insight into how texts are structured beyond sentence-level; how talk follows regular patterns in a wide range of different situations; how such complex areas as intonation operate in communication; and how discourse norms (the underlying rules that speakers and writers adhere to) and their realisations (the actual language forms which reflect those rules) in language differ from culture to culture. The aim of this book is to supply such insight in a condensed form.

Mine is not the first introduction to discourse analysis; Chapter 1 mentions several indispensable readings that anyone wishing to pursue the subject should tackle. But it is the first to attempt to mediate selectively a wide range of research specifically for the practical needs of language teachers. In this respect it is distinctly different from conventional introductions. It does not set out to report everything about discourse analysis, for not everything is of relevance to language teachers. Decisions have therefore been made along the way to exclude discussion of material that may be very interesting in itself, but of little practical adaptability to the language teaching context. For instance, within pragmatics, the study of how meaning is created in context (which thus shares an undefined frontier with discourse analysis), the conversational maxims of H. P. Grice (1975) have been very influential. These are a set of four common-sense norms that all speakers adhere to when conversing (e.g. 'be relevant'; 'be truthful'). In a decade of English language teaching since they first came to my notice, I have never met an occasion where the maxims could be usefully applied, although in my teaching of literary stylistics, they have helped my students understand some of the techniques writers use to undermine their readers' expectations. Grice, therefore, does not figure in this book. But, as with any introduction, the sifting process is ultimately subjective, and readers may find that things have been included that do not seem immediately relevant to their needs as teachers; others already well-tutored in discourse analysis will wish that certain names and areas of investigation had been included or given more attention. It is my hope, nonetheless, that most readers will find the selection of topics and names listed in the index to be a fair and representative range of material. I also hope that language teachers will find the structure of the book, a two-part framework based on (a) the familiar levels of conventional language description, and (b) the skills of speaking and writing, unforbidding and usable.

The book tries to illustrate everything with real data, spoken and written, in the true spirit of discourse analysis. In the case of spoken data, I have tried to mix my own data with that of others so that readers might be directed towards useful published sources if they have no access to data themselves. Because a lot of the data is my own, I apologise to non-British readers if it occasionally seems rather Brito-centric in its subject matter. The speakers and writers of the non-native speaker data do, however, include German, Italian, Hungarian, Turkish, Brazilian, Spanish, Chinese, Korean and Japanese learners.

The book does not stop at theory and description, but it does not go so far as telling its readers how to teach. This is because, first and foremost, discourse analysis is *not* a method for teaching languages; it is a way of describing and understanding how language is used. But it is also because there are as many ways of adapting new developments in description to the everyday business of teaching as there are language teachers. So, although I occasionally report on my own teaching (especially in Chapters 5 and 6), and present data gathered from my own EFL classes, it will be for you, the reader, ultimately to decide whether and how any of this array of material can be used in your situation.

In preparing a book of this complexity, many people have inevitably had a hand. The original inspiration came from eight years of responding to the insatiable intellectual curiosity of MA students at the University of Birmingham, most of whom were practising language teachers, and almost all of whom asked for more on discourse analysis whenever they had the chance. An equal number of undergraduates who studied language as part of their English degree also helped to shape the book.

In addition, several years of giving in-service courses for teachers in West Germany and Finland have suggested new areas and sharpened the reader activities, which have been tried out on course participants. In particular, the enthusiasm of the PILC groups of the Language Centres of the Finnish Universities in the years 1987–9 must be mentioned as one of the unfailing sources of inspiration to get the book done.

I must also mention my colleagues in the International Certificate Conference (ICC), whose annual pilgrimage to Chorley, Lancashire in the last few years has met with the penance of being subjected to the material as it developed; particular thanks here go to Tony Fitzpatrick of VHS Frankfurt, for his constant support.

Colleagues at the Universities of Birmingham and Nottingham who have encouraged and inspired me are almost too numerous to mention, but particular thanks go to David Brazil (who also checked the intonation in Chapter 4), Mike Hoey, Tim Johns, Martin Hewings and Malcolm Coulthard for comments at seminars and in informal chats at Birmingham, and to my new colleagues (but old friends and associates) at Nottingham, Ron Carter and Margaret Berry, who have already been subjected to some of the material and encouraged my work. My new students at Nottingham have also provided feedback on more recent versions of the material.

But above all, without the support of John Sinclair of Birmingham and his infinitely creative ideas and comments, the notion that there was ever anything interesting in language other than sentences would probably never have entered my head.

So much for the university environment that spawned the book. The most important, single influence on its final shape has been my editor, Michael Swan, whose good-humoured scepticism as to whether academics have anything worth saying to language teachers out there in the real world has been balanced by an open mind, razor-sharp comments on the text and an unflagging willingness to enter into intellectual debate, all of which have been a challenge and a reason to keep going to the bitter end.

Annemarie Young at CUP, who commissioned this book, has never complained when I have missed deadlines and has always made me feel that the enterprise was worth it. She too has made invaluable contributions to the book as it has taken shape. Brigit Viney, who has edited the manuscript, has also made many useful suggestions as to how it might be made more reader-friendly and has purged a number of inconsistencies and infelicities that lurked therein.

On the home front, my partner, Jeanne McCarten, has offered the professional expertise of a publisher and the personal support that provides a stable foundation for such an undertaking; her penance has been an unfair share of the washing up while I pounded the keys of our computer.

Liz Evans, Juliette Leverington and Enid Perrin have all done their bit of key-pounding to type up various versions of the manuscript, and I thank them, too.

But finally, I want to thank a primary-school teacher of mine, John Harrington of Cardiff, who, in the perspective of the receding past, emerges more and more as the person who started everything for me in educational terms, and to whom this book is respectfully, and affectionately, dedicated.

Cambridge, March 1990

1 What is discourse analysis?

'I only said "if"!' poor Alice pleaded in a piteous tone.

The two Queens looked at each other, and the Red Queen remarked, with a little shudder, 'She *says* she only said "if"—'

'But she said a great deal more than that!' the White Queen moaned, wringing her hands.'Oh, ever so much more than that!'

Lewis Carroll: *Through the Looking Glass*

1.1 A brief historical overview

Discourse analysis is concerned with the study of the relationship between language and the contexts in which it is used. It grew out of work in different disciplines in the 1960s and early 1970s, including linguistics, semiotics, psychology, anthropology and sociology. Discourse analysts study language in use: written texts of all kinds, and spoken data, from conversation to highly institutionalised forms of talk.

At a time when linguistics was largely concerned with the analysis of single sentences, Zellig Harris published a paper with the title 'Discourse analysis' (Harris 1952). Harris was interested in the distribution of linguistic elements in extended texts, and the links between the text and its social situation, though his paper is a far cry from the discourse analysis we are used to nowadays. Also important in the early years was the emergence of semiotics and the French structuralist approach to the study of narrative. In the 1960s, Dell Hymes provided a sociological perspective with the study of speech in its social setting (e.g. Hymes 1964). The linguistic philosophers such as Austin (1962), Searle (1969) and Grice (1975) were also influential in the study of language as social action, reflected in speech-act theory and the formulation of conversational maxims, alongside the emergence of pragmatics, which is the study of meaning in context (see Levinson 1983; Leech 1983).

British discourse analysis was greatly influenced by M. A. K. Halliday's functional approach to language (e.g. Halliday 1973), which in turn has connexions with the Prague School of linguists. Halliday's framework emphasises the social functions of language and the thematic and informational structure of speech and writing. Also important in Britain were Sinclair and Coulthard (1975) at the University of Birmingham, who developed a model for the description of teacher–pupil talk, based on a hierarchy of discourse units. Other similar work has dealt with doctor–patient interaction, service encounters, interviews, debates and business negotiations, as well as monologues. Novel work in the British tradition has also been done on intonation in discourse. The British work has principally followed structural–linguistic criteria, on the basis of the isolation of units, and sets of rules defining well-formed sequences of discourse.

American discourse analysis has been dominated by work within the ethnomethodological tradition, which emphasises the research method of close observation of groups of people communicating in natural settings. It examines types of speech event such as storytelling, greeting rituals and verbal duels in different cultural and social settings (e.g. Gumperz and Hymes 1972). What is often called *conversation analysis* within the American tradition can also be included under the general heading of discourse analysis. In conversational analysis, the emphasis is not upon building structural models but on the close observation of the behaviour of participants in talk and on patterns which recur over a wide range of natural data. The work of Goffman (1976; 1979), and Sacks, Schegloff and Jefferson (1974) is important in the study of conversational norms, turn-taking, and other aspects of spoken interaction. Alongside the conversation analysts, working within the sociolinguistic tradition, Labov's investigations of oral storytelling have also contributed to a long history of interest in narrative discourse. The American work has produced a large number of descriptions of discourse types, as well as insights into the social constraints of politeness and face-preserving phenomena in talk, overlapping with British work in pragmatics.

Also relevant to the development of discourse analysis as a whole is the work of text grammarians, working mostly with written language. Text grammarians see texts as language elements strung together in relationships with one another that can be defined. Linguists such as Van Dijk (1972), De Beaugrande (1980), Halliday and Hasan (1976) have made a significant impact in this area. The Prague School of linguists, with their interest in the structuring of information in discourse, has also been influential. Its most important contribution has been to show the links between grammar and discourse.

Discourse analysis has grown into a wide-ranging and heterogeneous discipline which finds its unity in the description of language above the sentence and an interest in the contexts and cultural influences which affect language in use. It is also now, increasingly, forming a backdrop to research in Applied Linguistics, and second language learning and teaching in particular.

1.2 Form and function

The famous British comedy duo, Eric Morecambe and Ernie Wise, started one of their shows in 1973 with the following dialogue:

(1.1)   Ernie: Tell 'em about the show.
         Eric (to the audience): Have we got a show for you tonight folks!
             Have we got a show for you! (aside to Ernie) Have we got a
             show for them?

This short dialogue raises a number of problems for anyone wishing to do a linguistic analysis of it; not least is the question of why it is funny (the audience laughed at Eric's question to Ernie). Most people would agree that it is funny because Eric is playing with a grammatical structure that seems to be ambiguous: 'Have we got a show for you!' has an inverted verb and subject. Inversion of the verb and its subject happens only under restricted conditions in English; the most typical circumstances in which this happens is when questions are being asked, but it also happens in exclamations (e.g. 'Wasn't my face red!'). So Eric's repeated grammatical *form* clearly undergoes a change in how it is *interpreted* by the audience between its second and third occurrence in the dialogue. Eric's inverted grammatical *form* in its first two occurrences clearly has the *function* of an exclamation, *telling* the audience something, not asking them anything, until the humorous moment when he begins to doubt whether they do have a show to offer, at which point he uses the same grammatical form to ask Ernie a genuine question. There seems, then, to be a lack of one-to-one correspondence between grammatical form and communicative function; the inverted form *in itself* does not inherently carry an exclamatory or a questioning function. By the same token, in other situations, an uninverted declarative form (subject before verb), typically associated with 'statements', might be heard as a question requiring an answer:

(1.2)   A: You're leaving for London.
         B: Yes, immediately.

So how we interpret grammatical forms depends on a number of factors, some linguistic, some purely situational. One *linguistic* feature that may affect our interpretation is the intonation. In the Eric and Ernie sketch, Eric's intonation was as follows:

(1.3)   Eric (to the audience): Have we got a SHOW for you tonight folks!
                 Have we got a SHOW for you! (aside to Ernie)
                 ↑ HAVE we got a show for them?

Two variables in Eric's delivery change. Firstly, the *tone contour*, i.e. the direction of his pitch, whether it rises or falls, changes (his last utterance, 'have we got a show for them' ends in a rising tone). Secondly, his voice jumps to a higher *pitch level* (represented here by writing *have* above the line). Is it this which makes his utterance a question? Not *necessarily*. Many questions have only falling tones, as in the following:

(1.4)   A: What was he wearing?
                 B: An anorak.
                 A: But was it his?

So the intonation does not *inherently* carry the function of question either, any more than the inversion of auxiliary verb and subject did. Grammatical forms and phonological forms examined separately are unreliable indicators of function; when they are taken together, *and* looked at in context, we can come to some decision about function. So decisions about communicative function cannot solely be the domain of grammar or phonology. Discourse analysis is not entirely separate from the study of grammar and phonology, as we shall see in Chapters 2 and 4, but discourse analysts are interested in a lot more than linguistic forms. Their concerns include how it is that Eric and Ernie interpret each other's grammar appropriately (Ernie commands Eric to tell the audience, Eric asks Ernie a question, etc.), how it is that the dialogue between the two comics is coherent and not gobbledygook, what Eric and Ernie's roles are in relation to one another, and what sort of 'rules' or conventions they are following as they converse with one another.

Eric and Ernie's conversation is only one example (and a rather crazy one at that) of spoken interaction; most of us in a typical week will observe or take part in a wide range of different types of spoken interaction: phone calls, buying things in shops, perhaps an interview for a job, or with a doctor, or with an employer, talking formally at meetings or in classrooms, informally in cafés or on buses, or intimately with our friends and loved ones. These situations will have their own formulae and conventions which we follow; they will have different ways of opening and closing the encounter, different role relationships, different purposes and different settings. Discourse analysis is interested in all these different factors and tries to account for them in a rigorous fashion with a separate set of descriptive labels from those used by conventional grammarians. The first fundamental distinction we have noted is between language forms and discourse functions; once we have made this distinction a lot of other conclusions can follow, and the labels used to describe discourse need not clash at all with those we are all used to in grammar. They will in fact complement and enrich each other. Chapters 2, 3 and 4 of this book will therefore be concerned with examining the relationships between language forms (grammatical, lexical and phonological ones), and discourse functions, for it is language forms, above all, which are the raw material of language teaching, while the overall aim is to enable learners to use language functionally.

Reader activity 1 🗝

Form and function

Can you create a context and suggest an intonation for the forms in the left-hand column so that they would be heard as performing the functions in the right-hand column, *without changing their grammatical structure*?

1. did I make a fool of myself   (a) question   (b) exclamation
2. you don't love me   (a) question   (b) statement
3. you eat it   (a) statement (b) command
4. switch the light on   (a) command   (b) question

1.3   Speech acts and discourse structures

So far we have suggested that form and function have to be separated to understand what is happening in discourse; this may be necessary to analyse Eric and Ernie's zany dialogue, but why discourse analysis? Applied linguists and language teachers have been familiar with the term *function* for years now; are we not simply talking about 'functions' when we analyse Eric and Ernie's talk? Why complicate matters with a whole new set of jargon?

In one sense we *are* talking about 'functions': we are concerned as much with what Eric and Ernie are *doing* with language as with what they are *saying.* When we say that a particular bit of speech or writing is a *request* or an *instruction* or an *exemplification* we are concentrating on what that piece of language is *doing, or* how the listener/reader is supposed to react; for this reason, such entities are often also called *speech acts* (see Austin 1962 and Searle 1969). Each of the stretches of language that are carrying the force of requesting, instructing, and so on is seen as performing a particular act; Eric's exclamation was performing the act of informing the audience that a great show was in store for them. So the approach to

9

communicative language teaching that emphasises the functions or speech acts that pieces of language perform overlaps in an important sense with the preoccupations of discourse analysts. We are all familiar with coursebooks that say things like: 'Here are some questions which can help people to remember experiences which they had almost forgotten: "Have you ever . . . ?", "Tell me about the time you . . . ?", "I hear you once . . . ?", "Didn't you once . . . ?", "You've . . ., haven't you?"'*. Materials such as these are concerned with speech acts, with what is *done* with words, not just the grammatical and lexical forms of what is *said*.

But when we speak or write, we do not just utter a string of linguistic forms, without beginning, middle or end, and anyway, we have already demonstrated the difficulty of assigning a function to a particular form of grammar and/or vocabulary. If we had taken Eric's words 'have we got a show for you' and treated them as a *sentence*, written on a page (perhaps to exemplify a particular structure, or particular vocabulary), it would have been impossible to attach a functional label to it with absolute certainty other than to say that in a large number of contexts this would most typically be heard as a question. Now this is undoubtedly a valuable generalisation to make for a learner, and many notional–functional language coursebooks do just that, offering short phrases or clauses which characteristically fulfil functions such as 'apologising' or 'making a polite request'. But the discourse analyst is much more interested in the process by which, for example, an inverted verb and subject come to be heard as an informing speech act, and to get at this, we must have our speech acts fully contextualised both in terms of the surrounding *text* and of the key features of the situation. Discourse analysis is thus fundamentally concerned with the relationship between language and the contexts of its use.

And there is more to the story than merely labelling chains of speech acts. Firstly, as we have said, discourses have beginnings, middles and ends. How is it, for example, that we feel that we are coming in in the middle of this conversation and leaving it before it has ended?

(1.5)   A: Well, try this spray, what I got, this is the biggest they come.
        B: Oh . . .
        A: . . . little make-up capsule.
        B: Oh, right, it's like these inhalers, isn't it?
        A: And I, I've found that not so bad since I've been using it, and it doesn't make you so grumpy.
        B: This is up your nose?
        A: Mm.
        B: Oh, wow! It looks a bit sort of violent, doesn't it? It works well, does it?

(Birmingham Collection of English Text)

---

* L. Jones: *Functions of English*, Cambridge University Press, 1981 ed., p. 22.

Our immediate reaction is that conversations can often begin with *well*, but that there is something odd about 'try this spray ...'. Suggesting to someone 'try X' usually only occurs in response to some remark or event or perceived state of affairs that warrants intervention, and such information is lacking here. Equally, we interpret B's final remark, 'It works well, does it?' as expecting a response from A. In addition, we might say that we do not expect people to leave the question of whether something is a fitting solution to a problem that has been raised dangling in the air; this we shall return to in section 1.10 when we look at written text.

The difficulty is not only the attaching of speech-act labels to utterances. The main problem with making a neat analysis of extract (1.5) is that it is clearly the 'middle' of something, which makes some features difficult to interpret. For instance, why does A say *well* at the beginning of his/her turn? What are '*these* inhalers'? Are they inhalers on the table in front of the speakers, or ones we all know about in the shops? Why does A change from talking about '*this* spray' to *that* in a short space of the dialogue?

The dialogue is structured in the sense that it can be coherently interpreted and seems to be progressing somewhere, but we are in the middle of a structure rather than witnessing the complete unfolding of the whole. It is in this respect, the interest in whole discourse structures, that discourse analysis adds something extra to the traditional concern with functions/ speech acts. Just what these larger structures might typically consist of must be the concern of the rest of this chapter before we address the detailed questions of the value of discourse analysis in language teaching.

Reader activity 2 🔑

What clues are there in the following extract which suggest that we are coming in in the middle of something? What other problems are there in interpreting individual words?

> A: I mean, I don't like this new emblem at all.
> B: The logo.
> A: Yeah, the castle on the Trent, it's horrible.
> C: Did you get a chance to talk to him?
> A: Yeah.
> C: How does he seem?

(Author's data 1989)

1.4   The scope of discourse analysis

Discourse analysis is not only concerned with the description and analysis of spoken interaction. In addition to all our verbal encounters we daily consume hundreds of written and printed words: newspaper articles, letters, stories, recipes, instructions, notices, comics, billboards, leaflets pushed through the door, and so on. We usually expect them to be coherent, meaningful communications in which the words and/or sentences are linked to one another in a fashion that corresponds to conventional formulae, just as we do with speech; therefore discourse analysts are equally interested in the organisation of written interaction. In this book, we shall use the term *discourse analysis* to cover the study of spoken and written interaction. Our overall aim is to come to a much better understanding of exactly how natural spoken and written discourse looks and sounds. This may well be different from what textbook writers and teachers have assumed from their own intuition, which is often burdened with prejudgements deriving from traditional grammar, vocabulary and intonation teaching. With a more accurate picture of natural discourse, we are in a better position to evaluate the descriptions upon which we base our teaching, the teaching materials, what goes on in the classroom, and the end products of our teaching, whether in the form of spoken or written output.

1.5   Spoken discourse: models of analysis

One influential approach to the study of spoken discourse is that developed at the University of Birmingham, where research initially concerned itself with the structure of discourse in school classrooms (Sinclair and Coulthard 1975). The Birmingham model is certainly not the only valid approach to analysing discourse, but it is a relatively simple and powerful model which has connexions with the study of speech acts such as were discussed in section 1.3 but which, at the same time, tries to capture the larger structures, the 'wholes' that we talked about in the same section. Sinclair and Coulthard found in the language of traditional native-speaker school classrooms a rigid pattern, where teachers and pupils spoke according to very fixed perceptions of their roles and where the talk could be seen to conform to highly structured sequences. An extract from their data illustrates this:

(1.6)   (T = teacher, P = any pupil who speaks)

T: Now then . . . I've got some things here, too. Hands up. What's that, what is it?
P: Saw.

T: It's a saw, yes this is a saw. What do we do with a saw?
P: Cut wood.
T: Yes. You're shouting out though. What do we do with a saw? Marvelette.
P: Cut wood.
T: We cut wood. And, erm, what do we do with a hacksaw, this hacksaw?
P: Cut trees.
T: Do we cut trees with this?
P: No. No.
T: Hands up. What do we do with this?
P: Cut wood.
T: Do we cut wood with this?
P: No.
T: What do we do with that then?
P: Cut wood.
T: We cut wood with that. What do we do with that?
P: Sir.
T: Cleveland.
P: Metal.
T: We cut metal. Yes we cut metal. And, er, I've got this here. What's that? Trevor.
P: An axe.
T: It's an axe yes. What do I cut with the axe?
P: Wood, wood.
T: Yes I cut wood with the axe. Right . . . Now then, I've got some more things here . . . (etc.)

(Sinclair and Coulthard 1975: 93–4)

This is only a short extract, but nonetheless, a clear pattern seems to emerge (and one that many will be familiar with from their own schooldays). The first thing we notice, intuitively, is that, although this is clearly part of a larger discourse (a 'lesson'), in itself it seems to have a completeness. A bit of business seems to commence with the teacher saying 'Now then . . .', and that same bit of business ends with the teacher saying 'Right . . . Now then'. The teacher (in this case a man) in his planning and execution of the lesson decides that the lesson shall be marked out in some way; he does not just run on without a pause from one part of the lesson to another. In fact he gives his pupils a clear signal of the beginning and end of this mini-phase of the lesson by using the words *now then* and *right* in a particular way (with falling intonation and a short pause afterwards) that make them into a sort of 'frame' on either side of the sequence of questions and answers. *Framing move* is precisely what Sinclair and Coulthard call the function of such utterances. The two framing moves, together with the question and answer sequence that falls between them, can be called a *transaction*, which again captures the feeling of what is being done with language here, rather in the

13

way that we talk of a 'transaction' in a shop between a shopkeeper and a customer, which will similarly be a completed whole, with a recognisable start and finish. However, *framing move* and *transaction* are only labels to attach to certain structural features, and the analogy with their non-specialist meanings should not be taken too far.

This classroom extract is very structured and formal, but transactions with framing moves of this kind are common in a number of other settings too: telephone calls are perhaps the most obvious, especially when we wish to close the call once the necessary business is done; a job interview is another situation where various phases of the interview are likely to be marked by the chairperson or main interviewer saying things like 'right', 'well now' or 'okay', rather in the way the teacher does. Notice, too, that there is a fairly limited number of words available in English for framing transactions (e.g. *right, okay, so,* etc.), and notice how some people habitually use the same ones.

Reader activity 3 🗝

1. How many other situations can you think of where framing moves are commonly used to divide up the discourse, apart from classrooms, telephone calls and job interviews?
2. Complete the list of what you think the most common framing words or phrases are in English and make a list of framing words in any other language you know. Do framing words translate directly from language to language?
3. What is your favourite framing word or phrase when you are teaching, or when you talk on the phone?

If we return to our piece of classroom data, the next problem is: does the question–answer sequence between the teacher and pupils have any internal structure, or is it just a string of language forms to which we can give individual function or speech-act labels? Sinclair and Coulthard show clearly that it does have a structure. Looking at the extract, we can see a pattern: (1) the teacher asks something ('What's that?'), (2) a pupil answers ('An axe') and (3) the teacher acknowledges the answer and comments on it ('It's an axe, yes'). The pattern of (1), (2) and (3) is then repeated. So we could label the pattern in the following way:

1. Ask   T
2. Answer   P
3. Comment   T

This gives us then a regular sequence of TPT–TPT–TPT–TPT, etc. So we can now return to our extract and begin to mark off the boundaries that create this pattern:

(1.7)   (/ = T/P/T   // = TPT//TPT//TPT)

> T: Now then . . . I've got some things here, too. Hands up. What's that, what is it? /
> P: Saw. /
> T: It's a saw, yes this is a saw. // What do we do with a saw? /
> P: Cut wood. /
> T: Yes. You're shouting out though. // What do we do with a saw? Marvelette. /
> P: Cut wood. /
> T: We cut wood. // And, erm, what do we do with . . . etc.

We can now isolate a typical segment between double slashes (//) and use it as a basic unit in our description:

(1.8)   T: // What do we do with a saw? Marvelette. /
           P: Cut wood. /
           T: We cut wood. //

Sinclair and Coulthard call this unit an *exchange*. This particular exchange consists of a question, an answer and a comment, and so it is a three-part exchange. Each of the parts are given the name *move* by Sinclair and Coulthard. Here are some other examples of exchanges, each with three moves:

(1.9)   A: What time is it?
           B: Six thirty.
           A: Thanks.

(1.10)   A: Tim's coming tomorrow.
           B: Oh yeah.
           A: Yes.

(1.11)   A: Here, hold this.
           B: (takes the box)
           A: Thanks.

Each of these exchanges consists of three moves, but it is only in (1) that the first move ('What time is it?') seems to be functioning as a question. The first move in (2) is heard as giving information, and the first move in (3) as a command. Equally, the second moves seem to have the function, respectively, of (1) an answer, (2) an acknowledgement and (3) a non-verbal response (taking the box). The third moves are in all three exchanges functioning as feedback on the second move: (1) to be polite and say thanks, (2) to confirm the information and (3) to say thanks again. In order to capture the similarity of the pattern in each case, Sinclair and Coulthard

(1975: 26–7) call the first move in each exchange an *opening move*, the second an *answering move* and the third a *follow-up move*. Sinclair and Brazil (1982: 49) prefer to talk of *initiation, response* and *follow-up*. It does not particularly matter for our purposes which set of labels we use, but for consistency, in this book the three moves will be called *initiation, response* and *follow-up*. We can now label our example exchanges using these terms:

Move	Exchange 1	Exchange 2	Exchange 3
Initiation	A: What time is it?	A: Tim's coming tomorrow.	A: Here, hold this.
Response	B: Six-thirty.	B: Oh yeah.	B: (takes the box)
Follow-up	A: Thanks.	A: Yes.	A: Thanks.

In these exchanges we can observe the importance of each move in the overall functional unit. Every exchange has to be initiated, whether with a statement, a question or a command; equally naturally, someone responds, whether in words or action. The status of the follow-up move is slightly different: in the classroom it fulfils the vital role of telling the pupils whether they have done what the teacher wanted them to; in other situations it may be an act of politeness, and the follow-up elements might even be extended further, as in this Spanish example:

(1.12)   A: Oiga, por favor, ¿qué hora es?
           B: Las cinco y media.
           A: Gracias.
           B: De nada.

Here A asks B the time, B replies ('half past five'), A thanks B ('gracias'), and then B says 'de nada' ('not at all'). Many English speakers would feel that such a lengthy ritual was unnecessary for such a minor favour and would omit the fourth part, reserving phrases such as 'not at all' for occasions where it is felt a great service has been done, for example where someone has been helped out of a difficult situation. The patterns of such exchanges may vary from culture to culture, and language learners may have to adjust to differences. They also vary from setting to setting: when we say 'thank you' to a ticket collector at a station barrier as our clipped ticket is handed back to us, we would not (in British society) expect 'not at all' from the ticket collector (see Aston 1988 for examples of how this operates in Italian service encounters in bookshops).

In other cases, the utterance following a response may be less obviously a follow-up and may seem to be just getting on with further conversational business:

(1.13)   A: Did you see Malcolm?
           B: Yes.

> A: What did he say about Brazil?
> B: Oh he said he's going next month.
> A: Did he mention the party?
> B: No.
> A: Funny . . . (etc.)

Different situations will require different formulae, depending on roles and settings. The teacher's role as evaluator, for example, makes the follow-up move very important in classrooms; where the follow-up move is withheld, the pupils are likely to suspect that something is wrong, that they have not given the answer the teacher wants, as in our extract from Sinclair and Coulthard's data:

(1.14)   T: What do we do with a hacksaw, this hacksaw?
         P: Cut trees.
         T: Do we cut trees with this?
         P: No. No.

The pupils know that 'cut trees' is not the right answer; it is only when one pupil says 'metal' that the full follow-up occurs ('We cut metal. Yes we cut metal'); the question 'Do we cut trees with this?' is simply recycling the initiating move, giving the pupils a second chance.

Reader activity 4 ⚓

1.   Can you put the moves of this discourse into an order that produces a coherent conversation? The conversation takes place at a travel agent's. What clues do you use to establish the correct order? Are there any moves that are easier to place than others; and if so, why?

> 'You haven't no, no.'
> 'No . . . in Littlewoods is it?'
> 'I'm awfully sorry, we haven't . . . um I don't know where you can try for Bath actually.'
> 'Can I help you?'
> 'Okay thanks.'
> 'Yeah they're inside there now.'
> 'Um have you by any chance got anything on Bath?'
> 'Um I don't really know . . . you could try perhaps Pickfords in Littlewoods, they might be able to help you.'
>
> (Birmingham Collection of English Text)

2.   Think of a typical encounter with a stranger in the street (e.g. asking the way, asking for change). What is the minimum number of moves necessary to complete a polite exchange in a language that you know other than English?

The three-part exchanges we have looked at so far are fascinating in another sense, too, which relates back to our discussion in section 1.3 on speech acts, in that, taken out of context and without the third part, it is often impossible to decide exactly what the functions of the individual speech acts in the exchange are in any completely meaningful way. Consider, for example:

(1.15)   A: What time is it?
           B: Five past six.
           A:

What could fill the third part here? Here are some possibilities:

1. A: Thanks.
2. A: Good! Clever girl!
3. A: No it isn't, and you know it isn't; it's half past and you're late again!

'Thanks' suggests that A's question was a genuine request for information. 'Clever girl!' smacks of the classroom (e.g. a lesson on 'telling the time' with a big demonstration clock), and 'No it isn't . . . etc.' suggests an accusation or a verbal trap for someone who is to be reproached. Neither of the last two is a genuine request for information; teachers usually already know the answers to the questions they ask of their pupils and the reproachful parent or employer in the last case is not ignorant of the time. These examples · underline the fact that function is arrived at with reference to the *participants*, *roles* and *settings* in any discourse, and that linguistic forms are interpreted in light of these. This is not to say that all communication between teachers and pupils is of the curious kind exemplified in (1.15); sometimes teachers ask 'real' questions ('How did you spend the weekend?'), but equally, a lot of language teaching question-and-answer sessions reflect the 'unreal' questions of Sinclair and Coulthard's data ('What's the past tense of *take*?'; 'What does *wash basin* mean?'). Nor do we wish to suggest that 'unreal' classroom questions serve no purpose; they are a useful means for the teacher of checking the state of knowledge of the students and of providing opportunities for practising language forms. But in evaluating the spoken output of language classrooms we shall at least want to decide whether there is a proper equilibrium or an imbalance between 'real' communication and 'teacher talk'. We would probably not like to think that our students spent all or most of their time indulging in the make-believe world of 'you-tell-me-things-I-already-know'.

1.6 Conversations outside the classroom

So far we have looked at talk in a rather restricted context: the traditional classroom, where roles are rigidly defined and the patterns of initiation, response and follow-up in exchanges are relatively easy to perceive, and where transactions are heavily marked. The classroom was a convenient place to start, as Sinclair and Coulthard discovered, but it is not the 'real' world of conversation. It is a peculiar place, a place where teachers ask questions to which they already know the answers, where pupils (at least younger pupils) have very limited rights as speakers, and where evaluation by the teacher of what the pupils say is a vital mechanism in the discourse structure. But using the classroom is most beneficial for our purposes since one of the things a model for the analysis of classroom talk enables us to do is evaluate our own output as teachers and that of our students. This we shall return to in Chapter 5. For the moment it is more important to examine the claim that the exchange model might be useful for the analysis of talk outside the classroom. If it is, then it could offer a yardstick for the kind of language aimed at in communicative language teaching and for all aspects of the complex chain of materials, methodology, implementation and evaluation, whatever our order of priority within that chain.

Conversations outside classroom settings vary in their degree of structuredness, but even so, conversations that seem at first sight to be 'free' and unstructured can often be shown to have a structure; what will differ is the kinds of speech-act labels needed to describe what is happening, and it is mainly in this area, the functions of the parts of individual moves, that discourse analysts have found it necessary to expand and modify the Sinclair–Coulthard model. Let us begin with a real example:

(1.16) (Jozef (J) is a visiting scholar from Hungary at an English department in a British university. He has established a fairly informal and relaxed relationship with Chris (C), a lecturer in the department. He pops into Chris's room one morning.)

C: Hello Jozef.
J: Hello Chris . . . could you do me a great favour.
C: Yeah.
J: I'm going to book four cinema tickets on the phone and they need a credit card number . . . could you give me your credit card number . . . they only accept payment by credit card over the phone.
C: Ah.
J: I telephoned there and they said they wouldn't do any reservations⌐
C: ⌊without a card.
J: Yes and I could pay you back in cash.
C: Yes . . . sure . . . no problem at all.
J: Yes.

C: Mm . . . I've got this one, which is an Access card.
J: And I just ⌈ tell them your number.
C: ⌊ You tell them my number . . . this one here.
J: And they tell me how much.
C: That's right . . . that's all . . . that's my name there and that number.
J: Yes . . . and I can settle it.
C: Yes and bring it back when you're done.
J: Yeah . . . I'll just telephone then.
C: Right . . . okay.
J: Thanks Chris.
C: Cheers.
(Jozef leaves the room.)

(Author's data 1988)

This is not like the classroom. Jozef and Chris are more or less equals in this piece of interaction, therefore each will enjoy the right to initiate, respond and follow up in their exchanges. It is not merely a question-and-answer session; sometimes they inform each other and acknowledge information. But their talk is not disorganised; there are patterns we can observe. The sequence begins and ends with framing mechanisms not entirely unlike the 'right' and 'now then' of the classroom: after the initial greeting, Jozef pauses and his voice moves to a higher pitch:

                    could you do me . . . (etc.)
(1.17)   J: Hello Chris . . . ↑

We shall return in greater detail to this use of pitch in Chapter 4. For the moment it is sufficient to record it as a signal of a boundary in the talk, in this case marking off the opening from the main business of the conversation. Starting the main business, Jozef then begins a long sequence, all of which is concerned with eliciting a favour from Chris. He does not immediately ask his question but in his initiating move gives the background to it first ('I'm going to book four . . . etc.'). This speech act we shall call a *starter*, after which comes the main part of the elicitation ('could you give me . . . etc.'). Jozef expands his elicitation with several comments ('they only accept payment . . . etc.'), during which he is supported by a sort of grunt from Chris ('ah') and an occasion where Chris completes Jozef's words for him, as if he has predicted what Jozef wanted to say ('without a card'). Jozef's long elicitation ends with 'and I could pay you back in cash'. Chris then responds "Yes sure . . . etc.') and Jozef follows up with 'yes'. The fact that Jozef says so much in asking the favour is because he is potentially inconveniencing Chris, and he thus has to prepare the ground carefully; this relationship between what is said and factors such as politeness and sensitivity to the other person is taken up in section 5.2.

So, complex though it is, we have initiation–response–follow-up sequences here that form meaningful exchanges just like the classroom ones. What we have here, which we would not expect in the classroom, are Chris's verbal supports; we should be very surprised to hear in a classroom of young children:

(1.18)   T: Now . . . I have some things here.
         Ps (in chorus): Oh yes . . . ah-ha.
         T: Used for cutting things.
         Ps: Oh, really?

But we can pare Jozef and Chris's exchange down to its basics:

(1.19)   J: // Could you give me your credit card number and I'll pay you in cash. /
         C: Yes sure no problem. /
         J: Yes. //

It now begins to look a little more manageable, and in it we can see the difference in complexity between a simple speech act and elaborated ones of the kind demanded by politeness, which can be difficult for the learner with limited linguistic resources in an L2. We can also see the difference between bare exchanges of the kind often found in coursebooks and the way, in natural discourse, that speakers support and complete one another's moves, how they follow up and acknowledge replies, and other features that we have not yet discussed. It is in this way, by using descriptive categories such as the exchange and its sub-components, that discourse analysis enables us to describe actual performances, to delimit targets more accurately in language teaching and to evaluate input and output in the teaching/learning process.

This extract also serves as a reminder of the form and function problem raised in section 1.2. Some of Jozef's declarative forms are heard by Chris as questions requiring a confirmation (or correction if necessary):

(1.20)   J: And I just ⌈ tell them your number.
         C: ⌊ You tell them my number . . . this one here.
         J: And they tell me how much.
         C: That's right . . . that's all . . . (etc.)

They are heard as questions since Chris is the person with the knowledge that Jozef is seeking to have confirmed (at least Jozef assumes that he is). Chris will not suppose that Jozef is telling him something he (Chris) already knows, and so will assume he is being asked to confirm.

Equally, we can observe the same kinds of exchange boundaries occurring in the middle of speaker turns as we did in the classroom data:

(1.21)   J: // And they tell me how much. /
         C: That's right . . . that's all . . . that's my name there and that number. /
         J: Yes // . . . and I can settle it. /

> C: Yes and bring it back when you're done. /
> J: Yeah // . . . I'll just telephone then.

The double slashes in Jozef's turns come after the follow-ups to Chris's answers and before new initiating moves. The conversation finally ends with a framing move similar to the teacher's ('right . . . okay'), and an expression of thanks.

Obviously there are numerous other features in the conversation (intonation, gesture, etc.) which make us more confident in our analysis, and we shall return to the most central of these later, but this short conversation should at least serve to illustrate that even apparently loosely structured talk adheres to norms and is regularly patterned. It is this type of patterning that can be as useful to the language teacher as the regular patterns of syntax are in clauses and sentences.

So far we have looked only at one model for the analysis of spoken interaction, the Sinclair–Coulthard 'Birmingham' model. We have argued that it is useful for describing talk in and out of the classroom; it captures patterns that reflect the basic functions of interaction and offers a hierarchical model where smaller units can be seen to combine to form larger ones and where the large units can be seen to consist of these smaller ones. The bare bones of the hierarchy (or *rank scale*) can be expressed as follows:

TRANSACTION
↕
EXCHANGE
↕
MOVE
↕
ACT

The lowest rank is what we have referred to as 'speech acts'; Sinclair and Coulthard simply call them *acts*, but for our general purposes, any fine distinction the terminology might suggest is unimportant. Sinclair and Coulthard's model is very useful for analysing patterns of interaction where talk is relatively tightly structured, such as between doctors and patients (see Coulthard and Ashby 1975), but all sorts of complications arise when we try to apply the model to talk in more informal, casual, and spontaneous contexts.

1.7 Talk as a social activity

Because of the rigid conventions of situations such as teacher talk and doctor–patient talk, it is relatively easy to predict who will speak when, who will ask and who will answer, who will interrupt, who will open and close the talk, and so on. But where talk is more casual, and among equals, everyone will have a part to play in controlling and monitoring the discourse, and the picture will look considerably more complicated.

Reader activity 5 ☛─Ө

Consider the problems which arise when we try to analyse the following extract from the point of view of exchange and transaction boundaries. Are there straightforward initiating, responding and follow-up moves? Decide where each move begins and ends and try to label some of the more obvious speech acts (e.g. *elicitations*, *replies*, *comments* and so on). There are complications here, not least because there are more than two people talking. Do you feel this extract is more or less tightly structured than the classroom talk or the conversation between Jozef and Chris? What extra problems does this sort of transcript raise for discourse analysts?

(1.22)   (University lecturer (L) at a student bar where he has just ordered drinks for a group of students (S1, S2, etc.). The barman (B) is attending to the order and the group are standing at the bar.)

L: Well, that should blow a hole in five pounds, shouldn't it?
S1: It's quite cheap actually.
L: (laughs)
S1: What's the um lecturers' club like, senior, senior, you know.
L: └ Ah it's very cosy and
     sedate and, er, you know, nice little armchairs and curtains . . .
     there are some interesting characters who get there.
S2: Is that the one where they have the toilets marked with er
     gentlemen, no, 'ladies and members'? ┐
L: └ Oh, oh ┐
S2:   └ Yeah it was one
     of the other lecturers who pointed it out, he ┌ thought it was quite
     amusing.   │
L: └ Yeah, I hadn't
     noticed that, yeah, might well be, yeah.
B: Four sixty-seven please.
L: Is that all, God, I thought it would cost more than that (pays)
     . . . thank you . . . I thought it would cost more than that.
S1: ┌ It's quite cheap.
S2: ├ I wouldn't argue with that one.
S3: └ No, it's quite good.
L: Now, how are we going to carry all these over?

(Author's data 1989)

B

There are features which can be handled by the Sinclair–Coulthard exchange structure model (the lecturer's 'now' at the end seems to be a typical boundary marker, and his laugh at the beginning of the talk could be seen as a follow-up to the student's remark), but there are many complications. The student who asks about the toilets does not get a proper answer from the lecturer, and, if anything, answers her own question; the barman comes in and disrupts the continuity of the talk, and, at one point, three people are talking at once. If this were a classroom, many would consider that the lecturer had lost all control over the discourse, and that people were behaving 'out of turn'.

Complications of this kind have led many discourse analysts to devote their attention more to observing how people behave and how they cooperate in the management of discourse, rather than to a concern with building elaborate models of structure (see Levinson 1983: 286). Observing conversational behaviour close to has been the preoccupation of a school of analysts roughly grouped under the name *ethnomethodologists*, though sociologists, anthropologists and psychologists have also made significant contributions. This approach has been largely, but not exclusively, an American phenomenon, and it has concentrated on areas of interest such as how pairs of utterances relate to one another (the study of *adjacency pairs*), how turn-taking is managed, how conversational openings and closings are effected, how topics enter and disappear from conversation, and how speakers engage in strategic acts of politeness, face-preservation, and so on. The emphasis is always on real data, and observing how people orient to the demands of the speech event. We shall look more closely at this kind of conversational analysis in Chapter 5, but the student–lecturer data extract above exemplifies some of the ways in which data can be dealt with.

Because the lecturer and his group are not in the classroom, students, as well as lecturer, feel free to raise new topics. S1 asks about the staff club, but he is hesitant, and stutters somewhat in his question; such hesitancy is a significant detail, and is a typical signal of deference. The lecturer feels free to overlap with his answer before the student has finished speaking. Turn-taking rights are exercised, with people taking turns at talk when they feel they have the right to say something. For example, the barman considers his right to continue the purchasing transaction to override the group's conversation, and the three students all feel they have an equal right to comment on the lecturer's remark about the price of the drinks. However, we might also observe that the talk is all directed at the lecturer, rather than student to student. Is this because the lecturer is seen as 'dominant speaker', a hangover from the classroom, which the group have only recently left? It is to answer such questions that ethnomethodologists examine large amounts of data to observe regular patterns of behaviour that might indicate adherence to underlying norms or 'rules' of conversation. In Chapter 5 we shall look at some of their findings concerning the issues our extract has raised, as well as others of a similar type. This is not to say that such findings must automatically have any implications for language teaching, but some of them may.

1.8   Written discourse

With written texts, some of the problems associated with spoken transcripts are absent: we do not have to contend with people all speaking at once, the writer has usually had time to think about what to say and how to say it, and the sentences are usually well formed in a way that the utterances of natural, spontaneous talk are not. But the overall questions remain the same: what norms or rules do people adhere to when creating written texts? Are texts structured according to recurring principles, is there a hierarchy of units comparable to acts, moves and exchanges, and are there conventional ways of opening and closing texts? As with spoken discourse, if we do find such regularities, and if they can be shown as elements that have different realisations in different languages, or that they may present problems for learners in other ways, then the insights of written discourse analysis might be applicable, in specifiable ways, to language teaching.

In Chapter 2, we shall consider some grammatical regularities observable in well-formed written texts, and how the structuring of sentences has implications for units such as paragraphs, and for the progression of whole texts. We shall also look at how the grammar of English offers a limited set of options for creating surface links between the clauses and sentences of a text, otherwise known as *cohesion*. Basically, most texts display links from sentence to sentence in terms of grammatical features such as pronominalisation, ellipsis (the omission of otherwise expected elements because they are retrievable from the previous text or context) and conjunction of various kinds (see Halliday and Hasan 1976). The resources available for grammatical cohesion can be listed finitely and compared across languages for translatability and distribution in real texts. Texts displaying such cohesive features are easy to find, such as this one on telephones:

(1.23)   If you'd like to give someone a phone for Christmas, there are *plenty* to choose from. *Whichever you* go for, if *it*'s to be used on the BT [British Telecom] network, make sure *it*'s approved – look for the label with a green circle to confirm *this*. Phones labelled with a red triangle are prohibited.

(*Which?* December 1989: 599)

The italicised items are all interpretable in relation to items in previous sentences. *Plenty* is assumed to mean 'plenty of phones'; *you* in the first and second sentence are interpreted as the same 'you'; *whichever* is interpreted as 'whichever telephone'; *it* is understood as the telephone, and *this* as 'the fact that it is approved'. These are features of grammatical cohesion, but there are lexical clues too: *go for* is a synonym of *choose*, and there is lexical repetition of *phone*, and of *label*.

Reader activity 6 🗝

Pick out the cohesive items between clauses and sentences in this text extract in the same way as was done for the telephone text:

(1.24)   British men are a pretty traditional bunch, when it comes to shaving; two out of three use a blade and soap, rather than an electric shaver. *Which?* readers are more continental in their tastes; around half of you use an electric shaver, about the same proportion as in the rest of Europe.

      For women, shaving is by far the most popular method of removing body hair. 85 per cent of the *Which?* women readers who removed body hair told us that they used a shaver.

      (*Which?* December 1989: 613)

Notice that, when talking of cohesion in the telephone text, we spoke of interpreting items and understanding them. This is important because the cohesive items are clues or signals as to how the text should be read, they are not absolutes. The pronoun *it* only gives us the information that a non-human entity is being referred to; it does not necessarily tell us which one. *It* could potentially have referred to *Christmas* in the phone text, but that would have produced an incoherent reading of the text. So cohesion is only a guide to coherence, and coherence is something created by the reader in the act of reading the text. Coherence is the feeling that a text hangs together, that it makes sense, and is not just a jumble of sentences (see Neubauer 1983: 7). The sentences 'Clare loves potatoes. She was born in Ireland.' are cohesive (*Clare/she*), but are only coherent if one already shares the stereotype ethnic association between being Irish and loving potatoes, or is prepared to assume a cause–effect relationship between the two sentences. So cohesion is only part of coherence in reading and writing, and indeed in spoken language too, for the same processes operate there.

1.9   Text and interpretation

Markers of various kinds, i.e. the linguistic signals of semantic and discourse functions (e.g. in English the *-ed* on the verb is a marker of pastness), are very much concerned with the *surface* of the text. Cohesive markers are no exception: they create links across sentence boundaries and pair and chain together items that are related (e.g. by referring to the same entity). But reading a text is far more complex than that: we have to interpret the ties and make sense of them. Making sense of a text is an act of *interpretation* that depends as much on what we as readers bring to a text as what the author puts into it. Interpretation can be seen as a set of *procedures* and the approach to the analysis of texts that emphasises the mental activities involved in interpretation can be broadly called *procedural*. Procedural approaches emphasise the role of the reader in actively building the world of the text, based on his/her experience of the world and how states and events are characteristically manifested in it. The reader has to activate such knowledge, make inferences and constantly assess his/her interpretation in the light of the situation and the aims and goals of the text as the reader perceives them. The work of De Beaugrande and Dressler (1981) is central to this approach. If we take a text which is cohesive in the sense described above, we can see that a lot more mental work has to go on for the reader to make it coherent:

(1.25)   The parents of a seven-year-old Australian boy
          woke to find a giant python crushing and trying
          to swallow him.
             The incident occurred in Cairns, Queensland
          and the boy's mother, Mrs Kathy Dryden said:
          'It was like a horror movie. It was a hot night
          and Bartholomew was lying under a mosquito
          net. He suddenly started screaming.
             'We rushed to the bedroom to find a huge
          snake trying to strangle him. It was coiled
          around his arms and neck and was going down
          his body.'
             Mrs Dryden and her husband, Peter, tried to
          stab the creature with knives but the python bit
          the boy several times before escaping.

(from *The Birmingham Post*, 12 March 1987, p. 10)

This text requires us to activate our knowledge of pythons as dangerous creatures which may threaten human life, which strangle their prey and to whose presence one must react with a certain urgency. More than this we make the cognitive link between 'a hot night' and the time of the event (this is implicit rather than explicit in the text). The boy's screaming must be taken to be a *consequence* of the python attacking him (rather than, say, prior to the arrival of the python). The 'creature' must be taken to be the python rather than the boy (which 'creature' could well refer to in another text), since parents do not normally stab their children in order to save their lives. All this is what the reader must bring to any text. What we are doing in making these cognitive links in the text is going further than just noting the semantic links between cohesive items (e.g. *creature* = general superordinate, *snake* = genus/superordinate, *python* = species/hyponym); we are creating coherence (see De Beaugrande and Dressler 1981: 6–12, 31–47). The various procedures that mediate between cohesion and coherence will be returned to in greater detail in sections 6.4–7, as this area of text analysis is obviously crucial in any discourse-based approach to reading and writing.

Another level of interpretation which we are involved in as we process texts is that of recognising *textual patterns*. Certain patterns in text reoccur time and time again and become deeply ingrained as part of our cultural knowledge. These patterns are manifested in regularly occurring functional relationships between bits of the text. These bits may be phrases, clauses, sentences or groups of sentences; we shall refer to them as textual *segments* to avoid confusion with grammatical elements and syntactic relations within clauses and sentences. A segment may sometimes be a clause, sometimes a sentence, sometimes a whole paragraph; what is important is that segments can be isolated using a set of labels covering a finite set of functional relations that can occur between any two bits of text. An example of segments coinciding with sentences are these two sentences from a report on a photographic exhibition:

(1.26)   The stress is on documentary and rightly so. Arty photographs are a bore.

(*The Guardian*, 27 October 1988: 24)

The interpretation that makes most sense is that the relationship between the second sentence and the first is that the second provides a *reason* for the first. The two segments are therefore in a *phenomenon–reason* relationship with one another. An example of a segment consisting of more than one sentence can be seen in extract (1.27), where the relationship between the first segment (sentence 1) and the second segment (sentences 2–5) is one of *phenomenon–example*; all of sentences 2–5 have to be read as part of the act of exemplification for the text to make sense.

(1.27)   Naturally, the more people pay for their houses, the more they want to rename their neighbourhoods. Suppose you've just coughed up £250,000 for an unspectacular house on the fringe of Highgate – an area with loads of cachet. The estate agent tells you it's Highgate. You've paid a Highgate price. There's no way you're going to admit that it's in Crouch End.

(Simon Hoggart, *The Observer Magazine*, 11 March 1990: 5)

The interpretation of relations between textual segments is a cognitive act on the part of the reader, who might be supposed to be asking questions of the text as it unfolds, such as (for extract 1.26) 'The stress is on documentary; why?' In this sense, reading the text is like a dialogue with the author, and the processing of two segments could be seen as analogous to the creation of an exchange in spoken discourse. Whether this dialogue with the author is a reality or an analytical construct is not a question that can be easily answered here, but a model which suggests this kind of interaction between reader and text or author might be able to capture difficulties readers experience in text processing and offer ways of attacking them.

The approach to text analysis that emphasises the interpretive acts involved in relating textual segments one to the other through relationships such as *phenomenon–reason*, *cause–consequence*, *instrument–achievement* and suchlike is a *clause-relational* approach, and is best exemplified in the work of Winter (1977, 1978) and Hoey (1983). The *phenomenon–reason* relation which united the two sentences of extract (1.26), along with *cause–consequence* and *instrument–achievement*, can be brought under the general heading of *logical sequence* relations. When segments of a text are compared or contrasted with one another, then we may talk of *matching* relations, which are also extremely common. *Logical sequencing* and *matching* are the two basic categories of the clause-relational approach. This view of text is dynamic; it is not just concerned with labelling what are sometimes called the *illocutionary acts* (a bit like speech acts) which individual clauses, sentences and paragraphs perform in a text, but is concerned with the relationships the textual segments enter into *with one another*.

It would of course be wrong to suggest that all texts are like the two sentences from the photo exhibition text and that the whole operation of reading was some sort of perverse guessing-game where authors made life difficult for readers. Texts often contain strong clues or *signals* as to how we should interpret the relations between segments; these are not absolutely deterministic but are *supporting evidence* to the cognitive activity of deducing the relations. For example, we may find in a text a sentence such as: 'Feeling ill, he went home', and here we would note that the sub-ordination of one element to another by the grammatical choice of joining a main clause to a subordinate one is a characteristic device of cause–consequence relations; it is a signal of the likely relation, which would have to be reinterpreted if the sentence were 'Going home, he felt ill'. Equally, an author might help us with a conjunction: '*Because* he felt ill, he went home', or else use items of general vocabulary to signal the same relation: '*The reason* he went home was that he was feeling ill'. Other types of signals include repetition and syntactic parallelism (using the same syntax in two or more different clauses to draw attention to a comparison or contrast, for example). In the sentence 'The politicians were in a huff, the industrialists were in a rage, the workers were in the mood for a fight', the parallelism of the 'subject + *be* + prepositional phrase' underlines the comparison between the three groups of people. The clause-relational approach takes all this evidence into account in its analyses.

Reader activity 7 ⚷

Here are some extracts from real texts. Decide what kind of relation exists between segments separated by a slash (/) in each case, and note any supporting evidence such as syntactic parallelism.

1. The BBC has put off a new corporate advertising campaign due to be aired this month, extolling the virtues and values of both television and radio. / A BBC spokesman delicately suggests that this may not be the most appropriate time to be telling the audience how wonderful the Beeb is.

   (*The Observer*, 16 November 1986: 42)

2. In Britain, the power of the unions added an extra dread, / which made British politics a special case; / on the Continent, Margaret Thatcher was regarded as something of a laboratory experiment, rather like a canary put down a mine-shaft to see if it will sing.

   (*The Sunday Times Magazine*, 30 December 1979: 14)

1.10   Larger patterns in text

The clause-relational approach to text also concerns itself with larger patterns which regularly occur in texts. If we consider a simple text like the following, which is concocted for the sake of illustration, we can see a pattern emerging which is found in hundreds of texts in a wide variety of subject areas and contexts:

(1.28)   Most people like to take a camera with them when they travel abroad. But all airports nowadays have X-ray security screening and X rays can damage film. One solution to this problem is to purchase a specially designed lead-lined pouch. These are cheap and can protect film from all but the strongest X rays.

The first sentence presents us with a *situation* and the second sentence with some sort of complication or *problem*. The third sentence describes a *response* to the problem and the final sentence gives a positive *evaluation* of the response. Such a sequence of relations forms a *problem–solution* pattern, and problem–solution patterns are extremely common in texts. Hoey (1983) analyses such texts in great detail, as well as some other common text patterns, some of which we shall return to in Chapter 6.

These larger patterns which may be found in texts (and indeed which may constitute the whole text) are the objects of interpretation by the reader, just as the smaller clause-relation were, and in the same way, are often *signalled* by the same sorts of grammatical and lexical devices such as subordination and parallelism. In our concocted text, for instance, we have a conjunction (*but*) indicating an *adversative* relation, backward lexical reference to 'this problem' (damage caused by X rays) and a forward reference to the solution (lead-lined pouches). Both readers and writers need to be aware of these signalling devices and to be able to use them when necessary to process textual relations that are not immediately obvious and to compose text that assists the reader in the act of interpretation. The larger patterns such as the problem–solution pattern are culturally ingrained, but they are often realised in a sequence of textual segments which is not so straightforward as our concocted text suggests. The sequence situation–problem–response–evaluation may be varied, but we do normally expect *all* the elements to be present in a well-formed text; where the sequence is varied, signalling plays an even more important part in *signposting* the text, that is, showing the reader a way round it.

Reader activity 8 🔑

Identify the elements of the problem–solution pattern in these extracts from advertisements and note any signalling devices.

1.

DAMP WALLS, FLAKING PAINT, PEELING WALLPAPER, MUSTY SMELLS
could mean Rising Damp

Rising damp, if not treated effectively could in time cause extensive damage to the structure of your home, ruin decoration and furniture. Damp also causes repugnant mould and mildewy smells and could be a hazard to health.

Doulton Wallguard guarantee to cure rising damp

Doulton, the international specialists in ceramic technology have developed a unique ceramic tube that when installed in walls draws moisture out and ensures it stays out for good. This tried and tested process requires no structural work and is usually installed in just one day.

Guaranteed for 30 Years

⟫→

2.   **In engineering jargon there is a
phenomenon known as N.V.H. It
stands for noise, vibration and harshness.**

You can easily tell how badly your car suffers from N.V.H. by the volume at which you have to play your radio and the way that you feel after a long journey. It's very tiring.

The rudimentary cure is to fill the car with sound deadening material. Everybody does this to some extent, even Ford.

But we believe that prevention is better than cure. After all, with the technology that we have at our disposal, there are more scientific ways of reducing N.V.H.

At the Ford design and development centre we have a room which is known as the anechoic chamber. It's here, on the rolling road, that our acoustics engineers explore new techniques in sound proofing.

The result is a car that never feels as if it's trying. Even at Autobahn speeds, with the smooth V6 engine and all round independent suspension, the performance is effortless.

(from *The Sunday Times Magazine*, 30 December 1979, pp. 42, 49)

1.11 Conclusion

We have seen in this chapter that discourse analysis is a vast subject area within linguistics, encompassing as it does the analysis of spoken and written language over and above concerns such as the structure of the clause or sentence. In this brief introduction we have looked at just some ways of analysing speech and writing and just some aspects of those particular models we have chosen to highlight. There is of course a lot more to look at. For example, we have not considered the big question of discourse in its social setting. In subsequent chapters we shall return to this and mention the Hallidayan model of language as social action (see Halliday 1978), looking at types of meaning in discourse and their relationship with the notion of *register*, the linguistic features of the text that reflect the social context in which it is produced. This and further discussion of the approaches outlined here will form the background to a reassessment of the basics of language teaching as they are conventionally understood: the *levels* of language description (grammar, lexis and phonology) and the *skills* of language use (reading, writing, listening and speaking). There will also be suggestions concerning teaching materials and procedures whenever it seems that discourse analysis has some direct bearing on these matters.

Further reading

Coulthard (1985) is an indispensable introduction to discourse analysis, as is Stubbs (1983).

Brown and Yule (1983) is a thorough and detailed survey, but is harder going because of its less obvious structure.

Van Dijk's (1985) collection of papers covers a vast range of areas within discourse analysis; the introduction sets the scene, and the papers can be dipped into according to area of interest.

Levinson (1983), although concerned with the broader field of 'pragmatics', provides a balanced criticism of the British, exchange-structure school as against the American conversation analysis.

G. Cook (1989) is a more recent book at an introductory level.

For the original Birmingham discourse model, Sinclair and Coulthard (1975) is still unsurpassed, though extensions and modifications as described in Coulthard and Montgomery (1981) and Sinclair and Brazil (1982) should also be consulted.

Further extensions and modifications are to be found in Carter and Burton (1982), Francis and Hunston (1987), and, specifically on the follow-up move, Hewings (1987).

More introductory reading on acts and communicative functions, as well as on speech and writing may be found in Riley (1985).

Schenkein (1978) is a seminal collection of American conversational analysis.

On written text, Halliday and Hasan (1976) is essential for the notion of cohesion, De Beaugrande and Dressler (1981), though difficult in places, expands on the procedural approach, while Winter (1977 and 1978) and Hoey (1983) are the best works for the clause-relational model.

Hewings and McCarthy (1988) offer a summary of the clause-relational approach with some pedagogical applications.

Halliday (1978) contains much discussion on language in its social setting.

Widdowson (1979), De Beaugrande (1980), Van Dijk (1980), Neubauer (1983) and Tannen (1984) are all useful sources on cohesion/coherence.

Reddick (1986) argues for the importance of personal interpretation in the analysis of text structure.

2   Discourse analysis and grammar

'All right, so far,' said the King;
and he went on muttering over
the verses to himself. '"We
know it to be true" – that's the
jury, of course – "If she should
push the matter on" – that must
be the Queen – "What would
become of you?" – What,
indeed?'

**Lewis Carroll: *Alice's Adventures
in Wonderland***

2.1   Introduction

In this chapter we shall start on familiar ground. Much of the discussion
will use terms that are common in language teaching: *clause, pronoun,
adverbial, conjunction,* and so on, and we shall be using them in familiar
ways. But we shall attempt to relate them to a probably less familiar set of
terms: *theme, rheme, reference, anaphoric* and so on, in order to make the
link between grammar and discourse. Nothing we shall say will undermine
the importance of grammar in language teaching; on the contrary, this
chapter takes as a basic premise that without a command of the rich and
variable resources of the grammar offered by a language such as English,
the construction of natural and sophisticated discourse is impossible. But
we shall be arguing that structuring the individual utterance, clause and
sentence, structuring the larger units of discourse and creating textual
coherence are ultimately inseparable. We shall be looking at what discourse
analysts can tell us about contextualised uses of structures and grammatical
items, and considering whether grammar teaching needs to broaden or shift
its orientations to cover significant areas at present under-represented in
grammar teaching. We begin by looking at grammatical cohesion, the
surface marking of semantic links between clauses and sentences in written
discourse, and between utterances and turns in speech.

2.2 Grammatical cohesion and textuality

Spoken and written discourses display grammatical connexions between individual clauses and utterances. For our purposes, these grammatical links can be classified under three broad types: *reference* (or *co-reference*; see Brown and Yule 1983: 192), *ellipsis/substitution*, and *conjunction*.

2.2.1 Reference

Reference items in English include pronouns (e.g. *he, she, it, him, they,* etc.), demonstratives (*this, that, these, those*), the article *the*, and items like *such a*. A complete list is given in Halliday and Hasan (1976: 37–9).

The opening lines of a famous English novel, *Jude the Obscure*, by Thomas Hardy, show different types of reference at work:

(2.1)   *The* schoolmaster was leaving *the* village, and *everybody* seemed sorry. *The* miller at Cresscombe lent *him the* small white tilted cart and horse to carry *his* goods to *the* city of *his* destination, about twenty miles off, *such a* vehicle proving of quite sufficient size for *the* departing teacher's effects.

The italicised items *refer*. For the text to be coherent, we assume that *him* in 'lent *him* the small white tilted cart' is *the schoolmaster* introduced earlier; likewise, *his* destination is the schoolmaster's. Referents for *him* and *his* can be confirmed by looking *back* in the text; this is called *anaphoric* reference. *Such a* also links back to *the cart* in the previous sentence. The novel opens with *the* schoolmaster leaving *the* village. Which schoolmaster? Which village? On the previous page of the novel, the two words *At Marygreen* stand alone, so we reasonably assume that *Marygreen* is the name of *the* village, and that the character is (or has been) schoolmaster of that village. We are using more than just the text here to establish referents; the author expects us to share a world with him independent of the text, with typical villages and their populations (*everybody*), their schoolmasters and millers. References to assumed, shared worlds outside of the text are *exophoric* references. Because they are not text-internal, they are not truly cohesive, but because they are an equally important part of the reader/listener's active role in creating coherence, they will be included in our general discussion of factors which contribute to 'textuality', that is, the feeling that something is a text, and not just a random collection of sentences.

Now consider this example of reference with the pronoun *they*:

(2.2)   They pressed round him in ragged fashion to take their money. Andy, Dave, Phil, Stephen, Bob.

(Graham Swift, *The Sweet Shop Owner*, Penguin Books Limited, 1983: 13)

In this particular text, neither anaphoric nor exophoric reference supplies the identity of *they*; we have to read on, and are given their identities in the second sentence. Where referents are withheld in this way, we can talk of cataphoric reference. This is a classic device for engaging the reader's attention; referents can be withheld for quite long stretches of text.

LOOKING BACKWARD: ANAPHORIC REFERENCE

Exercises which involve looking back in texts to find the referent of, for example, a pronoun, have long been common in first and second language teaching and testing. Usually items such as *he/she* or *them* can be decoded without major difficulty; other items such as *it* and *this* may be more troublesome because of their ability to refer to longer stretches of text and diffuse propositions not necessarily paraphrasable by any direct quotation from the text. Problems can also arise where lower-level learners are so engaged in decoding the individual utterance, clause or sentence that they lose sight of the links back to earlier ones. But evidence of *local* difficulties hindering global processing at given points in the unfolding discourse should not automatically be read as inherent difficulties with processing at the discourse level. Only if intervention at the local level fails to solve larger processing problems might we begin to consider intervention in the form of training 'discourse skills' to build up the sort of pragmatic awareness as to how references are decoded, which must, after all, be the basis of effective reading/listening in the learner's first language too. Nonetheless, there will always be cases where first language skills are lacking or undeveloped, and teachers may find themselves having to intervene to make up such short-comings. That, however, is a problem area beyond the purview of this book.

Grammar teachers have long been aware of recurring interference factors with pronouns and reference, such as the Japanese tendency to confuse *he* and *she*, the Spanish tendency to confuse *his* and *your*, and so on, and there is not much discourse analysts can say to ease those evergreen problems. What can be (and often is not) directly taught about a system such as that of English is the different ways of referring to the discourse itself by use of items such as *it*, *this* and *that*, which do not seem to translate in a one-to-one way to other languages, even where these are closely cognate (cf. German, French, Spanish). Some examples of how reference items refer to segments of discourse follow in (2.3–5); the first is one given by Halliday and Hasan (1976: 52):

(2.3)   It rained day and night for two weeks. The basement flooded and
           everything was under water. *It* spoilt all our calculations.

Here *it* seems to mean 'the events of two weeks', or 'the fact that it rained and flooded', that is, the situation as a whole rather than any one specified entity in that situation.

Reader activity 1 🖛⛬

What does *it* refer to in these short extracts: a noun phrase in the text, or a situation?

1. A pioneering 'school-based management' program in Miami–Dade County's 260 schools has also put some budget, salary and personnel decisions in the hands of local councils, composed largely of teachers. '*It*'s a recognition that our voices and input are important,' says junior highschool teacher Ann Colman.

    (*Newsweek*, 17 October 1988: 23)

2. Like the idea of deterring burglars with a big, ferocious hound – but can't stand dogs? For around £45 you can buy an automatic dog barking unit – Guard God, or the Boston Bulldog, both available by mail order from catalogues like the ones you're sent with credit card statements. You plug *it* in near the front door and its built-in microphone detects sharp noises.

    (*Which?* October 1988: 485)

Matters become more complicated when we look at *this* and *that* in discourse:

(2.4)   You may prefer to vent your tumble dryer permanently through a non-opening window. *This* isn't quite as neat, since the flexible hose remains visible, but *it* does save knocking a hole in the wall.

(*Which?* October 1988: 502)

(2.5)   Only a handful of satellite orbits are known to be changing. Such changes are usually subtle and can be detected only by long-term observations. One exception is the orbit of Neptune's large moon Triton, which is shrinking quite rapidly. *That* is because it circles Neptune in the direction opposite to the planet's revolution, generating strong gravitational friction.

(*New Scientist*, 23 January 1986: 33)

These are written examples, but speech abounds in the same choices of *it*, *this* and *that*. Surprisingly, conventional grammars do not give satisfactory descriptions of such usage (e.g. see Quirk *et al.* 1985: 868). Discourse analysts have touched upon the area (see Thavenius 1983: 167–9), and the insights of different analysts have a certain amount in common.

It is helpful, for a start, to return to the notion of discourse segments as functional units, rather than concentrating on sentences (or turns in speech), and to see the writer/speaker as faced with a number of strategic choices as to how to relate segments to one another and how to present them to the receiver. A simple example is Linde's (1979) investigations into how people reacted when asked to describe their apartments. She observed that there were significant differences in the distribution of *it* and *that* in people's descriptions. One room or area was always a current 'focus of attention', i.e. was the entity being talked about, the *topic* of any particular moment; pronominal references to the focus of attention were almost always made with *it*, while references across different focuses of attention used *that*:

(2.6)   And the living room was a very small room with two windows that wouldn't open and things like that. And *it* looked nice. *It* had a beautiful brick wall.

(2.7)   You entered into a tiny little hallway and the kitchen was off *that*.

Extract (2.6) is all within one focus of attention (the living room), while (2.7) refers across from one focus (the kitchen) to another (the hallway).

This is not to say Linde's conclusions solve the whole of the discourse reference problem; it is simply to make the point that many unanswered grammatical questions can be resolved at the discourse level, and that much good discourse analysis recognises the links between discourse organisation and grammatical choice. As such, discourse-level investigations are often invaluable reading for teachers looking for answers to grammatical problems.

An example of an error in discourse reference from a non-native speaker may help us to resolve the still unconcluded issue of *it*, *this* and *that*. The writer is giving a chapter-by-chapter summary of his university dissertation, starting with the introduction:

(2.8)   Introduction: It traces the developments in dialectology in recent years.

          (Author's data 1989)

English here demands '*This* traces ...' or the full noun phrase *The Introduction* repeated. Neither *it* nor *that* will do. It seems that *it* can only be used when an entity has already been marked as the focus of attention, usually by using a deictic word (such as *a*, *the*, or *my*, or *this/that*), so that versions such as (2.9–11) are acceptable:

(2.9)   The introduction is lengthy: it covers 56 pages.

(2.10)   This introduction is fine. It is brief and precise.

(2.11)   My introduction was too short. It had to be rewritten.

We can now conclude that *it* cannot be used to refer back to an entity unless it is already the focus of attention, but *this*, as in the corrected version of

(2.8), *can* make an entity into the focus of attention and create new foci of attention as the discourse progresses. *That*, as in Linde's explanation, can be used to refer across foci of attention, and, as is suggested by (2.5), can push a proposition out of central focus and marginalise it in some way.

The discussion of this one question of discourse reference has been lengthy in order to exemplify the type of approach discourse analysts take to grammar, in that they look for patterned recurrences across different data and try to relate the separate levels of analysis in a meaningful way. Individual grammatical choices are seen as significant in the staging and organisation of the discourse as a whole, and not just as local problems to be resolved within the bounds of the capital letter and the full stop. And the same approach is valid not only for questions of reference, as we shall see when we look at word order and tense and aspect choices.

Reader activity 2 🗝

Collect some examples of *it*, *this* and *that* used as discourse reference items after the fashion of the examples discussed in this section (any English-language newspaper should provide plenty of data). Do they fit the general conclusion drawn above as to their usage in discourse? If not, try to 'rewrite' the rule.

LOOKING OUTWARD: EXOPHORIC REFERENCE

We have mentioned the possibility of referring 'outward' from texts to identify the referents of reference items when backward or anaphoric reference does not supply the necessary information. Outward, or exophoric reference often directs us to the immediate context, as when someone says 'leave *it* on *the* table please' about a parcel you have for them. Sometimes, the referent is not in the immediate context but is assumed by the speaker/writer to be part of a shared world, either in terms of knowledge or experience. In English the determiners often act in this way:

(2.12)   *The government* are to blame for unemployment.

(2.13)   She was using one of *those strimmers* to get rid of the weeds.

It would be odd if someone replied to (2.12) with the question 'Which government?'. It is assumed by the speaker that the hearer will know which one, usually 'our government' or 'that of the country we are in / are talking about'. The same sort of exophoric reference is seen in phrases such as *the Queen*, *the Pope*, *the army*, and in sentences such as 'We always take *the* car since we can just put *the* kids, *the* dog and *the* luggage into it.' A learner whose L1 has no exact equivalent to English *the* may need to have this central use of the article taught explicitly. On the other hand, speakers of languages with extended use of definite articles to cover general nouns in situations where these would not be marked as definite in English sometimes produce utterances which, to the English ear, seem to be making exophoric reference, such as 'Do you like the folk music?' when no music is to be heard (cf. 'Do you like folk music?').

Exophoric reference (especially in the press) is often to a 'world of discourse' connected with the discourse of the moment, but not directly. British popular newspaper headlines sometimes make references such as '*That* dress. Queen scolds Princess Di'. Here the reader is assumed to have followed certain stories in the press, and the reference is like a long-range anaphoric one, to a text separated in time and space from the present. Native speakers often have difficulties with such references even if they have only been away from the papers and radio or television for a week or two; the foreign learner may experience even greater disorientation.

An example of a text referring to such an assumed shared world is extract (2.14), which talks of '*the* entire privatisation programme'; readers are assumed to know that this refers to the British government's sell-off in 1989 of the entire public water service into private hands:

(2.14)   Eighty per cent of Britain's sewage works are breaking pollution
         laws, according to a report to be published this week.
             The cost of fulfilling a government promise to clean them up will
         run into billions, and put *the entire privatisation programme* at risk.

         (*The Observer*, 4 December 1988: 3)

Exophoric references will often be to a world shared by sender and receiver of the linguistic message, regardless of cultural background, but equally often, references will be culture-bound and outside the experiences of the language learner (e.g. British references to *the City*, *the Chancellor*, and so on). In these cases the learner will need to consult some source of encyclopaedic information or ask an informant. This aspect of language learning is a gradual familiarisation with the cultural context of L2. Language teachers and materials writers will need to monitor the degree of cultural exophoric references in texts chosen for teaching to ensure that the referential burden is not too great.

Reader activity 3 ⚡⚷

Find exophoric references in the following extract and consider whether they are likely to create cultural difficulties for a learner of English.

King trial jury adjourns with transcript

Dennis Johnson

THE JURY in the trial of three people accused of conspiring to murder the Northern Ireland Secretary, Mr Tom King, adjourned last night after more than seven hours' deliberation.

They spent the night within Winchester crown court buildings, where the trial is taking place. Five hours after they retired to consider their verdict, the judge recalled them to answer a question they had put to him in a note.

That question was "Can we convict if we think the information collecting was for several purposes, or does the one whole aim have to be murder?"

The judge said the Crown had to prove an agreement to murder so that the jury was sure. It was not sufficient to prove it as a possibility or probability, but it must be proved beyond reasonable doubt.

(from *The Guardian*, 27 October 1988, p. 20)

Exophoric reference directs the receiver 'out of' the text and into an assumed shared world. This idea of *a shared world* overlaps with the idea of a shared world built up by sender and receiver as any discourse unfolds, and for this reason, some linguists see no real distinction between anaphoric and exophoric reference (e.g. Brown and Yule 1983: 201), since both proceed on the basis of an assumption by the sender that the receiver is, at any point in time, availed of all the knowledge necessary to decode any reference items. But for practical purposes the distinction may be a useful one to retain as it enables us to evaluate to what extent any discourse is self-contained, supplying its referents internally, or to what extent it depends heavily on external, culture-specific real-world referents.

LOOKING FORWARD: CATAPHORIC REFERENCE

Consider these opening lines of a news article:

(2.15)   She claims Leo Tolstoy as a distant cousin. Her grandfather was
           Alexei Tolstoy – the famous 'Red Count' who sided with Lenin's
           revolutionaries. Now, Tatyana Tolstaya has put pen to paper, in her
           case to demonstrate that someone from the family can write
           compactly. In her stories of ten to twelve typewritten pages, 'I

somehow try to show the whole life of a person from birth to death,' she says.

(*Newsweek*, 21 September 1987: 12)

We do not establish who *she* is until the second sentence. Forward-looking or cataphoric reference of this kind often involves pronouns but it can involve other reference items too, such as the definite article:

(2.16)   *The* trip would hardly have been noteworthy, except for *the* man who made it. In mid-July a powerful American financier flew to Mexico City for a series of talks with high-level government officials, including President Miguel de la Madrid and his finance minister, Gustavo Petricioli.

(*Newsweek*, 21 September 1987: 44)

Both examples of cataphoric reference were found in the same issue of *Newsweek*, which underlines the most characteristic function of cataphoric reference: to engage and hold the reader's attention with a 'read on and find out' message. In news stories and in literature, examples of cataphoric reference are often found in the opening sentences of the text.

Reader activity 4 🔑

Identify the cataphoric reference item and its referent in this extract:

It has often been compared to New Orleans's Mardi Gras as an outdoor celebration. Certainly New York's Mulberry Street and surrounding blocks have been as crowded over the last few days as Royal and Bourbon Streets in the French Quarter are for the Mardi Gras. More than three million people are estimated to have celebrated the 61st annual Feast of the San Gennaro down in Greenwich Village since it began on Thursday.

(*The Guardian*, 15 September 1987: 23)

Cataphoric reference is the reverse of anaphoric reference and is relatively straightforward, but language learners may lack awareness or confidence to put it into use in constructing texts, and may need to have the feature explicitly taught or exercised. There is, too, the danger of its overuse or its use in unnatural contexts. As always, it is a question of training the learner to observe features of language above sentence level where these might not necessarily be automatically transferred from L1, especially since, in English, reference often involves the definite article and demonstratives, which do not translate easily into many other languages.

2.2.2 Ellipsis and substitution

Ellipsis is the omission of elements normally required by the grammar which the speaker/writer assumes are obvious from the context and therefore need not be raised. This is not to say that every utterance which is not fully explicit is elliptical; most messages require some input from the context to make sense of them. Ellipsis is distinguished by the *structure* having some 'missing' element. If two people have to stack and label a pile of items and one says to the other 'you label and I'll stack', the fact that *label* and *stack* are usually transitive verbs requiring an object in the surface structure is suspended because the context 'supplies' the object. Another way of saying this is, of course, that structures are only fully realised when they need to be, and that ellipsis is a speaker choice made on a pragmatic assessment of the situation, not a compulsory feature when two clauses are joined together.

We shall concentrate here on the type of ellipsis where the 'missing' element is retrievable verbatim from the surrounding text, rather in the way that anaphoric and cataphoric references are, as opposed to exophoric references. For example:

(2.17)   The children will carry the small boxes, the adults the large ones.

where 'will carry' is supplied from the first clause to the second. This type of main-verb ellipsis is anaphoric; in English we would not expect:

(2.18)   *The children the small boxes, the adults will carry the large ones.

though some kind of analogous structure does seem possible in Japanese (see Hinds 1982: 19 and 48). Ellipsis as a notion is probably a universal feature of languages, but the grammatical options which realise it in discourse may vary markedly. For instance, English *does* have the kind of cataphoric ellipsis suggested by our rejected example (2.18), but usually only in front-placed subordinate clauses (see Quirk *et al.* 1985: 895):

(2.19)   If you could, I'd like you to be back here at five thirty.

English has broadly three types of ellipsis: nominal, verbal and clausal. Nominal ellipsis often involves omission of a noun headword:

(2.20)   Nelly liked the green tiles; myself I preferred the blue.

The Romance and Germanic languages have this kind of nominal ellipsis and it should not present great difficulties to speakers of those languages learning English.

Ellipsis within the verbal group may cause greater problems. Two very common types of verbal-group ellipsis are what Thomas (1987) calls *echoing* and *auxiliary contrasting*. Echoing repeats an element from the verbal group:

(2.21)   A: *Will* anyone be waiting?
            B: Jim *will*, I should think.

Contrasting is when the auxiliary changes:

(2.22)   A: *Has* she remarried?
            B: No, but she *will* one day, I'm sure.

Thomas also makes the point that in English, varying degrees of ellipsis are possible within the same verbal group:

(2.23)   A: Should any one have been told?
            B: John | should.
                    | should have.
                    | should have been.

These variants are not directly translatable to other languages and will have to be learnt.

With clausal ellipsis in English, individual clause elements may be omitted; especially common are subject-pronoun omissions ('doesn't matter', 'hope so', 'sorry, can't help you', etc.). Whole stretches of clausal components may also be omitted:

(2.24)   He said he would take early retirement as soon as he could and he has.

For this type of sentence, many languages will require at the very least some kind of substitute for the main verb and an object pronoun such as to produce a form roughly equivalent to 'He said he would take early retirement as soon as he could and he *has done it.*'

Ellipsis not only creates difficulties in learning what structural omissions are permissible, but also does not seem to be readily used even by proficient learners in situations where native speakers naturally resort to it (see Scarcella and Brunak 1981).

Reader activity 5 🗝

Identify examples of ellipsis in these extracts:

1. Most students start each term with an award cheque. But by the time accommodation and food are paid for, books are bought, trips taken home and a bit of social life lived, it usually looks pretty emaciated.

    (Advertisement for Barclays Bank, *University of Birmingham Bulletin*, 5 December 1988: 5)

2. 'You like watching children . . . ?' her tone seemed to say: 'You're like a child yourself.'
    'Yes. Don't you?' His cheek was full of cheese sandwich. She

didn't answer; only looked at the swings with anxiety.

'I sometimes wish,' he said, trying hard to empty his mouth, 'I could join in myself.'

'But you wouldn't?'

'Why not?'

He saw the sudden challenge in her eyes. And was that a smile somewhere in that held-aloft face?

'Well, if you feel that way . . . ?'

' — why *don't* you?'

'Why don't I?'

(Graham Swift, *The Sweet Shop Owner*, Penguin Books Limited, 1986: 27)

Other aspects of ellipsis that are difficult for learners occur in the area where ellipsis overlaps with what is often treated under the *grammar of coordination* (e.g. 'goats' milk and (goats') cheese', 'he fired and (he) missed the target', etc.). Once again, specific rules of realisation may not overlap between languages.

Substitution is similar to ellipsis, in that, in English, it operates either at nominal, verbal or clausal level. The items commonly used for substitution in English are:

One(s): I offered him a seat. He said he didn't want one.

Do: Did Mary take that letter? She might have done.

So/not: Do you need a lift? If so, wait for me; if not, I'll see you there.

Same: She chose the roast duck; I chose the same.

Most learners practise and drill these items in sentence-level grammar exercises. They are not easily and directly translatable to other languages. Many common, everyday substitutions tend to be learnt idiomatically (e.g. responses such as 'I think/hope so'). While it is easy to formulate basic rules for substitution, at more advanced levels of usage, subtleties emerge that may be more difficult to explain and present. For example, there are restrictions on reduced forms which might otherwise cause stress to fall on the substitute *do*, which is normally never prominent when it stands alone, as opposed to auxiliary *do* in ellipsis, which can be stressed (e.g. 'Did you win?' 'Yes, I DID!'):

(2.25)   A: Will you unlock the gate?
         B: I HAVE done already.
            * I've DONE already.

Where the speaker does wish to give prominence to the substitute *do*, then *so* is used as well:

(2.26)   I went to lock the gate. When I got there, I found somebody had already DONE so.

Our examples of ellipsis and substitution have included a number of spoken exchanges. This is because ellipsis and substitution assume a lot from the context; they proceed on the basis that omitted and substituted elements are easily recoverable, and are therefore natural in speech situations where a high degree of contextual support is available. We shall return to them briefly in section 5.9, when we discuss what constitutes natural speech.

It is sometimes difficult to separate the various types of cohesion, and it may seem questionable at times why linguists separate such words as the pronoun *it* and the substitute *one*. There are reasons for such categorisations: for example, substitutes can be modified ('a red one', 'the one in the corner') and as such are true substitution, while pronouns, unable to be modified in this way, (* 'a red it', * 'the it in the corner') *co-refer* but do not really *substitute* for noun phrases. However, in language teaching, there may be good reasons to bring different categories together, for instance, to contrast backward reference to an indefinite antecedent ('Do you need a pencil? Yes, I need one.') with reference to a definite antecedent ('Do you need the pencil? Yes, I need it.').

Reader activity 6 ⚏—ᕛ

The sentence below occurred in a letter of reference for someone applying for a job, written by a non-native speaker. What mistake has the writer made, and what explanation might a language teacher offer to help the writer avoid the error in future?

> If you require further information on the applicant, I would be pleased to do so.

(Author's data 1989)

2.2.3 *Conjunction*

We include conjunction here in our discussion of grammatical contributions to textuality even though it is somewhat different from reference, ellipsis and substitution. A conjunction does not set off a search backward or forward for its referent, but it does presuppose a textual sequence, and signals a relationship between segments of the discourse.

Discourse analysts ask the same sorts of questions about conjunctions as they do about other grammatical items: what roles do they play in creating discourse, do the categories and realisations differ from language to language, how are they distributed in speech and writing, what restrictions on their use are there which are not reflected purely through sentence analysis, and what features of their use are inadequately explicated in conventional grammars?

In fact it is not at all easy to list definitively all the items that perform the conjunctive role in English. Single-word conjunctions merge into phrasal and clausal ones, and there is often little difference between the linking of two clauses by a single-word conjunction, a phrasal one, or a lexical item somewhere else in the clause, a fact Winter (1977) has pointed out. For example, (2.27–30) signal the cause–consequence relation in several ways:

(2.27)   He was insensitive to the group's needs. *Consequently* there was a lot of bad feeling.   (single word conjunction)

(2.28)   He was insensitive to the group's needs. *As a consequence* there was a lot of bad feeling.   (adverbial phrase as conjunction)

(2.29)   *As a consequence of* his insensitivity to the group's needs, there was a lot of bad feeling.   (adverbial phrase plus nominalisation)

(2.30)   The bad feeling was *a consequence of* his insensitivity to the group's needs.   (lexical item within the predicate of the clause)

There are clearly differences in the way the speaker/writer has decided to package the information here. Note how (2.29) and (2.30) enable the information to be presented as one sentence, and how (2.30) enables the front-placing of 'bad feeling', a feature we shall return to in section 2.3 below. A true discourse grammar would examine the options for using 'X is a consequence of Y', as opposed to 'Y occurred; as a consequence, X occurred'. We would almost certainly find ourselves in the realm of information structure and the speaker/writer's assessment of what needed to be brought into focus at what point, and so on (see the discussion of theme and rheme below).

Halliday (1985: 302–9) offers a scheme for the classification of conjunctive relations and includes phrasal types as well as single-word everyday items such as *and*, *but*, *or*, etc. Here is a simplified list based on Halliday's three category headings of *elaboration*, *extension* and *enhancement*:

Type	Sub-types	Examples
elaboration	apposition	in other words
	clarification	or rather
extension	addition	and/but
	variation	alternatively
enhancement	spatio-temporal	there/previously
	causal-conditional	consequently/in that case

The full list appears in Halliday (1985: 306), and contains over forty conjunctive items; even that is not exhaustive. So the task for the language teacher is not a small one. However, when we look at natural data, especially spoken, we see that a few conjunctions (*and, but, so,* and *then*) are overwhelmingly frequent. We can also observe the wide use of *and,* where the reader/listener can supply additive, adversative, causal and temporal meanings, depending on contextual information, as in (2.31–34):

(2.31)   She's intelligent. And she's very reliable.   (additive)

(2.32)   I've lived here ten years and I've never heard of that pub.
          (adversative: *but* could substitute)

(2.33)   He fell in the river and caught a chill.   (causal)

(2.34)   I got up and made my breakfast.   (temporal sequence)

Equally, the possible choices of conjunction will often overlap in meaning, with little overall difference:

(2.35)   A: What about this meeting then?
          B: I may go, | and | I may not; it all depends.
                       | or |
                       | but |
                       | though |
                       | then |

Reader activity 7

Look at the text on the opposite page and find conjunctions linking sentences to one another. Using the simplified categorisation below, based on Halliday and Hasan (1976), can you say what type of conjunctive relation is being signalled in each case?

Categories:

1.   *Additive* (e.g. *and, in addition*)
2.   *Adversative* (e.g. *but, however*)
3.   *Causal* (e.g. *because, consequently*)
4.   *Temporal* (e.g. *then, subsequently*)

Wind power. Wave power. Solar power. Tidal power.

Whilst their use will increase they are unlikely to be able to provide large amounts of economic electricity. Generally, the cost of harnessing their power is huge.

However, there is a more practical, reliable and economical way of ensuring electricity for the future.

And that is through nuclear energy.

It's not a new idea, of course. We've been using nuclear electricity for the last 30 years.

In fact, it now accounts for around 20% of Britain's electricity production. And it's one of the cheapest and safest ways to produce electricity we know for the future.

What's more, world supplies of uranium are estimated to last for hundreds of years, which will give us more than enough time to develop alternatives if we need to.

So, while some people might not care about their children's future.

We do.

(Advertisement for British Nuclear Forum from *The Guardian*, 7 October 1988, p. 17)

When we look at a lot of natural spoken data, we find the basic conjunctions *and*, *but*, *so* and *then* much in evidence, and used not just to link individual utterances within turns, but often at the beginning of turns, linking one speaker's turn with another speaker's, or linking back to an earlier turn of the current speaker, or else marking a shift in topic or sub-topic (often with *but*). In this sense, the conjunctions are better thought of as *discourse markers*, in that they organise and 'manage' quite extended stretches of discourse.

An interesting example of differences in data comes from Hilsdon (1988). She compared spoken discourse of adult native speakers, young native speakers and Zambian young adult learners of English, and found in her Zambian subjects almost a complete absence of the use of *and* and *but* in the characteristic ways we have just described that native speakers use them. The reasons for the absence of this otherwise very common feature of spoken discourse in her Zambian data may be cultural, Hilsdon suggests.

Because is very frequent in spoken English, not just to express the cause–effect relationship, but also to express the reason relationship and as a speech-act marker signalling a 'this is why I am saying this' function, as in remarks such as 'this one's better quality, because we'll have to get one that will last', where the quality of the item being discussed is not an effect of the speaker's need to buy durable goods, but is simply a justification for making the remark. Firth (1988) made a study of the distribution of such 'reason' markers in the speech of a mixed native and non-native speaker group. He found that the non-native speakers exclusively used *because* to signal the reason/justification relation, while the native speakers varied the signal, using *because*, *'cos*, *like* and *see*, as in this extract from a conversation about smoking in public places:

(2.36) A: Once you start infringing upon the benefits of the other people, that's
        when your personal right is lost . . . just *like*, y'know, you have
        rights but yet y'know you can't kill anybody . . . *because* obviously
        it's infringing upon somebody else's rights . . . you don't need a
        majority for something to go wrong, you only need a small minority
        . . . *see*, that's where I mean that's just not right . . . *'cos* smoke just
        fills the room.

    (Firth 1988)

Differences in performance data of these kinds are often the reason why even quite advanced-learner output can seem unnatural. One of the major contributions of discourse analysis has been to emphasise the analysis of real data, and the significance in communicative terms of small words such as common everyday markers. In previous linguistic approaches these were too often dismissed as unimportant features of 'performance' which distracted from the business of describing underlying 'competence'.

Reader activity 8 🔑

Consider the following conversational extract from the point of view of the use of common, everyday conjunctions. What roles do they play in organising and managing the discourse?

> (A and B have been recounting a series of stories to C about getting lost while driving.)
>
> A: And another time, I forget where the village was, but there was a
>   sharp turn at the end of this village, and we says to him 'You turn
>   left here', so he turned left, into a school yard.
> B: Up a road into a school yard . . . ⌈ they were all following me.
> A: ⌊ it wasn't so bad that, but they
>   all followed behind us you see.
> B: Them that were behind me followed me.
> C: Yeah.
> B: See I should have gone on another ⌈ twenty yards.
> A: ⌊ But it was getting back
>   into the traffic stream that was the difficulty.
> B: I should have gone a few yards further on and then turned left.
> C: Aye, aye.
> B: There's a T-road.
> A: Oh.
> B: And you see with them saying 'turn left'.
> C: Yeah (laughs).
>
> (Author's data 1989)

In this section we have considered devices under a general heading of grammatical cohesion and textuality. Other grammatical choices at the clause level have implications for the organisation of the overall discourse, not least the *ordering* of elements in clauses and sentences, and it is to this we now turn.

2.3   Theme and rheme

Most learners, when learning the grammar of a foreign language, spend time assimilating the structure of clauses in that language, i.e. where subjects, objects and adverbials are placed in relation to the verb, and what options are available for rearranging the most typical sequences. Discourse analysts are interested in the implications of these different structural options for the creation of text, and, as always, it is from the examination of natural data that patterns of use are seen to emerge. Some of the structural options frequently found in natural data are ignored or under-played in language teaching (especially those found in spoken data, which are often dismissed as degraded or bad 'style'), probably owing to the continued dominance of standards taken from the written code. If the desire is to be faithful to data, grammar teaching may have to reorient some of its structural descriptions, while others already dealt with in sentence-level exercises may be adequately covered in traditional teaching and simply adjusted to discourse-oriented approaches.

English is what is often called an 'SVO' language, in that the declarative clause requires a verb at its centre, a subject before it and any object after it. This is simply a labelling device which enables comparisons to be made with declarative realisations in different languages, some of which will be 'VSO' or 'SOV' languages. This pattern is often recast in English, not least in interrogative structures, where the verbal group is split by the subject ('*Does* she *like* cats?'), and in cases where the object is brought forward:

(2.37)   *The Guardian*, Joyce reads.   OSV   *Object-fronted*

There are in English a variety of ways in which the basic clause elements of *subject, verb, complement/object, adverbial* can be rearranged by putting different elements at the *beginning* of the clause, as illustrated in (2.37) to (2.42). These ways of bringing different elements to the front are called *fronting devices.*

(2.38)   Sometimes Joyce reads *The Guardian.*
          ASVO   *Adverbial-fronted*

(2.39)   It's *The Guardian* Joyce reads.
          It + be + C/O + SV   *It-theme*, or *cleft* (*The Guardian* here seems to
          operate simultaneously as complement of *is* and as object of *reads*)

(2.40)   What Joyce reads is *The Guardian.*
            Wh- + SV + *be* + C/O   *Wh-pseudo-cleft*

(2.41)   She reads *The Guardian,* Joyce.
            S(pronoun) VOS(noun)   *Right-displaced subject*

(2.42)   Joyce, she reads *The Guardian.*
            S(noun) S(pronoun) VO   *Left-displaced subject*

Structures such as (2.41) and (2.42) are far from infrequent in spoken data, but are often, for no obvious reason, not presented in books claiming to describe grammatical options for the learner. Other variations of word order are also present in data, though some types may be rarer (e.g. complement-fronting: 'rich they may be, but I don't think they're happy'). If we look again at our examples from the point of view of how the information in them is presented, we can see how different options enable us to focus on or highlight certain elements: (2.37) seems to be saying something 'about' *The Guardian* rather than 'about' Joyce; (2.41) and (2.42) seem to be telling us something 'about' Joyce. This 'aboutness' is the sort of notion discourse analysts are concerned with, for it is a speaker/writer choice made independently of the propositional content of the message; the speaker/writer decides how to 'stage' the information, where to start, so to speak, in presenting the message.

In English, what we decide to bring to the *front* of the clause (by whatever means) is a signal of what is to be understood as the *framework* within which what we want to say is to be understood. The rest of the clause can then be seen as transmitting 'what we want to *say* within this framework'. Items brought to front-place in this way we shall call the *themes* (or *topics*) of their clauses. In what has been called the Prague School of linguistics, the relationship of the theme to the rest of the sentence is viewed as part of *communicative dynamism*, that is the assessment of the extent to which each element contributes to the development of the communication (see Firbas 1972). Alternatively, the theme can be seen as the 'point of departure' of the message (Halliday 1985: 38). For the moment, we shall take as the theme of a clause the subject noun-phrase, or, if this is not initial, then we shall include whatever comes before it. It seems that first position in the clause is important in many of the world's languages, and that creating a theme in the clause is a universal feature, though its realisations may vary from language to language.

Reader activity 9 🔑

Check that you are familiar with the devices for varying word order listed above in examples (2.37–42) by subjecting these two sentences to as many of them as possible (an example is given):

1. Bob takes the children out every Saturday.
   Example: Bob, he takes the children out every Saturday. (left displacement)

2. The gardener wants to cut down those bushes this spring.

We now turn to the relationship between these in-clause structures and the construction of text. There are clearly restrictions on where and when these devices may be used when they occur in real discourse. Both (2.43) and (2.44) sound odd:

(2.43)   Q: What time did you leave the building?
          A: What I did at five thirty was leave the building.

(2.44)   Dear Joan,
          Me, I'm sitting here at my desk writing to you. What's outside my window is a big lawn surrounded by trees and it's a flower bed that's in the middle of the lawn. When it was full of daffodils and tulips was in the spring. Here you'd love it. It's you who must come and stay sometime; what we've got is plenty of room.
                    Love, Sally

(2.43) is peculiar because 'leaving the building' is already 'given' in the question; it is therefore odd that it should be 'announced' again in the answer. (2.44) contains a string of grammatically well-formed sentences but it is highly unlikely that such a welter of low-frequency clause patterns would occur in one small piece of text. Moreover, it sounds as if the postcard writer is answering questions nobody has actually ever asked, such as 'Isn't it a pond that's in the middle of the lawn?' 'No, it's a flower bed that's . . .', or else implicit contrasts are being suggested without any apparent motivation: '*here* you'd love it', as opposed to 'somewhere where you might hate it'. Let us try getting rid of all the fronting devices and rewriting our postcard with subjects initial in every clause:

(2.45)   Dear Joan,
          I'm sitting here at my desk writing to you. A big lawn surrounded by trees is outside my window and a flower bed is in the middle of the lawn. It was full of daffodils and tulips in the spring. You'd love it here. You must come and stay sometime; we've got plenty of room.
                    Love, Sally

We probably now feel that the text is bland, a sort of flat landscape in which each bit of information is doled out without any overall sense of direction or organisation, and with equal weight given to all the elements of the message. Language teachers might recognise in this jejune version some of the characteristics of low-level learners' early attempts at letter- or essay-writing, hampered by impoverished grammatical resources, or the lack of confidence to transfer features from L1. What is missing from our postcard are strategic decisions to 'stage' the information and to put it into a discourse framework with the foregrounding of certain elements, such as is found in natural discourse. A third version, with discriminating use of fronting, seems more natural:

(2.46)   Dear Joan,
           I'm sitting here at my desk writing to you. Outside my window is a
           big lawn surrounded by trees, and in the middle of the lawn is a
           flower bed. It was full of daffodils and tulips in the spring. You'd
           love it here. You must come and stay sometime; we've got plenty of
           room.
                                                                   Love, Sally

In any spatial description of this kind, spatial orientation of the reader/ listener is important, and writers/speakers naturally give prominence to this function. The second sentence in (2.46) does this by front-placing location adverbials. The remaining sentences are neutral, with subjects in initial position. Linde and Labov's (1975) data of people describing their apartments also contain frequent front-placings of spatial adverbials, revealing the speakers' staging strategies.

In spoken narratives and anecdotes, speakers will often front-place key orientational features for their listeners. These are most obviously time and place markers ('once upon a time', 'one day', 'then, suddenly', 'at the corner', 'not far from here', etc.), but may also be foregrounding of key participants and information about them felt to be important for the listener. This is particularly noticeable in left-displaced structures, which are extremely common when a participant is being made the focus of attention as a main actor in the subsequent discourse, as in these extracts:

           (The extracts are from anecdotes about coincidences and from ghost
           stories.)

(2.47)   And the fellow who rang up from Spain that night, he's
           coincidence-prone . . .

(2.48)   That couple that we know in Portsmouth, I don't hear of her for
           months, and then, . . .

           (Author's data 1989)

But another version of left-displacement is also common: when one partici-pant is mentioned in the theme-slot, but only to provide a link with a new participant who will take the stage in the story (see (2.49) and (2.50)). The speaker can thus create a new topic or sub-topic framework, by activating different elements of the context, and using the theme-slot is one way of making a subject what we have called the 'focus of attention', the particular topic being addressed at any one time. Here are some examples from data:

(2.49)   One of the men, his wife was a swimming instructor, and she said to me . . .

(2.50)   This friend of mine, her son was in hospital, and he'd had a serious accident, and he . . .

(Author's data 1989)

Concentrating on the themes (or topics) of clauses does not tell us much about the rest of the clause, which may be called the *rheme* or *comment* of the clause. In fact, when we look at themes and rhemes together in connected text, we see further patterns emerging. We can divide our postcard text into themes and rhemes:

theme (topic)	*rheme (comment)*
1. I	'm sitting here . . .
2. Outside my window	is a big lawn . . .
3. In the middle of the lawn	is a flower bed.
4. This bed	was full of daffodils . . .
5. You	'd love it here.
6. You	must come and stay;
7. We	've got plenty of room.

Two different options can be seen to be realised here: (a) the *rheme* of sentence 3 contains an element (the flower bed) which becomes the *theme* of sentence 4; (b) the *theme* of sentence 5 is the same as the theme of sentence 6. These two textual options may be expressed thus:

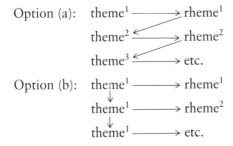

We can see these options at work in real texts:

(2.51)   As you will no doubt have been told, we have our own *photographic club* and darkroom. *The club* is called 'Monomanor' and there is an annual fee of £5. *The money* goes towards replacing any equipment worn out by use, or purchasing new equipment. Monomanor runs an annual *competition* with prizes, judging being done and prizes awarded at the garden party in the summer term. Besides *the competition*, we also have talks and/or film shows during the other terms.

(Advertisement for student camera club; author's data)

c

Extract (2.51) reflects option (a) quite strongly, where elements of rhemes become themes of subsequent sentences (relevant items are in italics). The next extract chooses predominantly option (b):

(2.52)

I am
Claudia Cassaigne
I live
rue Martel, Paris
I work
in the centre of Paris
I like
Classical ballet
English humour
Cooking Chinese food
Drinking Champagne
Keep fit exercises
Tall men with green eyes
Dressing up in the evening

I hate
Being badly dressed
Being broke
My perfume is
Feminine
Light
Very chic
For the evenings
Cavale. C'est Moi

(from *Cosmopolitan*, September 1985, p. 5)

Looking back at the camera club text, we see that sentences 2, 3 and 4 are slightly more complex than was suggested. The rheme of (2) contains *two* elements (*Monomanor* and *£5*) which are taken up as themes in the two separate subsequent sentences, giving us the pattern:

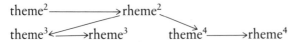

This third option is a hierarchical pattern. For further examples and discussions of theme–rheme patterns see Daneš (1974).

But are these patterns not simply questions of 'style' or 'rhetoric'? In a way, they are, insomuch as they are not truly structural, since no combinations are specifically forbidden by *rule*, and indeed, some of what was traditionally relegated to rag-bag categories such as 'style' has been taken over as the province of discourse analysis. It is hoped that the discussion so far has indicated the importance of thematisation as a means of creating topic frameworks and as an example of audience orientation. Further investigation would probably also discover links between certain patterns of theme and rheme and particular registers (e.g. many advertising texts use the option of returning to the same theme, usually the product name).

Reader activity 10 ⚿

Which pattern(s) of theme and rheme sequencing are predominant in these extracts? Consider too the author's choice in terms of topic frameworks, and the purpose and register of the texts.

1.

Cost of acid cleanup doubles

Fred Pearce

BRITAIN'S privatised electricity industry will face a bill for cleaning up acid pollution from its power stations that is more than double that so far admitted. The cost of meeting an EEC directive to combat acid rain, approved by ministers in June, will approach £3 billion, according to consultants who recently presented a study on strategies to reduce acid pollution to the Department of the Environment (DoE).

The study forms part of a broad review of technologies to combat acid rain, prepared at the request of the DoE by the Fellowship of Engineering.

The author of the study is Philip Comer of Technica, a consultancy. He told a meeting of the British Consultants Bureau in London last week that "with only a modest increase in electrical energy consumption, the DoE targets for pollution abatement will not be met . . . There is a divergence between stated policy and achievable objectives."

(from *New Scientist*, 22 October 1988, p. 29)

2. The brain is our most precious organ – the one above all which allows us to be human.

The brain contains 10 billion nerve cells, making thousands of billions of connections with each other. It is the most powerful data processor we know, but at the same time it is incredibly delicate. As soft as a ripe avocado, the brain has to be encased in the tough bones of the skull, and floats in its own waterbed of fluid. An adult brain weighs over 3lb and fills the skull. It receives one-fifth of the blood pumped out by the heart at each beat.

The brain looks not unlike a huge walnut kernel: it is dome-shaped with a wrinkled surface, and is in two halves joined in the middle. Coming out from the base of the brain like a stalk is the brain stem. This is the swollen top of the spinal cord, which runs on down to our 'tail'. Parts of the brain stem control our most basic functions: breathing, heart beat, waking and sleeping.

(from *The Observer*, 16 October 1988, p. 2)

Patterns of sequencing of theme and rheme are tendencies rather than absolutes. Very few texts (except perhaps highly ritualised ones such as religious litanies) repeat the same thematising patterns endlessly. We have suggested that low-level learners might be trapped in unnatural patterns owing to limited grammatical resources or lack of confidence in a new L2, but most advanced learners are likely to have a good feel for creating topic frameworks and orienting their audience. The grammatical structures that are underplayed in grammar books (e.g. left displacements, object-fronting) may be produced unconsciously by learners, but awareness and monitoring on the part of teachers is necessary to ensure that natural production using the wide resources of the grammar is indeed taking place.

So far, we have concentrated on thematising in clauses, but it should not be forgotten that sequencing choices of clauses within sentences, and sentences within paragraphs are of the same, discourse-related type. For instance, it has been observed that first sentences often tell us what the whole paragraph is *about*, a macro-level front-placing of an element signalling the framework of the message. Such sentences are often called *topic sentences*, and are considered important for skills such as skim-reading. It is often possible, just by reading the first sentence, to state what a paragraph is about (the paragraph theme), though it is not possible to state what the text is *saying* about its theme (the paragraph rheme). However, this does seem to be an oversimplification, and many paragraphs have initial sentences that do *not* tell us what the paragraph is about. Jones and Jones's (1985) study of cleft and pseudo-cleft sentences in discourse shows that the presence of a cleft structure, even if not paragraph-initial, is often a more reliable signal of paragraph topic, and anyway, relatively little is known about why writers make paragraph divisions where they do.

Finally, ideally, we should also consider sentences that contain more than one element other than the subject brought to front place, such as this very sentence you are reading. The first fronted element (*finally*) organises the text sequentially and tells you that the section is coming to a close (a *textual* function); *ideally* signals my attitude towards what I have to say, and has an *interpersonal* function. The next element, *we*, is part of the *content* or *ideational* meaning of the message, or, as Halliday (1985: 56) calls it, the *topical* theme. The unmarked (most frequent) order for complex themes can thus be stated as *textual + interpersonal + ideational*:

Themes	Textual	Interpersonal	Ideational
Examples	moreover	frankly	Joe Smith . . .
	likewise	obviously	burglars . . .
	for instance	personally	I . . .

(Adapted from Halliday 1985: 53–4)

A natural example of this ordering is seen in this sentence from a student essay on language and gender:

(2.53)   Conversely, possibly, females felt more at ease responding to a non-specific female address.

(Author's data 1989)

The notion of theme and how it is realised in English is an area where grammatical structure and discourse function seem most closely allied, and, if discourse analysis is to have an influence on how language is taught, then ways of presenting variations in clause structure in relation to discourse functions may be a good place to start. In the past, emphasis on invented sentences and on writing (in both theoretical and applied linguistics) has led to the relegation to the fringes of some structures found in natural talk. But natural data show that variations of standard SVOA order are much more frequent than might be thought. Furthermore, languages vary in how they deal with thematisation: Japanese has a particle *wa*, widely used to topicalise elements in clauses (Hinds 1986: 157), and Tagalog (the language of the Philippines) apparently topicalises at the *end* of clauses (Creider 1979). Other languages are similar to English; Duranti and Ochs (1979) give examples of left-displacement in Italian speech and discuss its functions in discourse management. Mixed nationality groups of learners may therefore present a variety of problems at various levels, just as is the case in conventional grammar teaching.

2.4 Tense and aspect

A great deal of attention has recently been paid to the relationship between tense–aspect choices and overall discourse constraints. By examining natural data, discourse analysts are able to observe regular correlations between discourse types and the predominance of certain tense and aspect choices in the clause. Equally, the emphasis in discourse analysis on interactive features of discourse such as speaker/writer perspective and standpoint, and the focusing or foregrounding of certain elements of the message, has led to reinterpretations of conventional statements about tense and aspect rules.

An example of the first type of approach is Zydatiss (1986), who looked at a number of text types in English where present perfect is either dominant or in regular contrast with past simple. Zydatiss observed that three basic functions of the present perfect, all under the general heading of *current relevance*, frequently recur over a wide range of text types. He names these functions: (1) conveying 'hot news', (2) expressing experiences, and (3) relating to present effects of changes and accomplishments.

'Hot news' texts are mostly found in broadcast and written news reports, but are also common in everyday speech. An example (taken from British television news) is: 'The government *has announced* a multi-million pound scheme to retrain the unemployed, but union chiefs *have pledged* all-out opposition to it.' This choice of tense and aspect will occur time and time again, and can be tapped as a rich source of illustrative material for language teaching (see for example, Swan and Walter 1990: 50, who use just such news events to illustrate present perfect usage). Letters-to-the-editor and agony-column letters, Zydatiss claims, contain frequent present perfects performing the 'experiences' and 'changes and accomplishments' functions. In hot news texts, present perfect regularly contrasts with past simple in the same text, where the topicalising sentence uses present perfect, while the details of the narrative are in past simple, for example: 'A British firm *has landed* a huge shipping contract in Brazil. The deal *was signed* at a meeting today in London.' Biographical sketches and obituaries are also a source of this shift of tense. Zydatiss lists many text types which seem to have such correlations. The usefulness of such investigations is not that they necessarily tell language teachers anything they did not already know or might conclude from intuition, but that they offer a short-cut to useful data sources and statistical back-up to intuition.

In specialist and academic texts such as scientific articles, correlations are often observable between discourse segments and tense and aspect choices. Medical research articles in journals such as the *British Medical Journal*, for instance, regularly use past simple in the *abstract* section, and shift to predominantly present perfect in the *introduction* section, at the end of which there is a shift back to past simple where the discourse begins its 'narrative' of the particular research experiment reported. Also in academic texts, one finds interesting correlations between the tenses used to cite other authors and the current author's standpoint: one might compare alternative citations such as 'Johnson (1975) suggests/has suggested/suggested/had suggested that . . .'.

Reader activity 11 ⚏

Consider this sentence taken from the *end* of an essay by a learner of English. In what way is her use of tense and aspect inappropriate? How would you correct it and what rule or guideline could you give her regarding tense and aspect in different sections of academic essays?

> *Conclusion*
> In this essay, I try to discuss the different types of information which the matrices give about words. Also some other information which matrices can convey are suggested in the last section.

(Author's data 1989)

A particular day-to-day context worth noting is the telling of stories, jokes and anecdotes. Schiffrin's (1981) data shows regular correlations between discourse segments and tense and aspect choices. Schiffrin considers principally the shifts from 'historic' present (i.e. using the present tense to describe actions and events in the past) to past simple in English oral anecdotes. She takes a model of narrative based on Labov (1972), in which the main elements are *orientation* (establishing time, place and characters), *complicating actions* (the main events that make the story), *resolution* (how the story reaches its end), and *evaluation* (comments on the events). Historic present tense verbs cluster in the *complicating action* segments, and, within those segments, particularly in the *middle* of the segment, and not typically in the initial or final clause. Historic present is also sometimes accompanied by changes from simple to progressive aspect where the time sequence seems to be broken and a particularly strong focus is given to actions. In the following extract, the speaker is recounting a ghost story; note the shifts in tense and aspect at crucial junctures:

(2.54)   A: Not all that long since, perhaps ten years ago, this friend of mine, her son was in hospital, and he'd had a serious accident and he was unconscious for a long time . . . anyway, she went to see him one day and she said 'Has anybody been to see you?', and he says 'No, but a right nice young lady came to see me,' he said, 'she was lovely, she stood at the foot of me bed, you know, she . . . had a little word with me.' Well eventually he came home, and they'd a lot of the family in the house, and Emma, this friend of mine, brought these photographs out, of the family through the years, and, passing them round, and he's looking at them and he said 'Oh! that's that young lady that came to see me when I was in bed.' She'd died when he was born . . . so.

B: Good God.

A: He'd never seen her.

B: No . . . heavens.

(Author's data 1989)

Note how 'he *says*' prefaces the significant event of the appearance of the 'lady'. Historic present occurs again, accompanied by progressive aspect (*he's looking*) at the highest moment of suspense in the tale.

In Schiffrin's data, historic present often occurs in segments where the episodes are understood by the listener as occurring in sequence and in the time-world of the story; therefore, to some extent, the grammatical marking of pastness may be considered redundant. Schiffrin compares these segments of narratives with sports commentaries, recipe commentaries (the speaker describing the process as it happens) and magicians' commentaries on their tricks. The historic present in anecdotes is really an 'internal evaluation device', focusing on the events that really 'make' the story.

The data for tense and aspect we have looked at can all be interpreted in the light of the speaker/writer's perspective and as projections of shifting perspectives. The tenses and aspects do not seem so much strictly bound to time as to issues such as the sender's purpose, the focus on different elements of the message, and the projection of a shared framework within which the receiver will understand the message.

Tense and aspect vary notoriously from language to language and are traditional stumbling-blocks for learners. The classic 'aspect' languages such as the Slavic tongues make choices of *perfective* and *imperfective* aspects which are quite at odds with the English notion of describing past events in terms of 'now-relevance' (present perfect) and 'break with the present' (past simple). However, some features, for example the use of historic present in anecdotes, seem widely distributed across languages (in Europe the Nordic and the Romance languages share this feature). Whether or not such features are transferred by learners without difficulty is another matter, and one worthy of close observation. Certainly in the genre-specific occurrences such as the medical articles discussed above, learners sometimes experience difficulties or show unawareness of the conventions of the genre.

2.5   Conclusion

This chapter has taken a selection of grammatical concepts and has attempted to show how discourse analysis has contributed to our understanding of the relationship between local choices within the clause and sentence and the organisation of the discourse as a whole. When speakers and writers are producing discourse, they are, at the same time as they are busy constructing clauses, monitoring the development of the larger discourse, and their choices at the local level can be seen simultaneously to reflect the concerns of the discourse as an unfolding production, with an audience, whether present or projected. A discourse-oriented approach to grammar would suggest not only a greater emphasis on contexts larger than the sentence, but also a reassessment of priorities in terms of what is taught about such things as word order, articles, ellipsis, tense and aspect, and some of the other categories discussed here.

If grammar is seen to have a direct role in welding clauses, turns and sentences into discourse, what of words themselves? What role does *vocabulary choice* play in the discourse process? It is to this question that we turn next.

Further reading

The most detailed work on grammar above clause level is Halliday (1985), but some prefer to treat this as a reference work rather than as reading.

Monaghan (1987) is an interesting, though sometimes difficult, collection of papers on different aspects of grammar and discourse.

For a detailed description of cohesion in English, Halliday and Hasan (1976) is unsurpassed, though Hasan's (1984) revision of lexical cohesion should also be taken into account.

The room descriptions in Dutch in Ehrich and Koster (1983) contain further examples comparable to Linde's.

Another interesting study of substitution is Jordan (1986).

Ellipsis in conversation is examined in detail in Ricento (1987).

More on expressing cause in conversation may be found in Schiffrin (1985a).

On the question of the significance of front position in the clause in the world's languages, see Fuller and Gundel (1987).

For word-order phenomena in various selected languages, see Givón (1984).

On front-placing in Spanish see Rivero (1980), and for French, see Barnes (1985).

Kies (1988) contains a good discussion on variations of word order in English data.

Discussion of the different theme–rheme patterns can be found in Daneš (1974), and further discussion of theme in P. H. Fries (1983).

For the distribution of theme–rheme patterns in written texts, see Eiler (1986) and Francis (1989).

Topic sentences in paragraphs are discussed by Grellet (1981: 96–8).

A good general survey of different treatments of 'given' and 'new' in relation to theme and rheme may be found in Allerton (1978).

A combined investigation of present progressive, deictic *that* and pronominalisation in spoken technical discourse can be found in Reichman-Adar (1984).

For more on tense in learned citations, see Riddle (1986).

Aspect in the Slavic languages is exemplified in Hopper (1979 and 1982) with reference to Russian discourse.

Aspect and discourse in French is dealt with by Monville-Burston and Waugh (1985) and Waugh and Monville-Burston (1986).

At the more advanced level, the papers in Schopf (1989) on tense in English are worth pursuing.

3 Discourse analysis and vocabulary

'When *I* use a word,' Humpty Dumpty said, in rather a scornful tone, 'it means just what I choose it to mean – neither more nor less.'

'The question is,' said Alice, 'whether you *can* make words mean so many different things.'

Lewis Carroll: *Through the Looking Glass*

3.1 Introduction

Bringing a discourse dimension into language teaching does not by any means imply an abandonment of teaching vocabulary. Vocabulary will still be the largest single element in tackling a new language for the learner and it would be irresponsible to suggest that it will take care of itself in some ideal world where language teaching and learning are discourse-driven. The vocabulary lesson (or part of a lesson) will still have a place in a discourse-oriented syllabus; the challenge is to bring the discourse dimension into vocabulary teaching alongside traditional and recent, more communicative approaches (e.g. Gairns and Redman 1986). Therefore, in this chapter we shall look at research into vocabulary in extended texts in speech and writing and consider if anything can be usefully exploited to give a discourse dimension to vocabulary teaching and vocabulary activities in the classroom. Most are already in agreement that vocabulary should, wherever possible, be taught in context, but context is a rather catch-all term and what we need to do at this point is to look at some of the specific relationships between vocabulary choice, *context* (in the sense of the situation in which the discourse is produced) and *co-text* (the actual text surrounding any given lexical item). The suggestions we shall make will be offered as a supplement to conventional vocabulary teaching rather than as a replacement for it.

3.2   Lexical cohesion

One recent attempt at studying vocabulary patterns above sentence level is
Halliday and Hasan's (1976) description of lexical cohesion. Related
vocabulary items occur across clause and sentence boundaries in written
texts and across act, move and turn boundaries in speech and are a major
characteristic of coherent discourse. The relations between vocabulary
items in texts described by the Halliday–Hasan model are of two principal
kinds: *reiteration* and *collocation*.

It is debatable whether collocation properly belongs to the notion of
lexical cohesion, since collocation only refers to the probability that lexical
items will co-occur, and is not a semantic relation between words. Here,
therefore, we shall consider the term 'lexical cohesion' to mean only exact
repetition of words and the role played by certain basic semantic relations
between words in creating *textuality*, that property of text which distinguishes it from a random sequence of unconnected sentences. We shall
consequently ignore collocational associations across sentence boundaries
as lying outside of these semantic relations.

If lexical reiteration can be shown to be a significant feature of textuality,
then there may be something for the language teacher to exploit. We shall
not suggest that it be exploited simply because it is there, but only if, by
doing so, we can give learners meaningful, controlled practice and the hope
of improving their text-creating and decoding abilities, and providing them
with more varied contexts for using and practising vocabulary.

Reiteration means either restating an item in a later part of the discourse
by direct repetition or else reasserting its meaning by exploiting *lexical
relations*. Lexical relations are the stable semantic relationships that exist
between words and which are the basis of descriptions given in dictionaries
and thesauri: for example, *rose* and *flower* are related by *hyponymy*; *rose* is
a *hyponym* of *flower*. *Eggplant* and *aubergine* are related by *synonymy*
(regardless of the geographical dimension of usage that distinguishes them).
In the following two sentences, lexical cohesion by synonymy occurs:

(3.1)   The meeting commenced at six thirty. But from the moment it began,
          it was clear that all was not well.

Here, *commence* and *begin* co-refer to the same entity in the real world.
They need not always do so:

(3.2)   The meeting commenced at six thirty; the storm began at eight.

In (3.2) *commence* and *begin* refer to separate events, but we would still
wish to see a *stylistic* relationship between them (perhaps to create dry
humour/irony). Decoding the co-referring relationship in (3.1) is an interpretive act of the reader, just as occurs with pronouns (see section 2.2). In
(3.3), cohesion by hyponymy occurs:

(3.3)   There was a fine old *rocking-chair* that his father used to sit in, a *desk* where he wrote letters, a nest of small *tables* and a dark, imposing *bookcase*. Now all this *furniture* was to be sold, and with it his own past.

The superordinate need not be an immediate superordinate in the family tree of a particular word; it can be a *general word* (see Halliday and Hasan 1976: Ch. 6). Instead of *furniture* we could have had all these *items/objects/things*, which are examples of general superordinates. Other general superordinates, covering human and abstract areas, include *people, creature, idea* and *fact*. Reiteration of this kind is extremely common in English discourse; we do not always find direct repetition of words, and very often find considerable variation from sentence to sentence in writing and from turn to turn in speech. Such variation can add new dimensions and nuances to meaning, and serves to build up an increasingly complex context, since every new word, even if it is essentially repeating or paraphrasing the semantics of an earlier word, brings with it its own connotations and history of occurrence. In the case of reiteration by a superordinate, we can often see a summarising or encapsulating function in the choice of words, bringing various elements of the text together under one, more general term. Reiteration is not a chance event; writers and speakers make conscious choices whether to repeat, or find a synonym, or a superordinate.

Discourse analysts have not yet given us any convincing rules or guidelines as to when or why a writer or speaker might choose a synonym for reiteration rather than repetition, though some research suggests a link between reiteration using synonyms and the idea of 're-entering' important topic words into the discourse at a later stage, that is to say bringing them back into focus, or foregrounding them again (see Jordan 1985). Other research claims correlations between boundaries of discourse *segments* (as opposed to sentences or paragraphs) and re-entering of full noun phrases instead of pronouns (see B. Fox 1987). We may also be dealing with a lexical parallel to the grammatical topicalisation discussed in section 2.3. In (3.4), we can observe the importance of the words *route* and *way* in the foregrounding of the topic in this short extract, which is *how to* or *ways of* getting a contract, as indicated by the headline:

(3.4)

HOW

to get a

contract

THE NORMAL route is to build up a following through live shows, send in tapes to record companies and then wait until someone "discovers" you. But there are other ways ...

(from *News on Sunday*, 14 June 1987, p. 22)

Such usage as this is very common in English discourse. However, in practice, since our knowledge is inadequate, language teachers must content themselves with observing each case as it arises and, for the moment, work on raising an awareness of such phenomena where awareness is lacking, and, most important of all, providing the lexical equipment in L2 and practice of the skills to enable learners to create texts that resemble naturally occurring ones themselves. It means that it *is* important to make learners aware that synonyms are not just ways of understanding new words when they crop up in class, nor are they some abstract notion for the organisation of lexicons and thesauri, but they are there to be used, just as any other linguistic device, in the creation of natural discourse.

Another implication for language pedagogy is that material writers who create their own texts or who simplify naturally occurring ones should remember that disturbing the lexical patterns of texts may lead to unnaturalness and inauthenticity at the discourse level; simplification may mean an unnatural amount of repetition, for example, compared with the variation between exact repetition and reiteration by other means found in natural texts.

An analysis of the following newspaper extract according to Halliday and Hasan's principles, shows lexical cohesion at work:

(3.5) **B**RITAIN'S green and pleasant meadows yesterday became "killing fields" with the start of the fox cub hunting season.

More than 6,000 young foxes enjoying their first flush of life will be hunted down in the next three months to give inexperienced young hounds a blood lust.

But the dogs will also suffer.

Anti-hunt campaigners estimate that 7,500 young hounds will be destroyed because they fail to make the grade.

And many experienced hounds will be killed because they are too old to hunt.

The cub hunting season is just a curtain-raiser to the traditional pastime of killing adult foxes.

(from *News on Sunday*, 2 August 1987, p. 10)

Fox cub is reiterated as the near-synonymous *young foxes*; *young hounds* is repeated, but also covered by the superordinate *dogs* in the third paragraph. *Destroyed* and *killed* are also synonymous in this context (paragraphs 3 and 4).

Learning to observe lexical links in a text according to Halliday and Hasan's model could be useful for language learners in various ways. For one thing, it encourages learners to group lexical items together according to particular contexts by looking at the lexical relations in any given text. One of the recurring problems for learners is that words presented by the teacher or coursebook as synonyms will probably only be synonymous in certain contexts and the learner has to learn to observe just when and where individual pairs of words may be used interchangeably.

   Little is known about the transferability of these lexical features of text
from one language to another. Some languages may have a preference for
repetition rather than linking by synonymy (such as is often said of literary
and academic styles in Spanish, for example); sometimes learners may find
the transfer of these skills to be easy and automatic. In either case the
learner may need to use a range of vocabulary that is perhaps wider than
the coursebook or materials have allowed for. Additionally, an awareness
of the usefulness of learning synonyms and hyponyms for text-creating
purposes may not always be psychologically present among learners; there
is often a tendency for such areas of vocabulary learning to be seen as word
study divorced from actual use, or at best only concerned with receptive
skills. Conventional treatments of vocabulary in published materials often
underline this word-out-of-context approach. Redman and Ellis's (1989
and 1990) vocabulary materials are exceptional in this respect.

Reader activity 1 ☜−0

Trace all subsequent lexical reiterations of the underlined words in the text
below. Are the reiterations in the form of near-synonyms, antonyms or
hyponyms/superordinates?

Cruise guards 'were asleep'

DOZING guards al-
lowed a group of
peace campaigners to
breach a missile se-
curity cordon yester-
day.

The women protesters
claimed to have walked
right up to cruise
launchers.

As sentries slept, they
tip-toed past sentries at
3am and inspected a
cruise convoy in a woody
copse on Salisbury Plain.

Greenham Common
campaigner Sarah
Graham said : "For the
sake of making things
more realistic, the copse
was protected by soldiers
dug into fox-holes.

"And there were dogs
rather than the usual
reels of barbed wire."

But, she claimed, the
American airmen were
dozing by the launchers.

"One was kipping ben-
eath one of the
vehicles," she added.

Eventually, one of the
airmen "woke up" and
spotted the women, who
had been trailing the
convoy from the
Greenham Common
base in Berkshire since
Tuesday.

The Ministry of De-
fence confirmed there
had been an incident.

Ten women had been
arrested, charged with
trespassing and released
on bail.

(from *News on Sunday*, 2 August 1987, p. 15)

3.3   Lexis in talk

There is no reason why the model of lexical relations in text outlined above
should not also be applied to spoken data (see Stubbs 1983: 22–3). When we

do this, we find that interesting observations can be made concerning how speakers reiterate their own and take up *one another's* vocabulary selections in one form or another from turn to turn and develop and expand topics in doing so. We shall refer to this phenomenon as *relexicalisation*. Let us look at a piece of data from Crystal and Davy (1975) and analyse it according to the general principles of the Halliday–Hasan model:

(3.6)   (Two women are talking about 'Bonfire Night', the night when many people in Britain have large bonfires and fireworks in their gardens.)

A: No, I don't think we can manage a large bonfire but the fireworks themselves er we have a little store of . . .

B: Oh yes, they're quite fun, yes.

A: Mm yes, the children like them very much so I think as long as one is careful, very careful (B: Oh yes) it's all right.

B: Mm.

A: But erm I ban bangers, we don't have any bangers (B: Yes) I can't stand those (B: Yes) just the pretty ones.

B: Sparklers are my favourites.

A: Mm Catherine Wheels are my favourites actually but er you know we have anything that's pretty and sparkly and we have a couple of rockets you know, to satisfy Jonathan who's all rockets and spacecrafts and things like this.

(Crystal and Davy 1975: 28)

In A's first turn, she concludes a few previous exchanges about bonfires and then shifts the topic to the closely associated *fireworks*. B accepts the topic and just says that fireworks are fun. A takes up B's use of *fun*, and relexicalises it as *like them* and then adds that one should be careful. B simply replies 'mm'. A (who seems to work hardest at this point in developing topics) returns to the fireworks themselves and talks of *particular* fireworks: *bangers* and *pretty ones*. B continues this with *sparklers*. A comes back with *Catherine Wheels*, then repeats *pretty* and *sparkly* and expands to *rockets*. At the same time she exploits the double association of *rocket* to bring in its near-synonym *spacecraft*, thus expanding the topic to talk about her child, Jonathan.

Meanwhile, other relexicalisations are discernible: *fun* in B's turn, which becomes *like* in A's, is taken up as *can't stand* in A's next turn, then as *favourites* by B, and finally as *favourites* again by A, representing, by moving from near-synonym to antonym and vice versa, the sub-topic of 'likes and preferences' with regard to fireworks. Another relexicalisation chain can be seen in the sub-topic of 'precautions and restrictions': *careful, ban, don't have* carry this strand over the turn boundaries. This small number of lexical chains accounts for *almost all the content items* in the extract. The intimate bond between topic development and the modification and reworking of lexical items already used makes the conversation develop coherently, seeming to move from sub-topic to sub-topic as a seamless whole. In this way the scope of the topics is worked out between the participants, with neither side necessarily dominating. This accords with the ethnomethodological approach to discourse analysis, which sees conversation as a *joint* activity that has to be worked at. Topics unfold interactively, rather than 'existing' as static entities; Wardaugh (1985: 139–40) refers to topic as a 'consensual outcome'. This is quite clearly so here. Speakers can throw topics into the ring, but whether they are taken up or die depends on the other speaker(s); if one speaker insists on pursuing his/her topics, ignoring the wishes of others, this is precisely when we recognise deviance into monologue or complain later to our friends that 'X was hogging the conversation'. Utterances by one speaker are an invitation to a response by another (see Goffman 1976); the initiating utterance puts an obligation on the responding speaker to make his/her turn both relevant to the previous turn and a positive contribution to the forward moving of the discourse (see Vuchinich 1977). Relexicalisation of some elements of the previous turn provides just such a contribution to relevance and provides other important 'I am with you' signals to the initiator.

Topics unfold, and the vocabulary used by the speakers offers openings for possible development, which may or may not be exploited. The 'conversation' class where topics are pre-set may be a straitjacket to this natural kind of development; a safer course of action might be to see pre-set topics merely as 'starters' and not to worry if the discourse develops its own momentum and goes off in unpredictable directions.

Reader activity 2 🔑

Look at this extract from Svartvik and Quirk's data and trace the repetitions and relexicalisations of the italicised items, in the way that was done for the fireworks text (the transcription is simplified here):

> A: You're *knitting* . . . what are you knitting, that's not a tiny *garment*.
> B: No (A: laughs) no it's for me, but it's very plain.
> A: It's a *lovely* colour.
> B: It's nice.
> A: Yeah, I never could take to knitting except on these double-O needles with string you know, that's my sort of knitting.
> B: Yeah.
> A: It grows quickly.
> B: Yeah I get very fed up.
> A: It's just the process though . . . do you sew? I used to sew a lot when . . .
> B: No I don't.

A: In the days when I was a human being.

B: I have aspirations to make marvellous garments you know.

A: Well it's so cheap you know, this is the thing.

B: Yes.

A: Particularly, I think you probably like the sort of clothes I like anyway, which is fairly simple, things like summer dresses which are just straight up and down you know, with a scoop neck.

B: Particularly with those shifts, I mean you're well away aren't you.

A: Yes, oh yes, terribly cheap.

(Svartvik and Quirk 1980: 83–4)

Other linguists' data, in analyses where they have been interested in discourse features such as agreement/disagreement patterns and everyday discussion, also show regularly recurring vocabulary patterns where speakers use synonyms, hyponyms and antonyms to perform conversational functions (see Pomerantz 1984 and Pearson 1986, for example). In Pearson's data, people did not typically agree or disagree with phrases such as 'I agree' or 'I disagree' (beloved of English coursebook writers); rather, there seemed to be a preference for simply using some sort of lexical relation between turns.

The way in which we can observe speakers moving from superordinates to hyponyms and from synonyms to antonyms and back again is a common feature of conversation and learners can be equipped to use this skill by regular practice. As with written texts, in English at least, speakers do not just repeat the same items endlessly. This may be so in all languages and the behaviour itself may be easily transferable (but see Hinds 1979, for interesting observations on the preference for direct repetition in Japanese conversation). However, to behave in this natural way in a foreign language, the learner needs to have a fairly rich vocabulary, and to have at his/her fingertips the synonyms, antonyms, etc. of the words that are 'in play'. Once again, the issue is how to relate abstract notions such as synonymy and hyponymy to discourse skills, rather than just teaching them as disembodied properties of word lists.

Encouraging recognition of the communicative value of these lexical relations can start at quite an early stage in language learning, as soon as the necessary vocabulary is encountered. Simple cue and response drills for pairwork can train the learner in immediately associating synonyms and antonyms, or a superordinate with its hyponyms, and vice versa (see Redman and Ellis 1989 for examples).

3.4 Textual aspects of lexical competence

A somewhat different type of lexical relation in discourse is when a writer or speaker rearranges the conventional and well-established lexical relations and asks us, as it were, to adjust our usual conceptualisations of how words relate to one another for the particular purposes of the text in question. In one way or another, our expectations as to how words are conventionally used are disturbed. A simple example is the following extract from a review of a book on American military planning:

(3.7)   The depressing feature of Allen's documents is the picture which
          emerges of smart but stupid military planners, the equivalent of
          America's madder fundamentalists, happily playing the fool with the
          future of the planet.

          (*The Guardian*, 13 November 1987: 15)

Here, two words, *smart* and *stupid*, frequently occurring in the language as antonyms, and therefore incompatible, are to be interpreted as compatible descriptions of the military experts. To do this we have to adjust our typical expectations of how the two words operate as a related pair. One reasonable interpretation would be that the experts are clever ('smart') but morally reckless ('stupid'); to interpret them as meaning 'intelligent but unintelligent' would clearly be a nonsense.

Similarly, groups of informants faced with the following advertisement text react with mild surprise if the last two words are first covered up and then revealed:

(3.8)   Just brush one generous
          coat of Hammerite di-
          rectly on to metal. Within
          15 minutes it's dried to
          a   smooth,   hammered-
          enamel finish that shrugs
          off dirt and water just like
          a non-stick pan. You get
          all of this in a choice of
          ten   attractive   colours.
          Plus black.   (from *Weekend*, 23–29 May 1984, p. 19)

In many situations *black* is an unexceptionable member of the 'colour' set of adjectives (such that the remark 'he/she wears really attractive colours, blacks and reds, you know . . .' would be quite normal). Here we are expected to place *black* outside of the range of 'attractive colours' and to consider it as a separate entity. Such an adjustment probably has no great permanent implications for the place of *black* in our mental lexicon (though we might be unconsciously on our guard and less surprised if we encountered the relationship of exclusion again, especially in the context of paints, perhaps) and, as in the case of *smart* and *stupid*, no necessary implications that such relations have language-wide validity.

Alongside these eye-catching disturbances of our lexical expectations are other, less obvious kinds of lexical readjustments. These are lexical relations that are valid in particular texts only, and whose interpretations may not correspond to dictionary definitions. The good reader/listener has to decide when words are being used as more or less synonymous (or in what Bailey (1985) calls 'functional equivalence') and, conversely, when those same words may be being used in a way that focuses on the *difference* in meaning-potential.

Discourse-specific lexical relations can be called *instantial* relations, borrowing the term from J. Ellis (1966) (see also Hasan 1984). They are found frequently in spoken and written texts, and are probably a universal feature in all languages. The problems learners tend to encounter with such uses are usually more psychologically-generated; it is not that they have never encountered ad hoc rearrangements of predictable lexical usage, but more that they come to texts (especially reading comprehension texts), with the expectation that words have rather fixed relationships with one another because they have correspondingly fixed meanings, and vice versa. The task of the teacher is mainly to raise an awareness that typical vocabulary relations are often readjusted in individual texts, and, of course, to assist learners where necessary in interpreting such reorderings. Instantial relations often represent important stylistic features in texts, either in the sense of creative lexical usage, or perhaps as devices of evaluation or irony or for particular focus (e.g. the *smart/stupid* relation); by definition, each case has to be interpreted individually.

Reader activity 3 🔑

Instantial relations

Financial and *economic* are very often used synonymously (e.g. 'The government has closed down the unit for financial/economic reasons'). How are they used in the following text? What possible interpretations could be put on the writer's choice of the words? (The writer is criticising a proposal to close a railway line in the north of England.)

> The accountants can produce as many figures as they like to prove that there are financial reasons for closing it. But there are no economic reasons. Already the campaign to keep the line has inspired many new initiatives along its length. It is an asset only now being fully appreciated in every sense.

(*Country Living*, May 1988: 19)

3.5   **Vocabulary and the organising of text**

A distinction is often made between *grammar* words and *lexical* words in language. This distinction also appears sometimes as *function* words versus *content* words, or *empty* words versus *full* words. The distinction is a useful one: it enables us to separate off those words which belong to *closed systems* in the language and which carry grammatical meaning, from those that belong to *open systems* and which belong to the major word classes of noun, verb, adjective and adverb. *This, that, these* and *those* in English belong to a closed system (as do the pronouns and prepositions) and carry the grammatical meaning of 'demonstratives'. *Monkey, sculpture, noise* and *toenail* belong to open-ended sets, which are often thought of as the 'creative' end of language. In between these two extremes is another type of vocabulary that has recently been studied by discourse analysts, a type that seems to share qualities of both the open and the closed-set words. Let us consider a paragraph taken from an article in a learned journal:

(3.9)   Here I want to spend some time examining this issue. First I propose
          to look briefly at the history of interest in the problem, then spend
          some time on its origins and magnitude before turning to an
          assessment of the present situation and approaches to its solution.
          Finally, I want to have a short peek at possible future prospects.

          (W. J. Kyle, *Annals of the GGAS*, University of Hong Kong, 1984, no. 12: 54–66)

What is this article *about*? Controlling pests on fruit trees? Designing examinations for secondary schools? The possibilities are countless. What we are lacking here is the vocabulary that would identify the *field* of discourse. These sentences tell us a lot about the structure of the article, but nothing about the author's subject matter. They tell us that the tenor is relatively formal (it is hardly likely that this is someone explaining informally to a friend why he/she has never liked boiled eggs), but with an element of informality ('a short peek'). They tell us that a problem and its possible solutions will be examined, and that one part of the text will deal with the past, another with the future. So the words in our example do quite a bit of lexical work (they are not as 'empty' as grammar words are often said to be), but, in another sense, we need to seek elsewhere in the text for their content, what we shall call their *lexicalisation*. In our mystery text, the *this* of 'this issue' tells us that we can look to the preceding text to find out what the issue is; the lexical meaning of *issue* tells us to look for something problematic, something that is a matter of public debate, etc. 'The problem' works in a similar way. *Assessment* will identify with a portion of the text where something is being judged or evaluated; *solution* will be matter which can be counterposed to the 'problem', and so on. So these words stand in place of segments of text (just as pronouns can); a segment may be a sentence, several sentences or a whole paragraph, or more. We, the reader, (or listener if our example had been, say, a lecture) match the words with the segments, and, if we have decoded the text correctly, can render an account of what 'the problem' is, or what 'the prospects' are, according to the author. We shall call words such as *issue*, *problem* and *assessment discourse-organising* words, since it is their job to organise and structure the argument, rather than answer for its content or field. They are examples of the general phenomenon of *signalling* discussed in Chapter 1. Further examples may be seen in this extract:

(3.10)   Week by week the amount of car traffic on our roads grows, 13 per cent in the last year alone.

Each day as I walk to work, I see the ludicrous spectacle of hundreds of commuters sitting alone in four or five-seater cars and barely moving as fast as I can walk.

Our traffic <u>crisis</u> now presents us with the classic conservation <u>dilemma</u> – too many people making too much demand on inadequate resources.

There are four possible <u>solutions</u>: One, provide more resources, in this case build more roads and car parks; two, restrict the availability of motorised transport by artificially raising the price of vehicles and fuel; three, license only those with a good reason for needing motorised transport and prohibit unnecessary use; four, reduce the average size of motor vehicles, especially those used for commuting purposes.

(from *Cambridge Weekly News*, 22 September 1988, p. 11)

The reader may be curious to know what extract (3.9) was about: in fact it is a study of the pollution of Hong Kong's streams, coastal waters and seashore. Pollution as a subject could be presented to the reader in a variety of ways; the author might have presented a series of claims and counter-claims about pollution, or perhaps a general statement about types of pollution and then details of these types. Our author chooses to present it as a *problem*, with *responses* ('approaches') to the problem and an *evaluation* ('assessment') of responses, in other words as a problem–solution text (see section 1.10). This is clearly signalled to the reader in our quoted extract. So, as well as representing text-segments, some of the discourse-organising words we are examining additionally give us indications of the larger text-patterns the author has chosen, and build up expectations concerning the shape of the whole discourse.

From this account of the work of certain words in organising discourses it will be apparent that the language learner who has trouble with such words may be disadvantaged in the struggle to decode the whole text as efficiently as possible and as closely as possible to the author's designs. If the discourse-organising words are seen as signals of the author's intent, then inability to understand them or misinterpretation of them could cause problems.

But just how many such words are there in a language like English? What is the size of the task facing the teacher and learner in this particular lexical area? Some linguists have attempted to provide answers, but probably no one has compiled a complete list. Winter (1977 and 1978) has provided checklists, which teachers and material writers may find useful, of what he calls *vocabulary 3*, a precisely delimited sub-set of this more general set of discourse-organising words. Here is a selection of the list from Winter (1978):

(3.11)　　achieve, addition, alike, attribute, basis, case, cause, change, compare, conclude, confirm, consequence, contrast, deny, depend, differ, distinction, effect, equal, exemplify, explanation, fact, feature, follow, form, general, grounds, happen, hypothetical, instance, instrumental, justification, kind, lead to, manner, matter, means, method, opposite, point, problem, real, reason, replace, respect, result, same, similar, situation, state, thing, time, truth, way, etc.

Francis (1986) focuses on what she calls *anaphoric nouns* and gives extensive examples of nouns that frequently occur to refer back to chunks of text in the way that 'this issue' did in our first example. Here is one of her lists:

(3.12)			
abstraction	analysis	approach	assessment
assumption	attitude	belief	classification
comparison	concept	concoction	confusion
consideration	deduction	diagnosis	distinction
distortion	doctrine	dogma	doubt
evaluation	evidence	examination	fabrication
falsification	fantasy	finding	formulation
hypothesis	idea	ideology	identification
illusion	inference	insight	interpretation
investigation	misinterpretation	misjudgement	misreading
notion	opinion	perspective	picture
pipedream	position	rationalisation	reading
realisation	reasoning	recognition	reflection
scenario	speculation	supposition	surmisal

tenet	theory	thinking	view
viewpoint	vision		

(Francis, 1986: 15)

Another useful source is Jordan (1984), which brings together a large number of texts and has a vocabulary index. These works are good sources for teachers and material writers interested in this area, but many teachers will find it as easy simply to collect examples of such words from the press, where non-narrative texts, of the type where the author is presenting views and arguments and where such vocabulary is most readily found, are plentiful. In vocational/specialist courses, the best sources are learners' own subject material.

It might, at this point, be worth reminding ourselves that discourse-organising words operate *predictively* in text as well as retrospectively: if a discourse organiser does not already have its lexicalisation in the earlier text we expect it to come later in the text and are on the lookout for it, at least the efficient reader is. In (3.10) above, *dilemma* and *solutions* point forward in the text and are lexicalised in the subsequent discourse.

Predictive skills are often emphasised in current reading skills materials (see, for example, Greenall and Swan 1986); the study of vocabulary and discourse organisation offers the possibility of a more structured approach to this kind of teaching and practice activity.

Reader activity 4 🗝

The italicised words in the following texts represent either preceding or subsequent segments of the discourse. Identify those segments by underlining the appropriate words:

1. I am always being asked to agree with the proposition that the British are the most anti-intellectual people in Europe. What other European language contains that withering little phrase 'too clever by half'? Where else do thinkers squirm when they are called intellectuals? Where else is public support for the institutions of intellectual culture – the universities and the subsidised arts – so precarious?
    Behind *these questions* lies a deep-seated inferiority complex in the post-imperial British middle-classes about the parochial philistinism of their culture, . . .

    (Michael Ignatieff, *The Observer*, 25 February 1990: 17)

2. *The issues* which emerge have beset the personal social services for generations – accountability, relationships with voluntary bodies, what their role is, for example, but the context is different.

    (*New Society*, 28 August 1987: ii)

Winter's work, and its extension in that of Hoey (1983), Jordan (1984) and Francis (1986), raises some interesting questions. First there is the question of whether it is possible to delimit a *procedural* vocabulary of such words that would be useful for readers/writers over a wide range of academic disciplines involving varied textual subject matters and genres. The notion of a procedural vocabulary is currently under debate in applied linguistics (see Widdowson 1983: 92–4; Robinson 1988). The procedural vocabulary is basically words that enable us to *do* things with the content-bearing words or *schematic* vocabulary. Another unanswered question is what happens if the most common signalling words are not known by the learner? Is coherent text-decoding seriously impaired or are such words the icing on the cake, especially in the case of production? Thirdly, if all languages have such text-organising vocabulary, can the teaching/learning process capitalise on transfer in some way? Are there direct and reliable translations for words like *point, argument, issue* and *fact* to and from other languages? Do languages with cognate words (e.g. French *problème*, Swedish *faktum*, Spanish *cuestión*) have an advantage here, or do they harbour false friends?

These questions cannot all be addressed in a book of this limited scope, but the vocabulary teacher and the learner can embark on their own research within their own situation as part of the 'learning-to-learn' process.

Reader activity 5 ⚷

Look back over the last few pages of text and note how many times I have used discourse-organising words to structure my text. Were you conscious of my use of them at the time of first reading? If so/not, what implications might this have for how language learners approach reading texts?

3.6   Signalling larger textual patterns

So far, the discourse-organising words we have looked at in greatest detail have been illustrated in their role of representing segments of text, parcelling up phrases and whole sentences. But we also noted in section 3.5 that they often have a broader textual function too, and that is to signal to the reader what *larger* textual patterns are being realised. We shall now look further at this phenomenon. In section 1.10, we saw an illustration of a *problem–solution* pattern. Discourse organisers often contribute to our awareness that a problem–solution pattern is being realised. In the following texts, items have been picked out in bold to exemplify this point. In the first example, only the headline, the first paragraph and the last paragraph of a rather long newspaper article are given to show how organising words have been used to 'wrap round' a long problem–solution text:

(3.13)   *Headline*   TV Violence: No Simple **Solution**

   Opening sentence   There is no doubt that one of the major **concerns** of both viewers and broadcasters is the amount and nature of violence on our television screens.

   (*main text*)

   Closing sentence   The chief 'lesson' of all our viewing, reading and discussion is that there is no simple **solution** to the **problem** of violence on television.

(*The Observer*, 16 November 1986: 42)

The words in bold predict (*solution* in the headline, *concern*) and reinforce (*solution*, *problem*) the problem–solution pattern of the longer text (omitted here for space reasons), in which various responses to the problem of television violence are discussed and evaluated.

(3.14)   In the past, the search for other worlds has been <u>hampered</u> by two factors. First, planets are tiny objects compared with stars: for instance, the sun, a typical star, is 300,000 times more massive than the Earth. Second, planets do not shine but only reflect light dimly from stars.   But Dr Campbell and his colleagues <u>got round</u> this <u>problem</u> by using high-resolution spectroscopy to measure accurately variations in a star's light. Slight differences in a star's light showed that many were being pushed and pulled out of their paths by unseen planets.

(from *The Observer*, 5 July 1987, p. 4)

Here both *problem* and *hampered* contribute to activating the problem–solution pattern, while *got round* indicates a positively evaluated response.

We can now begin to see that a number of vocabulary items characteristically cluster round the elements of larger patterns in texts. Words that often occur in the environments of the elements of problem–solution patterns include the following:

Problem   concern, difficulty, dilemma, drawback, hamper, hind(er/ance), obstacle, problem, snag

Response   change, combat (vb), come up with, develop, find, measure(s), respon(d/se)

Solution/result   answer, consequence, effect, outcome, result, solution, (re)solve

Evaluation   (in)effective, manage, overcome, succeed, (un)successful, viable, work (vb)

Likewise, other items characteristically cluster round the elements of claim–

counterclaim (or 'hypothetical–real') patterns, items such as *claim, assert, state, truth, false, in fact, in reality*, etc. Such words have been picked out in the following text:

(3.15)   Historians are generally <u>agreed</u> that British society is founded on a possessive individualism, but they have <u>disputed</u> the origins of that philosophy. Some trace it back to the middle ages, others link it to the rise of capitalism. But the <u>consensus</u> is that the cornerstone of this society has been the nuclear family – where man the breadwinner holds dominance over his dependent wife and children. The values of individual freedom, self-reliance, individual advancement and crucially, the obligation of family duty to look after one's own in time of need are central to its operation. Within strict limits and under careful regulation, helping those less fortunate than oneself has been <u>seen</u> as part of the individual's obligation to society.
　　But, although most would <u>accept</u> that these values have been dominant, they would also <u>acknowledge</u> that the development of capitalist society saw the parallel growth of another ideology. Against individualism with its emphasis on individual freedom has been <u>counterposed</u> collectivism with its egalitarian values, and stress on the <u>view</u> that one individual's freedom cannot be paid for by the denial of freedom to others. The 19th century growth of trades unions, the cooperative movement and organised socialist political movements are all <u>evidence</u> of this opposition to dominant ideology. Because of this recognition of collective rights and responsibilities, feminists have always <u>seen</u> the granting and safeguarding of women's rights as lying within this socialist tradition.

(from *New Society*, 28 August 1987, p. 10)

Jordan (1984) is a useful work for teachers/material writers wishing to look at how particular vocabulary items have a tendency to cluster in each different segment of text-patterns such as the problem–solution pattern. He gives reference lists for the many textual examples he presents in his book and has a coding system for whether particular words typically occur in the 'problem' section or wherever. Part of his word list for the claim and counterclaim (or hypothetical–real) pattern is listed below:

(3.16)   Whenever a writer needs to indicate doubt or uncertainty he uses a signal of hypotheticality to indicate this. Here are examples of such signalling words in the examples.

according to	estimated	might	seems
apparently	evidently	old wives' tale	should
appears	expected	perhaps	signs
arguably	forecast	potential	so-called
believes	imagine	probably	speculation
claimed	likely	promises to be	suggests
considered	look	reported	thought
could	may	says	

(Jordan 1984: 148)

These recurrent features of textual patterning may be exploited in vocabulary teaching/learning as a top–down phenomenon: once conscious of a larger text-pattern, the learner can be brought to an awareness of the rich vein of vocabulary that regularly realises it. As a bottom–up phenomenon, learners can bring together in their vocabulary records items that regularly occur in similar textual environments, e.g. the typical 'response' vocabulary of problem–solution patterns. Such lists can be added to over time to build up a rich, textually-based lexicon. It is yet another alternative to the random vocabulary list and the decontextualised, semantically-motivated list.

Reader activity 6 🔑

Pick out words in the following texts which are strongly associated with either the problem–solution pattern or the claim–counterclaim pattern:

1.   All western countries face a crisis in coping with the demands made on welfare provision by their growing elderly populations. The problem of resource scarcity is a real one. But perhaps not all countries have adopted so rigorously [as Britain] the view that care should be based on the family model.

   Scandinavia, for example, provides residential facilities for elderly people not wishing to remain at home or to live with their families, and those facilities are often available for use by local pensioners on a daily basis. Elderly people in the United States have developed communities of their own, supporting each other and running them by themselves, as their answer to increasing dependency. Some have argued against these 'age-dense' solutions, likening them to ghettos, but research suggests a high degree of consumer satisfaction.

   Examples from other countries demonstrate that there are alternative ways of tackling the issues of caring and dependency. The family model of care with the high demands made on women and lack of choice and frequent loneliness for the dependents is not the only solution.

(from *New Society*, 28 August 1987, p. 12)   ⟫→

2.   Local authorities believe strongly in the involve-
     ment of the public sector and the need for public
     planning. They think that it is more important to
     protect jobs which are already in their area than
     to attract more from outside. And since they hold
     that production is the key to economic revival,
     they think it is more important to sustain manu-
     facturing industry than to switch to alternatives,
     such as the service industry.

     Central government, on the other hand, places
     more faith in the private sector for its schemes,
     and it considers that public planning hinders
     rather than helps redevelopment. It usually dis-
     misses planning as 'red tape'. Government is
     also more interested in attracting new jobs than
     protecting old ones. Above all, it believes that the
     market decides what sort of jobs should and
     should not be done.

(from *New Society*, 28 August 1987, p. 20)

3.7   Register and signalling vocabulary

In claiming that particular vocabulary items tend to cluster round certain
elements of text patterns we are ignoring the important fact that *register*
(see page 32) is closely tied to lexical selection. Among the signals of the
problem element we proposed *problem*, *drawback* and *snag* (see page 79).
Clearly we might not expect to find *snag* occurring in this way in a formal
scientific report, nor perhaps *come up with* as a signpost for *response*
(*develop* would be a more predictable choice). Therefore, as in all matters,
the relationship between vocabulary and register needs to be brought out
when studying textual signalling. Lexical choice within the identified
clusters will depend on the context (textbook, mazagine, news report, etc.),
the author's assumptions about the audience (cultured/educated/readers of
the popular tabloid press, etc.) whether the style is to be read as 'written' or
'spoken', and so on. Most of the texts we have looked at so far have been
toward the 'written/formal/cultured' end of the spectrum. Here are two
more, this time with a more informal, colloquial tone. They are presented
to illustrate the fact that discourse-signalling words need not necessarily be
only rather 'dry' academic words taken from the Graeco-Latin vocabulary
of English. The relevant words are underlined:

(3.17) Put ordinary exterior varnish on your doors and window frames and in no
time at all <u>you'll wish you hadn't</u>.
   Wood shrinks and stretches when the temperature and humidity changes.
Ordinary varnish, doesn't, so it cracks.
   If you don't strip it off and start again <u>you'll be in real trouble</u>, your wood
will be open to attack from fungus and rot, and quite frankly, it will look
<u>awful</u>.

(Advertisement for Cuprinol from *The Observer*, 12 July 1987, p. 5)

Alongside more neutral items like *develop* and *reduce the risk* are informal,
direct addresses to the reader: *you'll wish you hadn't* and *quite frankly, it
will look awful* which create a pseudo-conversational register in which the
element of *problem* is realised.

(3.18) Decide to <u>tackle</u> that <u>troublesome</u> moss on your lawn and you could find yourself <u>going round and around in circles.</u> Or at least backwards and forwards to your local garden centre.
   Conventional moss treatments <u>simply won't</u> keep moss away for any length of time. You apply it and shortly afterwards your moss blackens and dies. <u>You think all of your worries are over. Far from it.</u> The little so and so's will <u>turn up again</u> as sure as <u>the proverbial bad penny.</u>

<u>You're back where you started.</u> And left with the choice of getting down on your hands and knees to weed it out or traipsing off to the shops for some more moss treatment.
   So if you want to <u>save yourself</u> heartache, backache and a considerable amount of shoe-leather, insist on Lawnsman Mosskiller from ICI. You'll be <u>rewarded</u> with a moss-free lawn for the rest of the season.
   Mix the sachet with water, stir, and sprinkle over your lawn. <u>It's that simple.</u>

(from *The Observer Magazine*, 6 April 1986, p. 12)

Here idiomatic phrases are used as signals of the response and its occurrence after a previous negatively evaluated response ('conventional
treatments'). Idioms are often a problem for the teacher insomuch as it is
not always easy to find natural contexts in which to present them. Research
by Moon (1987) suggests that writers and speakers use idiomatic phrases to
organise their discourse and to signal evaluation, far more frequently than
previous linguistic studies of idiomaticity have suggested. Idioms are good
metaphors for the kinds of textual segments we have been looking at
(problem/response, etc.). Consider how some of the following could be
used in informal discourses to suggest the problem–solution pattern:

(to be) in a fix   *to be up against a brick wall*
to come up trumps   *(sth) does the trick*
to have a crack at (doing something)   *to have a brainwave*
(to be) up a gum tree

Speakers and writers use these in informal situations to perform the same
kind of organising and signalling functions that the more formal vocabulary does in written argumentation.

We can now begin to see just how important certain vocabulary items are in organising discourses. Admittedly, we have concentrated on reporting, expository and argumentative texts, but learners frequently have to tackle quite daunting and lengthy examples of these in their textbooks, and syllabus specifications often demand·that they be studied. They are precisely the types of text that come festooned with comprehension questions in coursebooks and exams, and are regularly cited as being 'difficult', 'boring' and 'demotivating' for students by teachers. They are the texts that are hardest to unpack. Significantly, the kind of discourse-organising vocabulary that has occurred in most of our example texts, the Graeco-Latin words found in argumentation and exposition, is typical of the kind of vocabulary that research has claimed produces a 'lexical bar', a serious obstacle to progress in education, for children learning their first language (see Corson 1985). We should not underestimate the difficulties second language learners may experience with these words, particularly those who do not come from a Romance- or Germanic-language background.

Discourse-organising words are best presented and practised in their natural contexts. Simply looking them up in a monolingual dictionary can lead to a circularity of abstract definitions. Note how even a good, modern learner's dictionary like the Collins COBUILD (1987) dictionary defines *problem* in terms of *difficulty*, and *difficulty* in terms of *problem*:

(3.19) **problem** /probləm/, **problems. 1 A problem** is **1.1** a situation or a state of affairs that causes difficulties for people, so that they try to think of a way to deal with it. EG. *...how families can try to solve these problems... ...the social problems in modern society... I think we may have a problem here... She has a weight problem... The problem is that she can't cook.*

difficulty /dɪfɪkə'lti¹/, **difficulties. 1 A difficulty** is something that is a problem for you. EG. *There are lots of difficulties that have to be overcome... The main difficulty is a shortage of time.*
2 If something causes **difficulty**, it causes problems because it is not easy to do or understand. EG. *This can cause difficulty... ...questions of varying difficulty.*

(from *Collins COBUILD English Language Dictionary*, pp. 1143, 391)

3.8 Modality

One contribution that the study of vocabulary in naturally occurring discourses has made is to point up the all-pervasiveness of modality in spoken and written language. Modality is often thought of as the province of the closed class of modal verbs (*must, can, will, may*, etc.) and treated as part of the grammar of English, but a large number of 'lexical' words (nouns, adjectives, verbs and adverbs) carry the same or similar meanings to the modal verbs. For this reason, modality is dealt with here in our chapter on vocabulary rather than in Chapter 2.

Two notable studies of modality in large amounts of discourse, Holmes (1983) and Hermerén (1978), show a wide range of uses of the traditional class of modal verbs and of a vocabulary of lexical items carrying modal meanings, from the classic *epistemic* modality (concerned with degrees of certainty and possibility) to the *root* modalities (volition, permission, obligation). Both Holmes's and Hermerén's data show that, put together, other word classes express modality more frequently than modal verbs. The vocabulary of modality includes verbs such as *appear, assume, doubt, guess, look as if, suggest, think*, adverbs such as *actually, certainly, inevitably, obviously, possibly*, and nouns and adjectives related to them (for a full list, see Holmes 1988). In terms of frequency, the verbs and adverbs are considerably more frequent than the nouns and adjectives.

All these words carry important information about the stance and attitude of the sender to the message; they are concerned with assertion, tentativeness, commitment, detachment and other crucial aspects of *interpersonal* meaning (as opposed to ideational, or content, meanings). In the Hallidayan model of register they form a part of the *tenor* of the discourse. If we take a later part of one of our earlier texts, extract (3.10), we can see how modal vocabulary represents another aspect of discoursal meaning over and above the organisational and more general signalling vocabulary already analysed. Modal items are picked out in bold:

(3.20)   **Inevitably**, objections will be raised to the promotion of the motor cycle as the saviour of our environment.
    It is dangerous: it **can** be but three-fifths of all serious motor cycling accidents are caused by cars. So, by transferring some drivers from cars to motor cycles, the risk **can** immediately be reduced.
    Department of Transport statistics have **shown** that a car driver is nine times more **likely** to take someone else with him in an accident than a motor cyclist, so riding a motor cycle is **actually** making a contribution to road safety.

(*Cambridge Weekly News*, 22 September 1988: 11)

Discourse analysts have demonstrated that modality is fundamental in the creation of discourse; *all* messages choose some degree of modality, even if it is only to make a *neutral* choice of bald assertion (e.g. 'The cat sat on the mat', as compared with the heavily modalised 'I suppose it's possible the cat just may have sat on the mat'). Language teachers have always paid attention to the modal verbs but, Holmes (1988) shows, in her survey of four ESL textbooks, that the larger vocabulary of modal lexical items is often under-represented in teaching materials, and there does seem to be a need to redress the balance in light of what natural data shows.

Reader activity 7 🗝

Underline words conveying modality in this text:

■FOOD AND HEALTH

Can citrus peel harm?

Did you know that lemon and orange peel is coated with wax and chemicals?

The skin of almost all citrus fruit sold in the UK is treated with fungicides to stop it going mouldy. And the glossy surface is the result of bathing the fruit in wax.

Could the fungicides used on citrus peel be harmful – particularly since there's some evidence from laboratory tests that, in sufficient quantities, they may produce cancers or mutations in animals?

The Government doesn't feel there is any need to worry because the levels of fungicide permitted are very low. The levels are based on the recommendations of UK and international advisory bodies for the amount that can be consumed daily without any significant effect.

(from *Which?* January 1989, p. 4)

3.9   Conclusion

The study of vocabulary in discourse is concerned with patterns in text generated by the vocabulary relations that are found over clause and sentence boundaries, the role of certain words in organising discourses and signalling their structure, and the relationship between these features of textuality and the register of the end product. Such an approach also offers an alternative motivation for the construction of word lists to supplement the traditional semantic-field orientation. Students themselves can be encouraged to collect items along discourse-functional lines, something which becomes more and more important as they embark on composition writing and argumentation in general, and something which can offer an organised backdrop in learning areas normally left to organise themselves. Once more, though, the whole enterprise depends on adapting what is useful in discourse analysis to current practices, and on teachers and material writers paying greater attention to the insights offered by naturally occurring data.

Further reading

The standard work on lexical cohesion is Halliday and Hasan (1976); Hasan has since revised their model (see especially 1984).

Overall, not much research has been done on vocabulary and discourse, but further discussion of instantial relations may be found in McCarthy (1987 and 1988), and in Carter and McCarthy (1988: Ch. 5).

Cruse's (1975 and 1977) papers on hyponymy are innovative in that they look at language in use, while P. H. Fries (1986) and Ellis (1987) look at instantial synonymy.

On the use of superordinates in discourse, Wisniewski and Murphy (1989) is interesting.

McCarthy (1990) looks at further vocabulary features that cluster around text-organising words, and Lindeberg (1986) links lexical relations with thematic development in text.

A further paper that considers the re-entering of full noun phrases as opposed to pronouns is Hinds (1979).

Benson and Greaves (1973: 54–68) offer practical suggestions for the analysis of lexical relations in texts, based on the idea of lexical sets, and their paper on 'field of discourse' (1981) ties up the Hallidayan idea of collocation with the topics and institutional focuses of texts.

For more on topics as negotiated by participants see Richards and Schmidt (1983), and Brown and Yule (1983: 89).

Hoey (forthcoming) contains a thorough analysis and a novel view of the functioning of lexical cohesion.

King (1989) takes further the discussion of discourse-organising vocabulary.

Stubbs (1986) is a good, general paper on modality in discourse.

For more on modality see Perkins (1983) and Westney (1986)

D

4 Discourse analysis and phonology

> Alice felt even more indignant at
> this suggestion. 'I mean,' she
> said, 'that one can't help
> growing older.'
>   '*One* can't, perhaps,' said
> Humpty Dumpty, 'but *two* can.'

> **Lewis Carroll: *Through the Looking
> Glass***

4.1 Introduction

Under the heading of phonology in this chapter we shall take a brief look at
what has traditionally been thought of as 'pronunciation', but devote most
of our attention to intonation. This is partly because the most exciting
developments in the analysis of discourse have been in intonation studies
rather than at the segmental level (the study of phonemes and their
articulation) and partly because intonation teaching, where it has taken
place, has proceeded on the basis of assumptions that are open to challenge
from a discourse analyst's viewpoint.

4.2 Pronunciation

Traditional pronunciation teaching has found its strength in the ability of
linguists to segment the sounds of language into discrete items called
phonemes which, when used in the construction of words, produce
meaningful contrasts with other words (e.g. the phonemes /p/ and /b/ in
English give us contrasts such as *pump* and *bump*, *pat* and *bat*, etc.). The
position and manner of articulation of phonemes in a language like English
are well described and can be presented and practised in language classes
either as isolated sounds, in words, in contrasting pairs of words or in
minimal contexts. Such features will probably long remain the stock-in-
trade of pronunciation teaching and, if well done, can undoubtedly help
learners with difficulties.

Seen from the viewpoint of connected stretches of naturally occurring discourse, the problem becomes more complex. When words follow one another in speech, phonemes may undergo considerable changes. A simple example is the difference between the normal spoken rendition of 'good evening' [gədiːvnɪŋ], and that of 'good morning' [gəbmɔːnɪŋ]. The /d/ of the *citation form* of *good* (the way the word is said when isolated, out of context) becomes more like a /b/ when it precedes the bilabial /m/ of *morning*. As G. Brown (1977: 57) puts it: 'every consonant and every vowel will be affected by its neighbouring consonants and vowels and by the rhythmic structure in which it occurs.' Brown lists many examples of such *assimilations*, and of *elisions* (where sounds from the citation form are 'missed out' in connected speech: 'most men' will be said without a /t/ in natural, conversational speech).

Reader activity 1 🔑

Assimilations and elisions

Consider how the following would be articulated in informal conversation in Standard British English (or, if you speak another variety, in that variety). What changes would take place to the way the pronunciation of the individual words in isolation are represented in dictionaries?

1. ten or eleven months ago
2. I asked him what went on
3. not her! not Mary!
4. considering my age, I ran miles

Good advanced learners of English use assimilations and elisions naturally, but a surprising number of quite advanced learners continue to articulate the citation-form phonemes of English words in casual, connected speech. This will not usually cause problems of communication but is undoubtedly a contributing factor in 'foreign accent', and there may be a case for explicit intervention by the teacher to train students in the use of the most commonly occurring assimilations and elisions by practising pronunciation in (at least minimal) contexts. Alternatively, the answer may be to tackle the problem simultaneously from a 'top–down' and 'bottom–up' approach, on the premise that articulation, rhythmicality (see below) and intonation are inextricably linked, and that good intonation will have a washback effect on articulation in terms of reduced and altered articulations of individual phonemes, alongside the specific teaching of phonemes and the most common altered and reduced forms.

In some respects the most neglected aspect of the teaching of pronunciation has been the relationship between phoneme articulation and other, broader features of connected speech. Pennington and Richards (1986) argue that pronunciation *is* important as an aspect of discourse-oriented language teaching and that three areas, or components, should be addressed: segmental features, voice-setting features, and prosodic (intonational) features. The segmental, or phoneme-based, view of teaching, they argue, needs to be supplemented by concern with 'general articulatory characteristics of stretches of speech'. These include voice-setting features, such as, for example, the general tendency towards retroflex articulation in Indian speakers of English, which can cause persistent difficulties for the non-Indian listener. The prosodic component consists of stress and intonation. Pennington and Richards see pronunciation as a *constellation* of features manifested not just in the articulation of particular phonemes but in the stream of connected speech that is natural discourse.

Things such as voice-setting features are difficult to tackle, and are largely ignored in present-day teaching materials, but advice to learners on the typical settings of the speech organs that give each language its unique character when heard can help to improve the overall sound of the learner's performance. In fact, Honikman (1964) advocates establishing the voice-setting first, and *then* the details of articulation, thus taking a top–down approach.

4.3 Rhythm

When we listen to a stretch of spoken English discourse, we often feel that there is a rhythm or regularity to it, which gives it a characteristic sound, different from other languages and not always well-imitated by foreign learners. The impression of rhythm may arise out of a feeling of alternation between strong and weak 'beats' in various patterned recurrences:

(4.1)   Most of the people were visitors.

(4.2)   A friend of mine has bought a boat.

(4.3)   A week at the seaside is just what I need.

Brown (1977) found such recurring patterns in her recordings of broadcast talk. But other natural speech is often not as regular as this, nor will the patterns necessarily recur in the same way at different times. If we dip at random into natural data, we find stretches such as:

(4.4)   and the speed limit was five miles an hour

$$\begin{array}{cccccc} - & -- & / & / - - & / & - - & /- \end{array}$$
(4.5)   there was a sharp turn at the end of this village

(Author's data 1989)

Sometimes, in order to capture a felt rhythmicality, we can mark *silent beats* to maintain the rhythm:

$$\begin{array}{ccccccc} - & - & / & -- & / & (--) & / & - & - \end{array}$$
(4.6)   there's a house over there,   isn't there

Another way of looking at this is to say that utterances can be divided up into groups of syllables that have more or less the same duration, called *feet* (a *foot* as a unit must contain one stressed syllable). Within each foot, syllables will be 'stretched out' or 'squeezed together', depending on how many there are, to maintain the rhythmic time span, as in:

$$\begin{array}{c|c|c|c} / \;-\; - & / \;- & / & / \end{array}$$
(4.7) | This is the | one that | Frank | bought |

where the first foot has two weak beats, the second has one, and the third and fourth have none, but where all the feet are perceived to be of more or less the same duration.

Reader activity 2

Imagine contexts for these utterances and then mark them with / for stressed beats and – for unstressed beats:

1. What's the matter with Mary?
2. I knew she would come in the end.
3. Put salt on those chips if you want to.
4. He works on a farm, doesn't he?

In fact, instrumental analysis may reveal that the 'beats' are anything but precisely regular in real time and as we shall see, there are problems with such an account of rhythm. Nonetheless, the overall experience of rhythm is often still present. This general feeling we shall refer to as *rhythmicality* (see Couper-Kuhlen 1986: 55).

Traditionally, rhythm has been considered an important element in the teaching of spoken English. This is probably due to two main factors. Firstly, there does seem to be rhythmicality in varying degrees in long stretches of speech, especially carefully considered deliveries such as broadcast talks, fluent reading aloud, speeches and monologues, as well as some ordinary conversation. Secondly, the concept of English as a *stress-timed* language, deeply rooted in theoretical and applied linguistics, has dominated approaches to the teaching of rhythm.

To take the second factor first, the notion that the languages of the world can be classified according to rhythmic criteria has persisted throughout this century. The principal distinction is made between *stress-timing* and *syllable-timing*. Broadly speaking, languages such as English and Arabic are said to have more or less equal time spans (or *interstresses*) between stressed syllables, so that any intervening syllables, the number of which may vary, are made to fit into the available space between stresses. Stressed syllables are longer in duration than unstressed ones. Languages such as French and Spanish, on the other hand, have regular syllable length for both stressed and unstressed syllables, and are thus timed according to their syllables, or *syllable-timed*. While this distinction may correspond to some strongly felt perception of the different characteristic rhythms of languages, there is little hard instrumental evidence for it. In fact, in recent years, quite a lot of convincing *counter*-evidence has been presented. Dauer (1983) examined data in English, Thai, Spanish, Italian and Greek, and concluded that interstress intervals were no more regular in English than in Spanish, a so-called syllable-timed language, and several other investigations similarly challenge the stress-timed/syllable-timed distinction (e.g. Borzone de Manrique and Signorini 1983). We are forced to conclude, therefore, that the notion that English is stress-timed is unproven, and that perceptions of rhythmicality may have their origins in other phenomena of connected speech. The lack of evidence anyway undermines those teaching approaches that advocate training in reproducing utterances according to carefully timed beats on stressed syllables, using metronomes, table-tapping or hand-clapping (e.g. Greenwood 1981).

Bolinger (1986: 37–45) attempts to simplify the timing of interstresses and to account for rhythmicality with a few basic rules, and his account has been advocated as a basis for the teaching of rhythm by Faber (1986). Bolinger's description is based on the idea that English has two kinds of vowels, *full* and *reduced*. The reduced vowels are schwa /ə/, /ɨ/ as in 'sill*i*ness', /ɵ/ as in 'soloist, and 'syllabic' consonants (e.g. 'rabb*le*'). Other vowels are full vowels. Full (F) and reduced (R) correspond to syllable types which can be called *long* (L) and *short* (S). For example:

(4.8)   an unforgettable person
           R F   R F R R   F R   (vowels)
           S L   S L S S   L S   (syllables)

Bolinger's rule is simple: if an F is followed by another F or by a pause, then the first F becomes 'extra'-long (LL); compare the syllable rhythms of *seller* and *sell-by*:

(4.9)   the seller's advice
             F R
             L S

(4.10)   the sell-by advice
             F   F
             LL L

It must be noted that Bolinger is talking about the *timing* of the whole syllable, not the extending or drawling of the vowel. Another way of articulating the rule is that LL is the norm for full-vowelled syllables, but when followed by any S, the S 'borrows' time from LL, making it only L, as in *hat-box* and *hatter*:

(4.11)   hat-box   hatter
             LL L   L   S

Reader activity 3

Analyse the following utterances according to Bolinger's principles, labelling them with F and R for vowel-types and LL, L and S for syllable-types. Then try a loud reading of the phrases. Does Bolinger's system produce a natural rendition?

1.   Which hat shall Jo wear to the drinks party?
2.   I met Bill Smith in town at lunchtime.
3.   A bottle of mineral water.

'Borrowing', as illustrated in (4.11), means that rhythmic groups of approximately the same duration are produced in connected speech. The theory is appealing in its relative simplicity, but it suffers from a worrying circularity in that reduced vowels are only reduced because they are unstressed, whereas Bolinger's rule tends to take the question of stress out of the equation. The traditional stress-timing view, despite its shortcomings, recognises that vowel length and quality are dependent on stress. It is also difficult to see how such rules could be transferred into the language class except in the form of practice in repeating small chunks of ready-made language of phrase- or clause-length in the hope that some underlying competence will develop that can be transferred to the situation of natural speech production. Faber's optimism on the classroom applicability of Bolinger's theory may be somewhat misplaced.

It seems then that there is some basis in the notion of rhythmicality, if only as an as yet ill-described characteristic of English, but it is difficult to see how the stress-timing notion can be of much direct use in the language class where the emphasis is on natural discourse.

Not enough is yet known about rhythmicality in talk, or what its functions, if any, might be, and speculation abounds. Some phonologists feel that, in spoken interaction, the rhythm a ˙speaker establishes and conforms to represents an underlying *tempo* (basically the pace or speed of speech, just like the relationship between rhythm and tempo in music), which governs interaction and which gives important clues to participants concerning things such as turn-taking (Scollon 1982). Others see a different organising function in rhythm, in the dividing of information into coherent chunks for the listener (Taylor 1981), and yet others have argued for the importance of the role of rhythm in the overall perception of stresses on the part of the listener (Gumperz 1982: 109). But none of these accounts is entirely convincing.

The idea of stress-timing has been reinforced by a phonological tradition concerned with analysing literary texts, careful readings, broadcast talks and the like. Natural conversation certainly does not lend itself to regular rhythm-tapping, even though the flow of talk is punctuated (often regularly) with perceived stresses, and the business of spontaneous speech production hardly gives time for careful rhythmic pre-planning and 'keeping the beat' (even more so for the non-native speaker struggling with all the other encoding difficulties). Rhythm training in the classroom can only work with textual *products* rather than the process of creating rhythmic talk, and, indeed, forcing learners to indulge in artificially 'cramming' stressed and unstressed syllables into a regular rhythm may take their attention away from the genuinely interactive aspects of stress, not least the *speaker's choice* as to what is to be stressed and what not. It is to the interactive arena of where and when stress is placed that we next turn.

4.4 Word stress and prominence

At this point, it is useful to change our terminology slightly and introduce the term *prominence*. Syllables which stand out in the flow of talk, because the speaker has uttered them with relatively greater intensity, or duration, or pitch variation compared with surrounding syllables (and our perception of this phenomenon will usually be due to a variety of such features), will be referred to as *prominent* syllables (see Brazil 1985a and b). It is helpful to have this special term, *prominence*, so as not to confuse *word stress*, which words bear in their citation forms (sometimes called their *isolate* pronunciations), with what concerns us most here: the *choice* of the speaker to make certain words salient by giving prominence to syllables. This is therefore a more precise use of the term *prominence* than is found in some sources (e.g. Cruttenden 1986: 7).

A word such as *Japanese* in citation form would have a word-stress profile of:

(4.12) $\overset{2}{J}$Apa$\overset{1}{N}$ESE

where 1 represents so-called *primary* stress, and 2 *secondary* stress. But it is clear that prominence can occur differently on these two syllables, or indeed not at all, depending on the speaker's choice as to where the main stress (the 'sentence stress', or 'tonic') is placed in the utterance; the main stresses are underlined.

(4.13)   ACtually, she's japa<u>NESE</u>

(4.14)   a JApanese <u>SHIP</u>-owner's been <u>KID</u>napped

(4.15)   i thought <u>SHE</u> was japanese, NOT <u>HIM</u>

So word stress, as it is traditionally understood, and prominence, as we shall use it here, are two distinct levels. Where they overlap, of course, is in the fact that prominences may not be distributed just anywhere in the word, but may only fall on certain syllables. Where two prominences can occur in the same word, as is often the case with a whole class of words such as *JApanESE, UNiVERsal, conGRAtuLAtions*, etc., the second will always be the stronger. Thus *Japanese* may commonly receive prominence on *JA* or *NESE* or both, but will rarely if ever be realised as *jaPAnese*. Many other polysyllabic words may only have one *prominence* but may still have primary and secondary word stress (e.g. $\overset{1}{C}$Ata$\overset{2}{l}$yst, $\overset{1}{C}$ON$\overset{2}{f}$iscate, $\overset{1}{W}$HERE$\overset{2}{a}$bouts). So, when describing a word in a dictionary entry we can state which syllables are prone to prominence and which are not:

(4.16)   UNemPLOYED   she's UNemPLOYED
                                          an UNemployed WORker
                         not: * she's unEMployed

                CONfiDENtial   this is VEry confiDENtial
                                          a CONfidential MEmo
                         not: * a conFIdential memo

For the learner of English, information about which syllables may be prominent is useful; it is a natural part of the lexical competence of native speakers. In this regard, the traditional distinction between primary stress and secondary stress (see above) may be misleading, and it may be more helpful simply to indicate to the learner which syllables are prominence-prone (as Brazil's system of annotation in the Collins COBUILD (1987) dictionary does, for example). Otherwise, the learner may be misled into thinking that primary and secondary stress must be maintained at all costs. Thus Swan and Walter's (1984: 9) citation-form stress patterns for nationality words such as *japaNESE* are all right when the word is spoken in isolation, or in a context such as (4.13), but not for (4.14) (see above).

Reader activity 4 🗝

For the following list of words, do as in the example: first mark primary and secondary word stress, and then indicate, by underlining, which syllable or syllables may be made prominent in discourse. For example:

confrontational   CON̲fron̲T̲A̲tional
(with marks: 2 over CON, 1 over TA)

1. disused
2. complicated
3. application
4. dinosaur

4.5   The placing of prominence

When and why do speakers attach prominence to syllables and, thereby, to the words that contain those syllables in their utterances? Consider the following:

(4.17)   a CUP of TEA

(4.18)   the THIRD of APril

(4.19)   WHERE'S the BREADknife?

The non-prominent words (*a*, *of*, *the*) are, as it were, taken for granted; they do not represent any choice from a list of alternatives: 'a cup of tea' is not an alternative to 'a cup by/from tea' in most conceivable circumstances. But, equally, 'the breadknife' is not in any real sense a selection from *my/your/a/Mrs Jones's breadknife* in most situations, since the speaker assumes, or *projects the assumption* that the missing knife is the one in normal use in the household and that it does not need to be specially identified more than by *the*. There will, of course, be circumstances in which speakers deem it necessary to make prominent items which in most other circumstances can be taken as understood, as in (4.20) and (4.21):

4.20   NO, it's part OF the course, NOT just an optional EXtra

(4.21)   i can TAKE you right TO the door if you WISH

In these two examples, words that are otherwise usually taken for granted are signalled as significant selections by the speaker. (4.21) could equally well have been rendered as 'RIGHT to the DOOR', but the speaker has chosen to highlight the preposition *to*. It is this that is meant by interactive choice as realised in prominence, as opposed to the relatively stable patterns of word stress. So when we consider prominence in discourse we are considering the extent to which speakers' and listeners' worlds converge, and what is signalled as prominent (i.e. selected by the speaker from a list of possible alternatives and projected as a significant element of the message), as against that which can be assumed as part of the taken-for-granted elements of the message.

Reader activity 5 🗝

Try and picture the contexts of the following utterances and decide which syllables the speakers will be most likely to make prominent. Here is an example:

(passenger to bus-driver)
Does this bus go to Parkside?
DOES this bus go to PARKside?
or: does THIS bus go to PARKside?

1.   (customer to waiter in restaurant)
     Does the soup contain meat?

2.   (you telephone a friend at 11.30 p.m.)
     Sorry to ring you so late.

3.   (at a car-hire office)
     Will you accept a cheque?

In doing the reader activity, you may have noticed that it was not only small, function-words that were being made non-prominent. The traditional statement that lexical words are stressed and grammar/function words are not is only a general statistical tendency, not a rule, even though some consider it a useful fact to impart to learners (e.g. Currie and Yule 1982). It is quite likely that *contain* (1), *ring* (2) and *accept* (3) will receive no prominence, as they are part of the taken-for-granted elements of the discourse. By the same token, grammar/function words may well be made prominent for a variety of reasons:

(4.22)   we WERE hoping to get there beFORE tea

(4.23)   she SAID to leave it HERE, but there's NOwhere TO leave it

(4.24)   Pupil: i aRRIVED to the AIRport at SIX
         Teacher: aRRIVED AT
         Pupil: AH, i aRRIVED AT the airport at six

This last example is a very typical one in the language classroom. For the purposes of the interaction (to signal to the pupil that a mistake has been made), the teacher makes prominent a word that would normally be a non-selected, taken-for-granted item. The teacher is reacting naturally to the situation, but there is a danger that, in correcting with prominence on *at*, the pupil might judge the teacher's rendition to be the normal one.

Words like *surprised*, *accept* and *contain*, when they are non-prominent, may still be heard to retain traces of word stress (so that even non-prominent *surprised* may be heard as *surPRISED* rather than *SURprised*), or they may lose their word-stress pattern altogether; phonologists call this 'the intermediate accent rule' (Knowles 1987: 124–6).

If a speaker makes a word prominent which would not normally be made prominent, listeners seek motivation for the prominence as part of the general desire of participants to find coherence in discourse. The listener may decide, for instance, that some contrast is being suggested; if someone says:

(4.25)   i STUdied IN London FIVE YEARS ago

they may be heard as suggesting some significance for the word *in* (chosen as opposed to *near*, or *outside of*, for example), which may be unintentional. Sometimes it is even more difficult to make a coherent interpretation of prominence, as in these attested non-native speaker examples:

(4.26)   my SISter HATES flying JUST as much as i DO

(4.27)   can i PAY by credit CARD?

Reader activity 6

Listen carefully to any non-native speaker that you know when he/she is speaking English naturally. Are any words made prominent at inappropriate or incomprehensible places? Is there any pattern in the misplacing of prominence?

Speakers of some languages have a tendency when speaking English to make the last element of an utterance prominent, regardless of whether it would normally be prominent in English. Other problems with prominence can sometimes be traced back to misunderstandings about word stress, especially in compound words, so that a 'marked' version of the item is produced in contexts where there is no reason to do so:

(4.28)   i've BROken a coffee CUP

(4.29)   i HÁVE to REgister at the police STAtion to STAY in ENGland

Teachers have first and foremost to train themselves to observe learners, listening carefully for any problems that might be consistently related to misplaced prominence. Many available language teaching materials give learners practice in deciding which words to make prominent in sentences and dialogues, though such exercises are generally conflated under the heading of *stress* with exercises aimed at practising the word stress of citation forms. Bradford's *Intonation in Context* (1988) specifically addresses prominence in the sense we are using it here (see the Teacher's Book: 3–4), though in the Student's Book the term *highlighting* is used instead.

4.6   Intonational units

Many phonologists believe that it is possible to divide speech up into small units in which each unit has at least one main, or *nuclear* prominence. This prominence will be marked by some variation in pitch, either predominantly rising or falling (see 4.7). The unit thus defined may then have other, non-nuclear, prominences (usually just one), and other, non-prominent syllables. The nuclear prominence is the last prominence in the unit, and such units are usually called *tone units* or *tone groups*. Typical tone groups would be (from now on we shall show the nuclear syllable in bold to distinguish it from prominent, non-nuclear syllables):

(4.30)   / she WORKS for the **GO**vernment /

(4.31)   / i KNOW the **FACE** / but i CAN't put a **NAME** to it /

(4.32)   / WHERE's that **FRIEND** of yours /

Tone groups often have a slight pause after them, and are claimed to correspond most frequently in natural data with grammatical *clauses* (Halliday 1967), as do our examples above. In actual fact, it is not at all easy to isolate tone groups in natural data, especially in rapid, casual speech, and some linguists have abandoned the attempt altogether, as we shall see below. But the tone group is central to the school of linguists who see intonation as being concerned with the *information structure* of utterances. Halliday (1985) is principal among these. For Halliday, tone groups are informational units; the speaker decides how to segment the information to be transmitted and encodes each segment as a separate tone group. The nuclear prominence, or *tonic* as we shall now call it, projects what the speaker decides is *new* (in the sense of 'newsworthy') in the tone group. So in example (4.30), the newsworthy focus was on *government*, in (4.31), on *face* and *name*, and in (4.32) on *friend*. The rest of the tone group may be said to be *given*, but only in the sense of 'the background or framework in which the newsworthy items operate' rather than 'given' meaning 'already mentioned or understood'; the terms used by linguists can often be confusing because of their non-specialist meanings.

In the Hallidayan system, the unmarked or neutral unit of information is the clause, with the tonic on the last lexical item. This is reminiscent of the grammatical idea of *theme* and *rheme* in the clause (see Chapter 2), where the rheme (the portion of the clause from the verb onwards) characteristically contains the newsworthy information:

	theme	*rheme*
(4.33)	i	've PUT it in the **FRIDGE**
(4.34)	you	PUSH that little **BU**tton

Many utterances will not follow this neutral, unmarked pattern, and the nucleus may be located in a number of different places; for example, the theme may occupy its own tone group for purposes of foregrounding or contrast:

(4.35)   / the **WINE** / was **AW**ful / but the **FISH** / was su**PERB** /

And the many cases of marked themes discussed in Chapter 2 will bring the nucleus on to those themes:

(4.36)   / the **CA**rrots / we GROW our**SELVES** / but the po**TA**toes / we BUY in the **MAR**ket /

(4.37)   / in the after**NOON** / we went **SWI**mming /

Reader activity 7 🔑

Imagine contexts for these utterances and decide on the division into tone groups. Then mark the tonic syllables and any other prominent syllables. If possible, compare your results with someone else's, but remember that there may be more than one possible contextualisation.

1.   I've lost my car keys.
2.   Suddenly a cat jumped out.
3.   It's Mondays I hate most.
4.   David I know quite well; his sister I don't know at all.

It is the speaker who decides how the information is to be distributed in tone groups and where the tonic is placed, and the decisions rest on an assessment of what needs to be highlighted for the listener. *New* and *given*, as stated above, are not simply a matter of what has already been mentioned and what has not; an entity already mentioned may be highlighted to reassert it as a topic in the conversation or to contrast it with another entity; on the other hand, an entity may be treated as *given* because it is obvious in the context, even though it has not been mentioned at all. Because all such decisions are in the hands of the speaker, it may be argued that the notion of an unmarked or neutral information structure (i.e. one that uses the single tone-unit clause in which the information is distributed as given + new and the tonic is on the last lexical item) is irrelevant, and that, in language teaching, to teach such a structure as if it were an automatic reflex upon which 'special' or marked decisions are overlaid is misleading, since the decision-making and assessment of the state of the interaction on the part of the speaker are constant.

The tone group is a powerful, basic structure for the analysis of talk. After all, we do not speak in sentences, and often not even in regular clause-length chunks, and so if we can isolate a unit whose basis is the tonic prominence and relate this to informativeness in talk, we can begin to formulate rules for a grammar of speech, in which the tone group is the minimal useful contribution to any discourse. Research on such grammars of speech, operating in tandem with, but not subordinate in any way to, the traditional grammar of clauses and sentences, is in its infancy.

However, not all linguists are agreed that it *is* a straightforward matter to isolate tone groups. Evidence shows that even trained native speakers find it very difficult to break talk up into such units and to identify tonics in speech (Brown and Yule 1983: 158). Brown and her colleagues have abandoned the tone group and instead prefer to work with longer 'pause-defined' units. Long and extended pauses may be seen as 'constituting boundaries of phonological units which may be related to information units' (*ibid.*: 164). They also abandon the tonic as the single focus of information and instead mark all prominences equally, thus doing away with the complexities of deciding exactly what is meant by *given* and *new*. Prominence then simply acquires a 'watch this!' function, and may be used to draw the listener's attention to a wide variety of phenomena in the discourse, including marking the beginning of a speaker's turn, a new topic, special emphasis or contrast, or new information.

Brown and her associates are concerned with how speakers manage large stretches of interaction, in terms of turn-taking and topic-signalling and how speakers use pitch level to interact. For instance, there seems to be a direct correlation in English between the beginning of a new *topic* in speech and a shift to a higher pitch (see also Menn and Boyce 1982; Cruttenden 1986: 129). Correspondingly, there is a tendency for the speaker to drop low in his or her pitch range at the end of a topic or sub-topic. These phenomena are particularly noticeable where one speaker has a long turn or series of long turns, and is likely to be less noticeable where there is multi-party talk where no speaker dominates, and where there are sequences of short turns (see Schaffer 1984). The evidence certainly seems convincing that this is a basic function of raised pitch in English, and one that can be directly taught if it is seen to be lacking in the learner's spoken production.

Brown and her associates work with a unit they call the *paratone*, defined as 'a short sequence of units beginning with a stressed peak high in the speaker's voice range'; the unit then shows a descending order of pitch height on subsequent prominent syllables till the final prominence, which is a fall from high to low pitch. Paratones are related to topic, rather than to information structure. A typical transcription of speech using this approach is reproduced here; Brown and her colleagues use three lines, rather like a simplified musical stave, on which changes in the speaker's pitch level and the direction of pitch movements can be plotted. The three lines represent the low, mid and high average bands of the speaker's pitch range. It should be noted that this is a transcript of Scottish (Edinburgh) English, which does not have the large pitch movements associated with Received Pronunciation.

(4.38)   I found my drink was a great problem with them because

at that time I drank whisky and lemonade + and I would

go and ask for whisky and lemonade and I would get

whisky and lemon + because you have to ask for whisky

or scotch and seven up + you know + I eventually

cottoned on to it + but + and they couldn't get over

the fact that I didn't like ice in whisky and of course

they either gave me ice whether I wanted it or not or

they stacked the glass up + right up to the level that

you would normally have if you had ice in your drink

```
                ⌢
          _        ⌐           ⌢   _
   _   _         _     ‾   _         _   _   _
```

(from Brown and Yule *Discourse Analysis* 1983, pp. 102–3)

Reader activity 8 ⚷

Consider the advantages and disadvantages of Brown's system of transcription compared with the Hallidayan one of tone units and tonic syllables, not so much in terms of which one accounts best for all the details of intonational features, but in terms of their pedagogical usefulness. Which system would learners be most likely to find usable and helpful? Are there other, more user-friendly ways of transcribing intonation?

Turn-taking is another important aspect of pitch level in this view of intonation. The speaker can signal a desire to continue a speaking turn by using non-low pitch, even at a point where there is a pause, or at the end of a syntactic unit, such as a clause. Equally, a down-step in pitch is often a good turn-yielding cue. The intonational cues interact with other factors such as syntax, lexis, non-verbal communication and the context itself, and are typical of how the different levels of encoding have to be seen as operating in harmony in a discourse-oriented view of language (see Schaffer 1983).

The approach to intonation characterised by the work of Brown and her associates need not necessarily contradict the Hallidayan, informational view. In terms of pedagogical usefulness, a Hallidayan approach using tone groups could be a useful framework for practising prominence at lower levels of language proficiency, and for practising different tones (see 4.7), both alone and in combination. The Brown approach to intonation undoubtedly has advantages from our point of view in its concern with the management of longer stretches of discourse and with turn-taking and topic-framing, and doing away with tone groups certainly avoids an analytical difficulty. The system of transcription, though, is not particularly user-friendly, and language teachers may want to adopt their own ways of indicating pitch level and prominences, using other types of visual. representation. What is more, the interactive approach outlined in 4.7.4 below could be taken as a global set of principles which subsume local phenomena such as yielding the turn or changing the topic.

4.7 Tones and their meanings

4.7.1 *Types of tones*

The prominent syllables in an utterance are the carriers of any significant variation in pitch that the speaker might use. At recognisable points in the utterance, the pitch level may rise, fall, or be carefully kept level. Phonologists disagree as to the number of discrete types of significant falling, rising and level tones that are used in English; some distinguish between as many as eight, others work with four or five. For our practical purposes five will be a useful number to consider. These are:

1. Fall $\searrow$
2. Rise–fall $\wedge\!\!\searrow$
3. Fall–rise $\vee\!\!\nearrow$
4. Rise $\nearrow$
5. Level $\longrightarrow$

It is worth noting that the tone contour can often spread itself out over more than one syllable or word (especially tones 2 and 3). Indeed, it will often be difficult to separate consecutive occurrences of a fall and a rise from a single fall–rise that spreads over several words, though speakers sometimes clearly indicate by running words together (often into the same tone group) in a broad 'sweep' of the voice that the tone is a complex one spread over word boundaries. In the following piece of natural data, speaker A utters the last part of his question in one sweep, and speaker B says the words *seen one* in a single sweep in her reply. But then B clearly and deliberately separates *seen* and *one* in her next utterance by making *one* the tonic (to emphasise that it was only *one*) and by placing the rise–fall on *one* only, making *seen* a non-tonic, level-toned prominence:

(4.39)   A: / are there MANY good REcord shops in town? /

B: / i DON'T know about MANy / but i've SEEN one /

A: / MM /

B: / WELL / i've SEEN ONE /

(Author's data 1989)

In our example utterances, it will be sufficient to mark the tone on our bold-face tonic syllable, with the understanding that other features of the delivery may extend the domain of the tone over more than that syllable.

Though opinions vary widely as to the functions of the different tones, most phonologists are agreed on a broad distinction between tones that end with a falling contour (fall and rise–fall), and tones which end with a rising contour (fall–rise and rise). What is more, the distinction seems to be a linguistic universal and to have some universally common functional contrasts attached to it (see Cruttenden 1986: 168–9). But such is the confusion amongst descriptive and applied phonologists as to just what particular tones mean that it is worth taking a close look at different views to see where they seem to be pointing, if indeed there is sufficient common ground to merit any general conclusions.

4.7.2 *Grammatical approaches*

One widely held view is that intonation has a grammatical function, that is to say, that there are 'correct' intonations for things such as questions, sentence-tags, subordinate clauses, and so on. Most common among these views is that 'yes–no' type interrogatives end in a rising tone, as in:

(4.40)   / IS it INteresting? /

(4.41)   / d'you feel ANGry? /

Conversely, *wh-* interrogatives are held to be uttered with a fall:

(4.42)   / WHAT'S the PROBlem? /

In fact, there seems to be little hard evidence that this *is* so, and much evidence to suggest that there is no one-to-one relationship between sentence-type and tone. C. C. Fries's (1964) data had 61 per cent of questions with a falling tone, and he concluded that 'there seem to be no intonation sequences on questions that are not also found on other types of utterances, and no intonation sequences on other types of utterances that are not found on questions'. Other researchers have come to just the same conclusion. Our opening example of the comedy sketch in Chapter 1 also underlined this lack of correspondence between grammatical form and discourse function, and it would seem open to question whether any direct intonational and grammatical correlates exist, whether for interrogatives or other grammatical structures. Tags, for instance, display that speaker-controlled variability that is the hallmark of interaction:

(4.43)   / it was BOB SMITH / < WASN'T it? /
                                      < WASN'T it? /

Both are interrogative *structures* (i.e. inverted verb and subject), but the choice of fall or rise seems to depend entirely on the speaker's assessment of the mutual state of knowledge between speaker and listener.

The more we look at intonation and grammar, the more we are forced to conclude that they are separate systems which work independently, but in harmony, to contribute to discourse meaning.

4.7.3 *Attitudinal approaches*

By far the most common view of intonation is that it is related to attitude and/or emotion, that some intonations express 'surprise', or 'detachment', and so on. This seems particularly so when we look at utterances such as:

(4.44)   / JOHN! / HOW nice to SEE you! / (high fall: surprise)

(4.45)   / he's COming on FRIday / ISn't that GOOD! / (rise–fall: excitement)

Very often, though, it is simply the lexis that misleads us: the selfsame intonation patterns can be used without any emotive implications, or else with completely different ones:

(4.46)   A: / CAN i invite my SISter? /

               B: / YES! / BRING her aLONG! / (high fall: enthusiasm? friendly acceptance?)

(4.47)   / the CHILD is BRILLiant / BEST in the CLASS / (rise–fall: purely informative? enthusiastic? sarcastic?)

We can see what a mess can be got into if we try to attach attitudinal or emotive labels to tones out of context, for it seems almost any emotion can be accompanied by any tone, and that without lexical or contextual information or other vocal clues we cannot reliably label a tone contour as displaying a particular attitude or emotion. The most we can say is that emotional intensification tends to be accompanied by wider pitch contrasts, but that is far from attributing particular emotions and attitudes to particular tone contours.

Reader activity 9 🔑

Try saying the utterances on the following page as they are labelled, and then try to change the words to any other words that fit the same pattern, but retaining the same tone contours, as in the example. How does your interpretation of the attitudinal or emotive aspect of the utterances change?

Example: / MARK / WHAT's the MATTer? /

           / YES / MAYbe FRIday /

           / POSSibly / i DON'T KNOW /

1. / he's a STUpid FOOL! /

2. / if you Opened your EYES / you'd SEE it! /

3. / JIM? / i DON'T beLIEVE it! /

The attitudinal/emotive approach to intonation is deeply entrenched in English language teaching. Boyle (1987) says that 'stress and intonation are employed in that area of language which deals with attitudes, moods, emotions'. Roberts (1983) suggests step-by-step intonational analysis of dialogues with students and considers the attitudinal analysis to be crucial, as seen in the instructions to teachers:

(4.48)   Step 3: This step must not be omitted. Pick a line or lines in which
           the attitude is very clear and where stress and intonation patterns are
           easily recognised; e.g. "what a beautiful day!".

           (Roberts 1983)

The teacher then utters this with level pitch which the students must 'correct' to a high falling pitch, because the speaker is 'happy', not 'sad'. The assumption is that level pitch would convey an attitude of sadness, and yet it is clear that level tone can be used by someone who is perfectly polite, happy and interested, as in this attested example of a telephone switchboard operator speaking to a caller:

(4.49)   / and YOU ARE MR . . . ? /

It is context, rather than the tone itself, which denotes whether someone is happy, sad, or whatever.

The point about attitude can be further underlined with two examples from teaching material by Thompson (1981): identical tone patterns in the two responses realise quite different attitudinal contexts:

(4.50)   (a) Alan: Sorry about the noise last night, Jo

           Jo: I should think so too

           (b) David: . . . Sorry to ring so late

           Jo: Not at all

We must conclude that it is probably a fruitless enterprise to teach intonation as 'attitude' or 'emotion'. How people express attitudes and emotions is a complex combination of vocal cues, intonation, lexis, non-verbal behaviour and contextual factors. Such matters may well be cultural universals; there is certainly not enough evidence to suggest major differences that warrant direct pedagogical intervention. When attitudinal cues are *mis*understood, as in judgements such as 'speakers of language X always sound arrogant in English', the reason is likely to be traceable to misleading signals concerning what assumptions the speaker has encoded by tone choice with regard to such things as the state of the hearer's knowledge, what is recoverable from context and what is 'newsworthy' or the centre of focus, that is to say, the interactive level of signalling that intonation can be shown to convey. L1 interference may also play a part: if a speaker has as L1 a language with a narrower pitch range than English (e.g. Danish), then he/she may well sound 'flat' and monotonous in English, or if L1 is a language with a tendency to 'jump' regularly in pitch (e.g. French), then the speaker may sound 'excitable'. But the remedies here would seem to be training in typical English pitch range and tone contours rather than anything to do with teaching learners how to express emotions.

4.7.4 Interactive approaches

The interpretation of tone choice that seems most reliable and which seems to make most sense, given what we have said about the fundamentally interactive nature of the other parts of the intonation system (prominence, tonic placement) is to see tones as fulfilling an interactive role in the signalling of the 'state of play' in discourse. The speaker has to judge how to deliver the tone group. Should it be delivered as open-ended, as incomplete in some way, as non-conducive with regard to a possible response (i.e. not restricting the possible field of response), as background to what is the main message, as referring to common ground? Or on the other hand, should it be delivered as possessing a finality or completeness, as 'telling' rather than simply referring to background, as conducive towards the response of the hearer, or as the main core of the message? Tone choice in English seems to fulfil these opposing functions, and Cruttenden (1981) has referred to a major distinction between *open* and *closed* meanings, while Brazil (1985a and b) talks of *referring* and *proclaiming* functions. In British Received Pronunciation, the open or referring functions are carried by tones ending in rises; the closed or proclaiming functions by those ending in falls. When there is no orientation on the part of the speaker to either of these functions, the tone is neutral or oblique, and is realised by a level pitch. Let us consider some examples:

(4.51)   / IF you ⟍LIKÉ / we can GO via ⟍MANchester /

(4.52)   A: / are YOU mr ⟍BLAKÉ? /

        B: / ⟍YÉS /

(4.53)   A: / NOW / YOU must be mr BLAKE? /

          B: / YES /

          A: / RIGHT / room TWENty-SIX /

(4.54)   A: / are YOU mr BLAKE? /

          B: / YES /

          A: / AH / the SECretary / would like a WORD with you /

          B: / OH /

In (4.51), 'if you like' is treated as background or subordinate information to the main message. But *subordinate* here is not intended in the grammatical sense; the speaker might have considered the *grammatically* subordinate clause to be the main message and the (grammatically) main clause to be the background or 'common ground' information:

.(4.55)   / we COULD go via MANchester / but ONLY if you WANT to /

In (4.52), 'Are you Mr Blake?' is an open-ended utterance: it calls for some completion or closing, in this case an answer that establishes the unknown polarity (a 'yes–no' question). Mr Blake's answer provides the finality that was missing. Speaker A in (4.53) is sure that this is Mr Blake, and so uses a closed and conducive tone. But in (4.54), Mr Blake is not satisfied that things *are* final and closed, and his rising-tone answer has an implicit 'why?' or 'who wants to know?' in it, and an incompleteness that is only closed by A's utterance, followed by a confirmation of the closure by Mr Blake's 'oh'.

Reader activity 10

Label the tonics (the main prominences in bold) in these utterances with either fall–rise ($\searrow\nearrow$) or falling ($\searrow$) tones, according to whether you judge them to be 'open/referring' meanings or 'closed/proclaiming' meanings:

1.   / IF you see **TIM** / CAN you ask him to **RING** me? /

2.   A: / i met JOsie **COLEman** / in **TOWN** /
     B: / JOsie **COLEman**? /
     A: / **YES** /

3.   A: / **IS** it five o'**CLOCK**? /
     B: / FIVE **TO** /
     A: / **AH**! / **GOOD**! / JUST in **TIME**! /

In this interactive view of tone choice, the speaker is constantly making assumptions as to what should be treated as background or common ground, what may be uttered with a conducive tone, what is open-ended, and what should be delivered as world-changing in the perception of the hearer.

Brazil (1985a and b) attaches a further interactive significance to the internal choice represented by rise–fall as opposed to fall, and rise as opposed to fall–rise. Rise–fall and rise are seen to be *dominant-speaker* choices; at any given point in a conversation, one speaker will typically exercise dominance, though dominance may change frequently in casual conversation among equals. Dominant speakers have the option of using the dominant tones *or* the non-dominant ones; non-dominant speakers will only use non-dominant tones. In a situation such as a classroom, it is most likely that the teacher will exercise the dominant-speaker option; pupils who do so may be misheard as insolent. The following is most likely to be a teacher giving the class information rather than a pupil answering a teacher question:

(4.56)   / it's TOOK / TOOK / is the past tense of TAKE /

The interactive approach to tone choice seems to be the most convincing of the explanations we have looked at in 4.7.2–4. Nonetheless, there are unresolved difficulties for pedagogical application. For instance, it is difficult to conceptualise why *wh-* questions are very often uttered with a falling tone, when they seem every bit as 'incomplete' and 'open-ended' as yes–no questions. One has to remind oneself that the choice of tone is independent of the choice of grammatical form, and that it is the speaker's assessment of the conducive (and therefore non-open) character of the question that is important. 'WHAT'S the **TIME**?', uttered with falling tone, invites the hearer to choose from a catalogue of possible alternatives, and can be seen to be conducive, but such explanations often seem to be pushing the interactive terminology to its limits, and may not sound convincing in class or in teaching materials. However, until we have more satisfactory terms for interactive functions, the interactive approach as a whole can be adapted and simplified for teaching purposes and used productively. Bradford (1988) offers just such an adaptation.

4.8 Key

The *relative* level of pitch between one part of an utterance and another can often be heard to change, to jump upwards, or to drop and trail off. We are all familiar with utterances where the speaker's pitch level suddenly rises, as in B's reply in (4.57), where we can show the jump by moving to the line above in our transcription:

(4.57)   A: / IS that COUsin of yours still here? /

B: / she's my SISter / NOT my COUsin! /

B seems to be expressing something contrary to A's expectations; there is a contrast between *cousin* and *sister*. Sometimes, though, the pitch level drops:

(4.58)   / WELL / THAT'S IT then / THAT'S FInished /

Here the speaker is indicating that 'that's finished' does not add anything new to the discourse, but rather that it is to be heard as functionally equivalent to 'that's it then', as saying more or less the same thing. These two choices Brazil (1985a and b) refers to as *high key* and *low key*, respectively. When speakers are speaking in the middle of their average pitch range, they are speaking in *mid-key*, and the utterance simply *adds* more to the ongoing discourse. These three functions, high for contrastiveness, mid for addition, and low for reiteration are the *key system* of English; they represent a further layer of speaker choice in intonation.

The jump to high key and the drop to low have also been seen as important cues in topic management, with high key marking the initiation of a topical segment, and low key its ending (see the remarks on paratones in 4.6). Bradford (1988) again provides useful pedagogical applications of Brazil's account of key choices.

Reader activity 11

Consider points where the speakers would be likely to jump to high key or to drop to low key in these utterances:

1. A: / i'll ASK CARlos / HE'S brazilian /

    B: / CARlos? / he's CHIlean / DIDn't you KNOW? /

2. A: / WELL / THANKS / you've been VERY HELPful /

    B: / WHO? / ME? / NOT at ALL! / it's my JOB! /

4.9 Pitch across speakers

A final observation needs to be made concerning how pitch-level choices operate across speaker turns. Matching or concord in pitch between speakers is a phenomenon noted by Brown, Currie and Kenworthy (1980: 23–4), and dealt with by Brazil (1985a and b) under the heading of *termination*. Brown's team show with their data how speakers sometimes begin a new topic by asking a question which begins high in the speaker's pitch range, and how this high pitch is echoed by the hearer with high pitch at the beginning of the answer. A typical topic-opening sequence might be:

(4.59)　A: / HAVE you ever been to　TURkey?　/

　　　　B: / NO / NEver /

　　　　A: / it's a GREAT COUNtry / REAlly /

This kind of 'termination' choice exercises constraints on the listener as to what sort of key will be used in the answer. In example (4.59), the speaker expects the hearer to produce a high-key, contrastive answer (a true yes–no polarity).

High-key concord is used not only at the beginning of topics; in (4.60), speaker A responds in high key to agree with B's assessment of a situation which is contrary to normal expectations:

(4.60)　(A and B have been discussing a photocopier which is always breaking down)

　　　　A: / SHOCKing things / AREN'T they /

　　　　B: / they ARE / YES / and THAT'S / a NEW one /

　　　　A: / YES /

　　　　(Author's data 1989)

If a speaker uses low termination, as B does in (4.61), the constraints on the hearer to continue are minimal:

(4.61)　A: / so THAT'S IT then /

　　　　B: / YEAH / THAT'S IT /

　　　　A: / RIGHT /

4.10 Summary

The picture we have painted of intonation may suggest a complexity that will never lend itself to straightforward pedagogy. However, the distinct advantage of an interactive description such as Brazil's, with discrete layers of choice, or, for that matter, any description that adequately separates the functions of prominence, tone and pitch level, is that separate parts of the system can be dealt with individually, while not losing sight of either the overall discourse significance of the different levels of choice or the unified sense of the importance of speaker choice and adjustment to the constantly changing state of play between participants in the talk. Interactive approaches to intonation, as well as being intuitively more satisfying, do away with much of the confusing labelling of attitudinal approaches and offer a more systematic framework for innovative pedagogy. Decisions will still have to be made about presentation and how to make a complex set of concepts appealing to learners, but good language teachers have never lacked the ability to translate new types of description into useful practice.

4.11 Conclusion

Should intonation be left to develop for itself, or should we *teach* it? There do seem to be some good arguments for the latter view. For one thing, while all languages seem to use intonation in some form or another, it is by no means certain that realisations are the same. Even within dialects and varieties of English, particular tones seem to have different functions. Some researchers claim to have found significant differences from English in the distribution of tones in other languages and how learners use English tones (e.g. for German, see Scuffil 1982, A. Fox 1984, and Rees 1986; for Dutch, see Willems 1982). But learners' problems may not all be explained away by contrastive analysis. Lower-level learners often have to encode utterances in L2 word-by-word, and under such conditions, appropriate tone-grouping, prominence, tone and key may simply not be realised. This fact might argue for giving learners the opportunity to practise intonation using words and phrases they are already familiar with and do not have to struggle too much with on the level of lexico-grammatical encoding. Or else other modes of spoken language such as scripted drama might be used; Johns-Lewis (1986) shows how quite wide pitch variation is found in acting situations (in comparison with conversation and reading aloud), and drama could offer a context for spotlighting intonation features.

There are certainly practical conclusions to be drawn from the interactive descriptions we have examined. For one thing, the simple fall and the fall–rise are definitely the most useful tones to present and practise first, since they fulfil such basic, everyday functions, and they can be presented in contrast with each other in the same utterance or exchange, as in examples (4.51–55). The key system is also relatively straightforward and easily graspable, and contextualised dialogues and situations can be devised to elicit different keys. Pitch rise and drops at topic and sub-topic boundaries can be practised in prepared talks and anecdote-telling. Such discrete-level practice is probably more manageable than trying to elicit the whole complex system of choices in one go.

Reader activity 12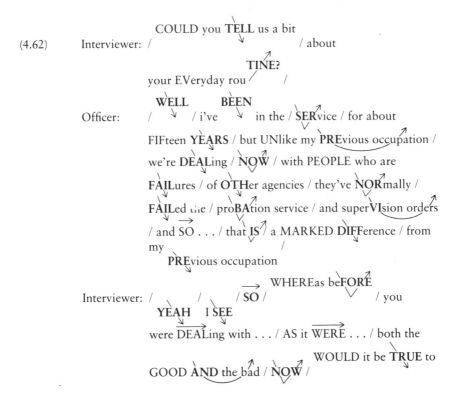

To finish this chapter, we might look at what a short piece of natural discourse looks like when transcribed for all its relevant features (prominence, tone and key) in the kind of transcription we have been using in this chapter. Do you think the transcription is pedagogically usable as it stands? Is it too complicated? Ought it to be changed in some ways, or might other types of transcription more effectively convey the same amount of information?

(The extract is taken from a recording of a senior prison officer in a British gaol talking about his job in an informal interview.)

(4.62) Interviewer: / COULD you TELL us a bit / about your EVeryday rou / TINE? /

Officer: / WELL / i've BEEN / in the / SERvice / for about FIFteen YEARS / but UNlike my PREvious occupation / we're DEALing / NOW / with PEOPLE who are FAILures / of OTHer agencies / they've NORmally / FAILed the / proBAtion service / and superVIsion orders / and SO . . . / that IS / a MARKED DIFFerence / from my PREvious occupation

Interviewer: / / / SO / WHEREas beFORE / you YEAH I SEE were DEALing with . . . / AS it WERE . . . / both the GOOD AND the bad / NOW / WOULD it be TRUE to

115

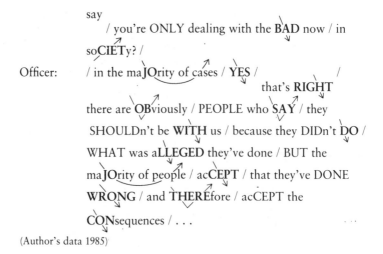

Officer:

(Author's data 1985)

This chapter ends the investigation of the contribution of discourse analysis to the three main levels of linguistic description which are already the basis of language teaching: grammar, lexis and phonology. The rest of the book will consider descriptions of speech and writing based on discourse models and will address the questions of how natural speech and writing can best be described and how such descriptions can be related to the concerns of language teachers, especially in the areas of speaking/listening and reading/ writing skills.

Further reading

The most accessible works that deal with intonation in discourse in general are
Brown and Yule (1983), Brazil (1985a and b) and Cruttenden (1986), but there
are many other sources dealing with particular features.

On the importance of relating articulatory and other broader features of speech see
Wong (1986), and for more on teaching voice quality settings, see Esling and
Wong (1983).

On the notion of feet see Abercrombie (1964).

The concept of stress-timing is explained in Pike (1945); also useful for the
arguments concerning rhythm and stress is Ladd (1980: 34–46).

Brazil, Coulthard and Johns (1980) and Coulthard and Brazil (1982) provide
further explanations of prominence, and a very interesting study of how teachers
use prominence in language classes is Hewings (1987).

For more on the relationship between tone groups and clauses, see Schubiger (1964)
and Lindstrom (1978), and for further examples of the Brown approach, see Yule
(1980a and b) and Brown (1983).

For intonation and turn-taking, see Brown, Currie and Kenworthy (1980: 24) and
Cutler and Pearson (1986).

On the lack of correlation between grammatical categories and tones, Stenström
(1984) and Geluykens (1988) are worth reading.

An example of a different distribution of tones in a non-RP variety of English is
Guy *et al.*'s (1986) study of Australian intonation.

Finally, for another discourse-oriented approach to teaching intonation, see the
very practical functional categories in V. J. Cook (1979).

5 Spoken language

'Speak when you're spoken to!'
the Queen sharply interrupted
her.
'But if everybody obeyed that
rule,' said Alice, who was
always ready for a little argument, 'and if you only spoke
when you were spoken to, and
the other person always waited
for *you* to begin, you see nobody
would ever say anything.'

**Lewis Carroll: *Through the Looking
Glass***

5.1 Introduction

So far in this book we have looked at discourse analysis in general and, in greater detail, at the way grammar, lexis and phonology have been approached by discourse analysts. Our task now is to look closer at various manifestations of discourse, in this chapter spoken and in the next written, with a view to potential applications in language teaching. We have already stated as our ongoing concern the establishment of as accurate a picture as possible of natural discourse, in order to have this as a yardstick for judging approaches to language teaching and for evaluating what goes on in classrooms and the output of learners.

Spoken language is a vast subject, and little is known in hard statistical terms of the distribution of different types of speech in people's everyday lives. If we list at random a number of different types of speech and consider how much of each day or week we spend engaged in each one, we can only roughly guess at some sort of frequency ranking, other than to say that casual conversation is almost certainly the most frequent for most people. The rest will depend on our daily occupation and what sorts of contacts we have with others. Some different types of speech might be:

telephone calls (business and private)

service encounters (shops, ticket offices, etc.)
interviews (jobs, journalistic, in official settings)
classroom (classes, seminars, lectures, tutorials)
rituals (church prayers, sermons, weddings)
monologues (speeches, stories, jokes)
language-in-action (talk accompanying *doing*: fixing, cooking, assembling, demonstrating, etc.)
casual conversation (strangers, friends, intimates)
organising and directing people (work, home, in the street)

Until large corpora of natural speech are assembled (and that is no small task given the problems of recording such data), we have to rely on intuition as language teachers to decide which forms of talk are most central and useful to investigate and practise with groups of learners. But we can be confident that such areas as casual conversation, language-in-action, monologues of various kinds, telephone calls, service encounters and, from the point of view of evaluating what goes on in classrooms, classroom talk, will all be worth investigating and understanding more clearly.

We have already touched on classroom talk as described by the Birmingham school of discourse analysts in section 1.5, and on conversation in section 1.7 in connexion with the ethnomethodological approach. Here we shall look closely at what has been said about the forms and patterns of different types of talk and consider whether there are things that can be taught or practised to assist language learning. We shall, as always, not necessarily assume that, because something can be described, it must therefore be taught. We shall begin with small units and work up to larger ones.

5.2   Adjacency pairs

Pairs of utterances in talk are often mutually dependent; a most obvious example is that a question predicts an answer, and that an answer presupposes a question. It is possible to state the requirements, in a normal conversational sequence, for many types of utterances, in terms of what is expected as a response and what certain responses presuppose. Some examples might be:

Utterance function	Expected response
greeting	greeting
congratulation	thanks
apology	acceptance
inform	acknowledge
leave-taking	leave-taking

E

Pairs of utterances such as *greeting–greeting* and *apology–acceptance* are called *adjacency pairs* (see Schegloff and Sacks 1973). The mutual dependence of such utterances is underlined by the fact that we can only be absolutely sure of the *function* of the initiating utterance (the *first pair-part* as it is usually called) when it is contextualised with the response it gets (the *second pair-part*), and vice versa (thus 'hello' in English could be a greeting, a request to a telephone caller to identify themselves, or an expression of surprise: 'Hello! What's this here?'). This is to reiterate the problem of form and function raised in section 1.2. In example (5.1) the imperative first pair-part can be classified functionally as an *informing move*, in light of the *acknowledging* second pair-part it receives:

(5.1)   (On a train)
           Ticket collector: (inspecting passenger's ticket) Change at
               Peterborough.
           Passenger: Thank you.

           (Author's field notes)

Reader activity 1 🔑

Look at these extracts from natural data and consider the different functions of *thank you* in each case. Follow-up moves such as 'not at all' / 'that's okay' / 'you're welcome' would *not* be appropriate here in British English; why not? Can you think of any culture or language where they *would* be realised?

1.   Bus conductor: One pound twenty.
     Passenger: (gives £1.20)
     Conductor: Thank you.
     Passenger: Thank you.

2.   (University seminar; lecturer is facing the class, using an
     overhead projector.)
     Student: It's not focused.
     Lecturer: Thank you (adjusts the projector).

Adjacency pairs are of different types. Some ritualised first pair-parts may have an identical second pair-part (*hello – hello, happy New Year – happy New Year*), while others expect a different second pair-part (*congratulations – thanks*). Equally, a second pair-part such as *thanks* will presuppose quite a wide range of first pair-parts (offers, apologies, informing moves, congratulations, commiserations, etc.). Other first pair-parts have various possibilities and generate further expectations too; take, for example, *invitation*:

(5.2)   A: Would you like to come over for a drink tomorrow?
           B: Yes, that would be nice.   (*accept*)
              Yes, if it could be after six.   (*accept with condition*)
              No.   (*reject*)

We probably react against the bald *No* answer; politeness codes demand a more elaborate structure for the response:

(5.3)   B: Thanks very much, but I'm afraid I'm booked up tomorrow night, what about . . . (etc.)

We can segment the polite refusal of the invitation into *appreciation* ('thanks very much'), *softener* ('I'm afraid'), *reason* ('I'm booked up') and *face-saver* ('what about . . .'). This pattern would typically be found between adult friends, colleagues, etc. in informal but polite situations. More intimate situations may well omit the 'softener'. Each of these elements will have several possible realisations, and these can be practised in language learning in a systematic way.

Different roles and settings will generate different structures for such adjacency pairs, and discourse analysts try to observe in natural data just what patterns occur in particular settings. Scarcella and Brunak (1981) compared native and non-native speakers' strategies for giving informal invitations. The native speakers *prefaced* their invitations (e.g. 'I was wondering, uh, we're having a party . . .'), while the non-natives were sometimes too formal or too blunt (e.g. 'I would like to invite you to a party'; 'I want you to come in a party'). Similarly, it seems that native speakers usually preface *disagreement* second pair-parts in English with partial agreement ('yes, but . . .') and with softeners (Pearson 1986). This sort of observation has direct implications for the design of role play and similar activities and what linguistic elements need to be pre-taught, where learners are instructed to behave in ways specified by the activity and where the goal is a simulation of 'real life' discourse.

Observation of the behaviour of native and non-native speakers is all-important, and differences in such behaviour can enable teachers to pinpoint linguistic deficiencies which can be made up by concentrating on particular areas and realisations. Trosborg (1987), for instance, who studied apology strategies, found that because of lower linguistic competence, her non-native speaker subjects resorted more to ritualised apology formulae than did native speaker subjects. The native speakers used other strategies such as 'repair offers' (e.g. 'oh dear, let me get you another one'), or even challenged the accusation. In short, the native speakers elaborated the apology, but one must have the linguistic equipment to do this in an L2. Again, this emphasises the importance of pre-teaching particular strategies and the language that realises them; otherwise, role plays can become no more than tests that learners are certain to fail.

Data-based observations of the kinds referred to above question the adequacy of formula-based 'functional' teaching of the type that swept into fashion in English language teaching in the late 1970s, and underline the wisdom of the trend towards a broader-based and eclectic lexico-grammatical input to enable the learner to 'behave' naturally. However, this is not to deny the usefulness of formulae as a survival kit at the most elementary levels, nor should we forget that much native-speaker language *is* formulaic; it is simply that the native speaker usually has a vastly greater range of formulae to call upon for use in a wider range of strategic domains, along with a flexible and adaptable lexicon of non-formula based items.

The principle of adjacency pairs and how they are realised in natural speech point to the importance of creating minimal contexts in the teaching of common communicative functions and the limited value of teaching single utterances. We have seen once again that the structure and elaboration of the adjacency pair is determined by role and setting, and that the functions of its component utterances depend on the co-presence of both parts. In Chapter 1 we additionally noted the importance of the *follow-up* move in signalling function. Considering the follow-up move as well brings us back to the notion of the exchange as a significant unit of discourse.

5.3   Exchanges

Chapter 1 described the exchange as the central unit in the Birmingham-type analysis of classroom talk, and showed that it could be applied outside of the classroom too (section 1.6). Exchanges are independently observable entities; adjacency pairs may be found within their boundaries, but first and second pair-parts do not necessarily coincide with initiating and responding moves. In (5.4) below, there is such a coincidence, but in (5.5) adjacency pairing occurs in the initiation and response (*statement of achievement – congratulation*), *and* in the responding and follow-up move (*congratulation – thanks*):

(5.4)   A: Congratulations on the new job, by the way.
         B: Oh, thanks.

(5.5)   A: I've just passed my driving test.
         B: Oh, congratulations.
         A: Thanks.

Particularly noticeable in the Sinclair–Coulthard data was the pattern of the three-part exchange in traditional classrooms, where the teacher made the initiation *and* the follow-up move, while pupils were restricted to responding moves. In a good many language classes this is still the pattern, especially in situations where large classes of perhaps 40 to 50 pupils is the norm. Where this happens, it is likely that pupils will have the chance to practise only a very impoverished range of utterance functions. In such language classrooms, learners rarely get the opportunity to take other than the responding role, and even in cases where students are encouraged to initiate, the follow-up move is often still in the hands of the teacher, and learners get little or no practice in this particular discourse function.

It is worth looking at some common follow-up moves in eliciting exchanges in everyday talk. While speakers outside classrooms do not usually behave like teachers and evaluate the *quality* of one another's utterances (in terms of correctness, fluency, etc.), they often evaluate (or at least react to) its content; we might compare what can sometimes happen in the classroom (5.6) with what is likely to happen in the real world (5.7):

(5.6)   Teacher: Now Maria, you ask Fumiko.
          Maria: What did you do at the weekend?
          Fumiko: I went to Wales.
          Teacher: Good, now Fumiko, you ask Marco, . . . (etc.)

(5.7)   Maria: What did you do at the weekend?
          Fumiko: I went to Wales.
          Maria: Oh, really? Where did you go?

Follow-up moves of this latter kind might include: *how nice, that's interesting, oh dear, how awful, lucky you, oh no, I see, did you, right*. These evaluations can also occur in the responding move in informing exchanges. They are of interest because they are often not directly translatable language to language (compare Swedish *säger du det?*, Spanish ¡ay! ¡qué horror!, with English realisations such as *really?* and *how awful!*). What is more, they are often noticeably absent from the learner's natural conversational discourse, where instead we may get a range of vocalisations or 'noises' that can be 'culturally peculiar' to the English ear (cf. the Japanese tendency to use an extended *o-o-o-o-h* in reply to a wide range of initiations and responses).

Reader activity 2 🔑

One possible way of getting learners to practise adjacency pairs and exchange structures in the classroom after the necessary realisations have been taught is to use *function–chain* activities. A sequence of functions is decided upon and role cards given to pairs of learners instructing them to play out a sequence of events calculated to generate the desired functions. On the following page there is a real example of two non-native speakers acting out their instructions, which are reproduced before the transcript. To what extent do you think the activity achieves its aims? Is the exchange structure natural, and are the adjacency pairs realised in natural ways?

Language for pre-teaching in the presentation segment of the lesson: asking for and giving topical information; saying one is unable to give information, etc. (e.g. 'What's been happening?'; 'catch up on sth'; 'Sorry, I can't tell you'; exciting events', 'be up to date', etc.).

Role card A:

You've just come back from a holiday abroad and are talking to a friend/colleague, B.

1. Try and catch up on the national news you've missed while away.
2. Try in particular to find out if anything important has happened on the *political* scene. Get as much detail as you can.
3. Find out about an important sporting event you know you have missed.

Role card B:

You are talking to your friend/colleague, A, who has just returned from a holiday abroad.

1. Tell him/her you are not really up-to-date either and explain why.
2. You *do* know of one important political event; tell him/her what it was.
3. Apologise for not knowing what's been happening in the world of sport, and explain why.

Sample transcript:

A: Well, what happened in this country in the last six weeks?
B: I really can't tell you, I haven't read any newspapers.
A: Wasn't there a big event in politics?
B: Yes, it turned out the Democrats got a new leader.
A: Oh, I see, that's interesting, can you tell me more about it?
B: Awfully sorry, I heard it on the radio but I was too tired and I don't remember.
A: Doesn't matter. What about Manchester United's game?
B: Sorry, I'm not interested in football.

(ICC data 1988–90)

There does often seem to be a need for encouraging learners to practise common follow-up strategies of the type we have looked at, and design of speaking activities will once again be crucial, especially the roles learners are to perform. Getting students to interview one another on given subjects should yield question–answer sequences with opportunities for the questioners to use follow-up moves, but if the questioner perceives his/her role as a 'journalistic' interviewer rather than learning about someone and *exchanging* information, then the journalistic role, with its typical *low* occurrence of follow-up moves, may be the one played out. There is evidence of this in the following piece of learner dialogue, where student A is interviewing student B. B is recounting his career:

(5.8)   B: Well, I studied theology and qualified as a priest.
           A: Oh!
           B: But after I saw this job, this job as a priest is nothing for me, I . . .
           A: Did you not like it?
           B: It was much too stressing.
           A: It . . . is it not a bit like a social worker?
           B: Yes, it's . . . most part of it is social work, but that, that troubles
              and the psychological troubles, they, they told to me, ah, I
              couldn't manage to, to stand all, you understand? And then I get
              sick, and my heart was and so . . .
           A: Became ill.
           B: Yes, ill, and, and I left the job. It wasn't, I wasn't able to stand it.
           A: Do you think you were too young?
           B: Perhaps, I thought, yes, perhaps this is . . . the, the young people
              didn't come to the church, and there were too less young people,
              and too ma . . . too mu . . . too many old peoples, and I felt I'm
              too young for this job, I, in ten years perhaps . . .
           A: You might go back?
           B: Or in fifteen I can go back, yes . . .

           (ICC data 1988–90)

The interview continues in this vein throughout. Only in her first turn in the extract does A evaluate B's utterance, with a simple 'oh!'; at other potential follow-up move slots she is concerned with helping B in his utterances ('became ill', 'you might go back'). We get none of the typical interactive follow-ups listed earlier that are found in natural conversation; speaker A is competently playing out the role of 'questioner' imposed by the interviewing situation, with the addition of giving support to her interlocutor.

Reader activity 3 🗝

Look at this further piece of learner–learner interview data on the following page and consider the follow-up moves (or lack of them). Taking also into consideration the initiating moves, what evidence is there of how the speakers perceive their roles?

(Student B is explaining his surname to student A.)

B: The name Akkad is a very, has a very long story, it goes back to at least 2,000 years. It was a state between Syria, Iraq and Jordan, they called it the the Akkada . . . and this is where my name been, ah, deriven from, you know . . . I'm not bluffing, but this is a small story about name.

A: It's quite interesting, and erm, so you, where are you from?

B: Syria, Middle East.

A: And you live here in Switzerland?

B: Yes, ah, for about 23 years.

A: Can you tell me a bit about you?

B: About myself, well, I . . .

A: About what, what . . .

B: What I've done here? Well, I've, erm, when I first came to Switzerland, I've studied first a little German language.

A: Yes.

B: I mean I learnt the German language, it was very difficult.

A: It's hard, isn't it?

B: Yes, particularly the Swiss German . . . (etc.)

(ICC data 1988–90)

Close examination of learner data can tell us a lot about how activity design affects output. The *absence* of a feature in learner talk may not necessarily mean that the feature has not been acquired; it may simply be that the activity does not generate its natural use. The intimate relationship between exchange structure and role and setting means that designing activities for speaking involves variables that will have an effect on the exchange patterns of the output. Interview-style patterns are fine if interview-language is the desired goal; they are a poor substitute for natural conversational patterns if that is the goal. Conversational data *do* contain stretches where initiate–respond–initiate–respond is the pattern, but rarely for long periods; such a pattern extended over a whole conversation would almost certainly lead the person on the receiving end of the questions to assess the event as having been 'like an interrogation'. This is not to underestimate the difficulty of designing activities which *will* generate natural conversational exchange patterns among learners, nor to say that such an enterprise is doomed to failure; it is simply to isolate one of the levels of difficulty involved. Discourse analysis can highlight problem areas; it cannot give simple solutions to the problems.

5.4   Turn-taking

Much has been made in discourse analysis of the study of turn-taking, and one can hardly write an introductory survey of discourse studies without noting the work done in this field. In the classic ethnomethodological way, discourse analysts have observed how participants organise themselves to take turns at talk. In any piece of natural English discourse, turns will occur smoothly, with only little overlap and interruption, and only very brief silences between turns (on average, less than a second). People take turns when they are selected or *nominated* by the current speaker, or if no one is selected, they may speak of their own accord (*self-selection*). If neither of these conditions applies, the person who is currently speaking may continue (Sacks *et al.* 1974). While the current speaker is talking, listeners are attentive to the syntactic completeness or otherwise of the speaker's contribution, and to clues in the pitch level that may indicate that a turn is coming to a close (see section 4.6). There are specific linguistic devices for getting the turn when one is unable to enter the normal flow of turn-taking or when the setting demands that specific conventions be followed. These vary greatly in level of formality and appropriacy to different situations ('If I may, Mr Chairman', 'I wonder if I might say something', 'Can I just come in here', 'Hang on a minute', 'Shut up will you, I can't get a word in edgewise'). There are also linguistic means of *not* taking the turn when one has the opportunity, or simply of making it clear to the speaker that we are attending to the message. These are usually referred to as *back-channel* responses, and consist of vocalisations such as *mm*, *ah-ha*, and short words and phrases such as *yeah*, *no*, *right*, *sure* (see Yngve 1970). Back-channel realisations vary interestingly from culture to culture (some languages have back-channel vocalisations that sound odd in English, such as *eh-eh*, or highly nasalised sounds). Another feature of turn-taking is the way speakers predict one another's utterances and often complete them for them, or overlap with them as they complete; we saw this happening to a certain extent in the way our student interviewer helped her partner in extract (5.8).

Natural conversational data can often seem chaotic because of back-channel, utterance-completions and overlaps, as in this extract:

(5.9)   (A and B are discussing domestic pets.)

A: Well, of course, people who go to the vet's ⌈ are
B: ⌊ Mm.
A: interested in the cats and dogs, ain't they?
B: ⌊ Yeah, but the people that first
     have pets kit—pets er don't ⌈ realise what's ⌈ involved, do they?
A: ⌊ care   ⌊ Well it sorts them
     out, you know, those that don't care that's it so . . . but
B: ⌊ Mm   ⌊ Mm

A: if you wanna, you know, somebody that's keen on having a pet
B: ⌐ Mm   ⌐ Mm
A: and want it in ⌐ good order.
B: ⌊ Done . . . done properly, that's right, yeah.

(Lawley data 1987)

This extract is not at all untypical. Such a transcript looks so messy that we would probably never dream of using it in an English language class as a dialogue for learners. Even on the rare occasions when authentic dialogue is transcribed in teaching materials, it is usually so 'cleaned up' that it bears little resemblance to raw data. Such real data are a reminder of how idealised are the representations of speech not only in teaching materials, but in novels, so-called 'verbatim' reports (such as reports of parliamentary debates), radio and television soap operas and drama in general. Raw data of this kind, if well-recorded, still have a use in extensive listening activities for more advanced learners, but we have to resign ourselves to the inevitability that most conversational data used in class or transcribed in materials will have ordered, non-overlapping turn-taking.

The traditional classroom, as observed by Sinclair and Coulthard, has very ordered turn-taking under the control of the teacher, and pupils rarely speak out of turn. More recent trends in classroom organisation, such as pair and group work, attempt to break this rigid turn-taking pattern, but do not always succeed in recreating more natural patterns. Often the problem lies, as before, in activity design. We are all familiar with role plays where individuals are so intent on formulating their contributions and making them at the 'right' moment as determined by the activity rubric, that they pay little attention to the contributions of others, and the natural patterns of back-channel, utterance completion, etc. simply do not occur. The looser the restrictions on what and when people may speak, the more naturally the turn-taking emerges. Extract (5.8), for all its faults, contains fairly natural turn-taking, as one would expect in an interview, and it also contains utterance completion, which one might not expect if the 'journalistic' role were fully dominant all of the time.

It is not a question of telling learners that speakers take turns; they know this naturally from their own language. The problem is to make sure that activities generate the natural sorts of turn-taking that occur in the target discourse type and so not inhibit typical turn-taking patterns. But two other problems might arise in connexion with turn-taking: one is the fact that dominant and garrulous speakers often grab too many turns (gender can be a factor here), and the other is the question of culture-specific conventions.

Problems of dominant speakers can be partially solved by giving people with such tendencies restricted roles in activities, and quieter learners will often rise to the challenge of a major speaker role in the comparative anonymity provided by role plays and similar activities. The culture-specific problems are more complex. For instance, in some cultures, silence has a more acceptable role than in others. Many teachers will be familiar with individuals or groups from cultures where longer silences seem to be tolerated in conversation (e.g. Finns), or where the 'thinking time' before a response is forthcoming seems agonisingly long (a tendency observable among Japanese learners). Discourse analysts have looked at such phenomena and try to describe the different norms that speakers from different cultures orient to during such behaviour. A set of norms in one culture might decree that talk must be kept going, whenever possible, even if only to 'buy time'; another culture might decree that face must be preserved wherever possible, and not put at risk by unconsidered talk. *Rule-conflicts* of this type are often seen to be the underlying cause of conversational breakdowns (e.g. for Japanese versus American norms, see Noguchi 1987). It is not easy to see how the language teacher can solve such problems, except to draw attention to the typical behaviour of the target culture, and to warn learners of the possible consequences of transferring L1 conventions to the L2 context.

Other features of how turns are given and gained in English may also prompt specific awareness training where necessary; these include body language such as inhalation and head movement as a turn-seeking signal, eye contact, gesticulation, etc., as well as linguistic phenomena such as a drop in pitch (see Chapter 4) or use of grammatical tags.

Lexical realisations of turn management can be taught directly. In addition to the range of phrases mentioned above for getting the turn and not being interrupted in formal and informal settings, there are conventional phrases for interrupting ('Can I interrupt for a moment?', 'Hang on a minute, I've got something to tell you', 'Sorry to butt in, but . . . '), for pre-planning one's turn ('I'll try to be brief, but there are a number of things . . . '; 'There were three things I wanted to say'; 'Just two things, Mary, . . . ') and for closing ('And just one last point'; 'One more second and I'll finish', 'One last thing, Bill', 'And that's it').

Our overall conclusion is that turn-taking in itself is something that may not need to be 'taught', but specific linguistic realisations can be presented and practised and significant cultural differences can at least be pointed out to the learner.

Reader activity 4

Look at this transcript of a natural conversation, which has the turn-taking transcribed just as it occurred naturally. 'Clean it up' (i.e. make it presentable as a dialogue to be read in class with a group of learners). Make the turn-taking sequential by removing overlaps and back-channel utterances and add any extra punctuation you feel is necessary. How does it now look? Does it still feel natural, or has it lost too much in the revision?

(B has just arrived, after a long car journey, at A's house.)

A: Sit down . . . you're all right then?

B: Yes okay Jack, I er I did a daft thing though, I planned the
    route out you know I had it all written out ⌐
C: └ Yeah ⌐
B: └ and
    unlike most people, you see a signpost Repley so I took ⌐ it.
C: └ Yeah.

B: And I came over Mistham ⌐ by the reservoirs, nice it was.
A: └ Oh, by Mistham, over the top
    . . . nice run.
B: Colours are pleasant, aren't ⌐ they.
C: ├ Yeah.
A: └ Nice run that.
B: Yeah, we enjoyed it . . . wasn't the way we intended ⌐ but as
A: └ No.
B: usual ⌐ . . . it was nice.
A: └ We were just talking about that.
B: Oh yes, it was all right.

(Author's data 1989)

5.5   Transactions and topics

5.5.1   *Transactions*

Here we are concerned with how speakers manage longer stretches of talk.
In Chapter 1, we looked briefly at transaction boundary markers and noted
that, although they are most marked in settings such as classrooms,
doctor's surgeries and formal interviews, they are also present in conversation, especially marking out openings and closings. We also considered
the question of realisations of markers in different languages.

The teacher can isolate, present and exemplify a set of useful transaction
markers such as *right, now, so, okay,* and so on, for example, by drawing
attention to how he/she uses markers to divide up a lesson. It is often
interesting to get learners to see if these translate directly into their L1, and
to ask them to consider what words L1 uses to mark such boundaries and to
compare these across languages if possible. But providing contexts in which
learners can then practise these markers is more difficult. If it was the
teacher who traditionally marked out the boundaries of chunks of business
in the classroom, then the most obvious way to hand over to the learner this
particular function is to generate activities where the learners themselves
are responsible for segmenting the business, and where activities need to be

opened and closed within a specified time limit. Task-based learning seems especially well suited to this sort of learner-management of the larger discourse, when groups and sub-groups have to achieve a specified goal, arrive at decisions or produce some other recognisable 'real-world' outcome as stages along the way of completing some preconceived task or set of tasks. One actual example from which the next data samples are taken is a task where advanced learners, in groups, have to decide on how to arrange a room for a school open day. They must make decisions on the disposition of the furniture and what extra furniture will be needed in order to write a note for the school caretaker to act upon (the next stage of the task). When observed in their discussions (there were no predetermined 'chairpersons'), various members of both sub-groups spontaneously used opening and closing markers with the characteristic falling intonation followed by a jump to high key for openings and a drop to low key for closing markers (see section 4.8). For example:

(5.10)   A: / RIGHT /   WHERE shall we have the TABLES?   /

(5.11)   B: / NOW /   WHAT about the REAding area?   /

(5.12)   C: / RIGHT /
                    THAT'S IT /

(Author's data 1989)

These were advanced learners, but it is the activity itself and their responsibility for its conduct rather than their level of English alone that generates the natural use of these transaction markers.

Another way of raising awareness of boundary markers and producing data for discussion is by using 'topping-and-tailing' activities. A dialogue is taken, and the beginning and end removed, so that what is left is clearly the 'middle' of a piece of talk (just as in extract (1.5) on page 10 and the reader activity that follows it). The instruction to the learners (in pairs or in groups) is to add a beginning and an end so that the dialogue represents a meeting between two friends who talk briefly and then have to part. This generates greeting and leave-taking adjacency pairs, but also produces a need for opening and closing markers (e.g. 'Hello, what's new?', 'Anyway, I must go', 'Well, I'll give you a ring soon', 'Look, I can't stop now').

5.5.2 *Topics*

Several questions arise around the notion of *topic*, not least, what *is* a topic? Another set of questions concerns how topics are opened, developed, changed and closed, and what linguistic resources are available for this.

The question 'What is a topic?' may strike many language teachers as otiose, but there are different ways of looking at topic. Topics could be defined, on the formal level, as stretches of talk bounded by certain topic and/or transactional markers, such as lexical ones (*by the way, to change the subject*), or phonological ones (changes in pitch). Or we could take a semantic framework, and try to express the content of different segments of talk according to single-word or phrasal titles (e.g. 'holidays', 'buying a house'), or else we could use interactive criteria and say that something is only a topic if more than one speaker makes an utterance relevant to it. We could equally take an overall pragmatic approach and say that topics are strings of utterances perceived as relevant to one another by participants in talk. Or we could take a purely surface cohesional view, and say that topics end where chains of lexical cohesion peter out (see section 3.3). All of these approaches are valid in some measure; the one that tends to dominate language teaching materials is the expression of topics as titles for the 'subject matter' of speech events. Here we hope to supplement that view with a consideration of structural and interactive features of topics.

Topics can be the reason for talk or they can arise because people are already talking. The former situation is exemplified in this extract, where A has put on some new clothes for a special occasion and B and C are casting an eye over his appearance, at A's request:

(5.13)   (A comes in holding his jacket.)

B: That looks very nice, put it on and let's have a look at you.
A: I don't like the two buttons, I didn't know it had two buttons, I
    thought it had three.
C: Well, it's the style of the coat, Ken.
B: Nick's has only got two ⌈ buttons.
C: ⌊ It's a ⌈ low cut.
A: ⌊ All right?
B: ⌊ Very ⌈ nice.
C: ⌊ It's beautiful.
B: Lovely, lovely.
A: Does it look nice?
B: Yeah, it goes very well with those trousers, there's a colour in the
    jacket that picks up the colour in the trousers.
C: Them others he wears are striped, but they clashed, too much
    alike.
A: ⌊ Two different stripes ⌉
C: ⌊ But not matching each other if you
    understand what I mean.
B: Yeah, yeah . . . ⌈ yeah.
A: ⌊ It's all right then, eh?
B: It's very nice, Dad, it looks very, very good.
A: I don't like the, I like three buttons, you see . . .
C: Ken, it's the style of the coat!

(Author's data 1989)

The talk has been occasioned by a set of actions and events taking place at that time, but there are different ways of describing the 'topic' here. We could take a pragmatic view, based on relevance criteria, and simply say 'whether A's coat is all right' is the topic. We could give it a semantic-field 'headline' such as 'trying on clothes', since all the utterances are relevant to that and the main lexical items belong to that semantic field, or we could make it more functional and call it 'convincing A that his clothes are nice', since the functions of most of the discourse acts are concerned with that end, and all three parties are collaborating on that subject. On the other hand, for A himself, it is clear that 'three-button versus two-button jackets' is an important 'topic', but if we consider it interactively, it gets short shrift from the others, especially from C, who interrupts and cuts dead A's attempt to revive the topic (there are further paralinguistic cues in C's final turn, such as exaggerated pitch range and extra intensity and diphthong length on *style*). We therefore conclude that 'three or two buttons' is a *sub*-topic, or merely a *speaker's topic* that never quite makes it to become a full *conversational topic* (see Brown and Yule 1983: 87–94).

Extract (5.13) was occasioned by particular events, and talk was an essential ingredient in achieving a specific goal, but in most casual conversations, we find topics being raised for a variety of reasons, often just to keep the talk going, simply because people are together and 'chatting'. It is on such occasions that we see most clearly how topics start, grow, shift, merge into one another and come to a close. In extract (5.14), a group of four people are having a New Year drink together, and A has been recounting the story of how his luggage got sent to the wrong airport on a recent skiing holiday:

(5.14)   A: . . . no bother to me, 'cos I happened to have in my side pack a
              spare vest and ⌈ socks you see.
          B: ⌊ Ah, I see, that was in your hand baggage
              ⌈ was it?
          A: ⌊ And I'd got my toilet equipment with me.
          B: Yeah, it's a good idea to take a few basic things in the hand
              baggage, isn't it, ⌈ I think in case of that.
          A: ⌊ Yeah, well it's usually the things you require
              first, you see, sometimes you don't have time to unpack all your
              luggage when you arrive.
          B: Still, pretty horrendous, though.
          A: Oh, it was very unsettling, . . . still, so many other unsettling
              factors I didn't know whether I was on my head or my heels that
              day.
          B: Mm . . .
          C: D'you do a lot of skiing then?
          A: I go each year, yes . . . it's my only chance of getting my weight
              down, you see, and it isn't the exercise that does it, it's the fact
              that the meals are so far apart.

C: (laughs)
D: Yeah?
A: Yes, I'm not joking . . . if we eat say, right, breakfast eight, lunch
   one, evening meal six, perhaps a snack after that then ⌈ you're
   eating four times a day, but
C: ⌊ You'd
   never get no skiing in would you?
A: Well, in these places, you breakfast at eight, well, half past eight,
   . . . (etc.)

(Author's data 1989)

Within a very short space of time the conversation has moved from losing
luggage at an airport to skiing, to weight-watching and exercise, to meal-
times at hotels. It remains coherent within the overall framework of 'A's
recent holiday', but how does it drift from sub-topic to sub-topic? Structural features are apparent. The speakers do give lexical and phonological
cues that they feel a particular sub-topic has been sufficiently explored: as
the first sub-topic is exhausted, B and A both use *still* (a typical boundary
marker, with falling intonation and a short pause), and both give a
summary or general evaluation of what has gone before, another typical
closing move. C introduces the new sub-topic, skiing, with the characteristic jump to high key we have noted elsewhere. Skiing has been an element
in A's lost luggage anecdote (it was a skiing holiday), and using an element
from a just completed story as the topic of subsequent conversation has
been observed to be a very common speaker behaviour (Jefferson 1978). A's
reply includes a drop in pitch on *yes*, then a pause, and then a shift to
talking about keeping his weight down, meals and exercise, which are
associatively linked sub-topics (see Stech 1982), triggered off by one
another, an extremely common feature in this kind of casual conversation.
We might also note that topic shifts occur in the vicinity of short silences,
indicated by ' . . . ' in the transcript; this has also been observed as a regular
feature of casual conversation (see Maynard 1980).

Reader activity 5 ⚷

Look at this extract from further on in the drinks conversation (5.14). The
talk has drifted to Christmas in the village where the speakers live, which
was the period that A was away on his skiing holiday. Analyse the
sub-topic shifts in terms of the linguistic features at their boundaries. High
and low key are not marked, but where might you expect them to occur?

B: No . . . it was generally very quiet and the weather was . . . what
   did it do, it just ⌈ it was quite sunny actually.
D: ⌊ It was quite sunny a couple of the days.

B: Christmas Day was quite sunny ⌜ we went for a walk, had a splendid walk.

D: ⌞ In the morning, it rained in the afternoon.

A: British Christmases rarely change, it's a time for gorging yourself and going for walks.

B: Yeah, that's right, and you never get any snow.

C: Yes, it was very sunny Christmas Day.

B: Mm.

A: Mm.

B: Mm . . . when are you heading off again, Bob?

A: A week today . . . I shall be off to Munich this time . . . so I'm just wondering where the luggage is going to go, and looking at my case now, I find that it's burst open, and whether it's fair wear and tear I don't know, because last time I saw it it was in perfect nick.

B: You reckon it might have suffered from its journey.

A: Oh, they get slung about you know, I never used to get a decent case, I buy a cheap one.

B: Mm.

A: Because they just get scratched.

B: Mm.

(Author's data 1989)

What implications, if any, does all this have for language teaching? Language teachers have always concentrated on the *vocabulary* of topics, and this makes good sense, for without a wide vocabulary it is impossible to talk on a topic, and, as we have noted, semantic and associative coherence between lexical items is an extremely common means of developing and changing topics. But the interactive features of topics can also be taught and practised, such as the use of markers, both opening ones (*by the way, incidentally, I meant to ask you, talking of X*) and closing ones (*still, anyway, so there we are*), or summarising a stretch of talk and reacting to it with an evaluation (*sounds awful, it was all rather unsettling, quite strange, really*). Listening activities can raise learners' awareness of how speakers mark topic shifts by means of activities focusing on points in the talk where speakers make summaries and evaluations, and on markers and pitch changes.

The design of classroom activities to replicate casual conversational settings is notoriously difficult; it is much easier to set up the sort of functional dialogue exemplified in (5.13) ('convincing X his/her clothes look nice'). However, activities where a short anecdote is recounted and partners or groups have to develop a conversation based on some element within the anecdote, or the game-type where a preordained list of topics has to be talked about in a set time with coherent links between each subject, can go some way towards creating the conditions wherein topic management arises naturally. As with other activities, the output can be evaluated against what we know about natural data, and design changes effected accordingly. Perhaps most important of all is to try to recreate the *reciprocity* that is typical of conversation; A tells B something about his/her life, feelings or experiences and, typically, B returns with things about his/her own life and experiences. The same tends to happen with stories: one story by one speaker is likely to trigger off a series of stories by others present. We saw how interview-type activities carry with them the danger that talk will be one-sided, with a questioner and a respondent trapped in their roles, and a lack of reciprocity. The activity design, or the teacher as monitor of the activity, should therefore build in some mechanism for ensuring reciprocity, such as activities where participants have to find out what they have in common or where they differ in terms of a specified list of features relating to opinions, biography, pastimes, etc. (e.g. see some of the speaking activities in Collie and Slater 1991).

5.6   Interactional and transactional talk

A distinction is often made by discourse analysts between transactional and interactional talk. Transactional talk is for getting business done in the world, i.e. in order to produce some change in the situation that pertains. It could be to tell somebody something they need to know, to effect the purchase of something, to get someone to do something, or many other world-changing things. Interactional talk, on the other hand, has as its primary functions the lubrication of the social wheels, establishing roles and relationships with another person prior to transactional talk, confirming and consolidating relationships, expressing solidarity, and so on. The group of speakers in extract (5.13) were engaged mainly in transactional talk (finalising someone's dress arrangements), while in (5.14) the speakers were engaged in primarily interactional talk, just chatting about someone's holiday and enjoying a social drink. The words *mainly* and *primarily* are used to underline the fact that talk is rarely all one thing or the other, and, in a sense, it is almost impossible to conceive of talk between two people that does not, in some small way, 'change the world', even if that only means getting to know someone a little better. Also, it is important to note that natural data show that even in the most strictly 'transactional' of settings, people often engage in interactional talk, exchanging chat about the weather and many unpredictable things, as in these exchanges: the first is in a British chemist's shop; the second is a university porter registering some newly arrived students at their campus accommodation:

(5.15)   Customer: Can you give me a strong painkiller for an abscess, or else a suicide note.
Assistant: (laughing) Oh dear! Well, we've got . . . (etc.)

(Author's field notes)

(5.16)   Porter: So, Foti . . . and Spampinato . . . (writes their names) are you Italians? I'm studying Italian Art, only part time, of course, I love it, I love Italian Art.
Student: (looking bewildered) Excuse me?

(Author's field notes)

The data in Aston (1988) of service encounters in Italian bookshops show a constant tendency for customers and assistants to engage in some sort of friendly chat either before or after the mainly transactional phase. This can, at times, be fairly unnerving for the foreign language learner who has carefully worked out what to say before engaging in a transactional encounter in L2, only to find it all thrown into confusion by unexpected friendly chat from the other party.

In illustrating with real data that the borders between transactional and interactional language are often blurred, discourse analysts are not saying anything blindingly new or contrary to most sensible intuition, but the point is certainly worth remembering in the design of speaking activities for the language classroom, and there is no doubt that some teaching materials are imbalanced between the two types of talk.

Belton (1988) criticises what he sees as a tendency in language teaching of the notional–functional school to overemphasise transactional language at the expense of interactional, and makes a plea for a better balance between the two. This implies that some sort of unpredictability be built in to activities such as service encounter role plays, or, perhaps most effectively, in listening activities. The general point also reflects the experience of many Languages for Specific Purposes (LSP) teachers who are told by course participants that it is the unpredictable social talk that throws them rather than talk in their specialist contexts.

5.7   Stories, anecdotes, jokes

Almost any piece of conversational data between friends will yield occasions where people engage in the telling of stories, anecdotes, jokes and other kinds of narratives. The ability to tell a good story or joke is a highly regarded talent, probably in all cultures. As with other types of language events, discourse analysts have sought to describe what all narratives have in common. Brief mention was made in section 2.4 of a model of narrative developed by Labov (1972). The Labov model, rather, like the problem–solution model we have referred to at various points in this book, specifies elements that are commonly found in normal narratives. They are:

	E
Abstract	*v*
	a
Orientation	*l*
	u
Complicating event	*a*
	t
Resolution	*i*
	o
Coda	*n*

Abstracts are short statements of what the story is going to be about ('I must tell you about an embarrassing moment yesterday'). *Orientation* sets out the time, place and characters for the reader/listener ('you know that secretary in our office, well, last week . . . '). *Complicating events* are the main events that make the story happen ('the xerox machine caught fire'). *Resolutions* are how the events sort themselves out ('and she got £2,000 compensation'), while *codas* provide a bridge between the story world and the moment of telling ('and ever since, I've never been able to look at a mango without feeling sick'). Not all stories have all these ingredients; abstracts and codas may be absent, but the other elements must be there for it to be a real story. In addition, there is what is termed *evaluation*, deliberately set vertically in our list to show it as an element that weaves in and out of the story constantly. Evaluation means making the story worth listening to/reading, either by directly telling one's audience ('you'll love this one'; 'it's not the world's funniest joke, but I like it') or by a number of devices internal to the story such as exaggeration ('he came in with this huge, gi-normous watermelon'), recreating noises, etc. ('and she went scr-r-r-u-u-nch, splat, right into the tree') or constantly evaluating individual events ('which amazed me really'). As always, the terms used in the model are simply labels, and may sometimes less than adequately describe the component referred to; Swan, for example, suggests that *validation* might be a better label than *evaluation* (personal communication).

All this would suggest that expecting a learner to tell a decent story in L2 is a tall order, and indeed it is; not everyone is an accomplished storyteller in their first language. Jokes are particularly difficult to tell in an L2. However, some things can be observed and taught and practised in relation to storytelling, and listening activities based on storytelling are a good way of raising awareness of narrative skills. Real data, as always, supplies a rich selection of realisations for the narrative elements, and markers of the elements will not necessarily translate from one language to another. Some common openers to spoken stories and jokes in English include:

I'll always remember the time . . .
Did I ever tell you about . . .
Then there was the time we . . .
I must tell you about . . .
Have you heard the one about . . .
You'll never guess what happened yesterday . . .
I heard a good one the other day . . .
I had a funny experience last week . . .

There are also regularly occurring markers for complicating events:

And then, suddenly/out of the blue . . .
Next thing we knew . . .
And as if that wasn't enough . . .
Then guess what happened . . .

Common codas include 'makes you wonder', 'so, there we are', 'and that was it, really', 'looking back it was all very . . .', 'and that was as true as I'm standing here'. Such useful language is never given in dictionaries, and is often absent from coursebooks too, though it is every bit as important as the written-text counterparts such as 'once upon a time', which tend to get more of an airing in teaching.

Two other things are notable when we look at real data. One is that stories are often told collaboratively, by more than one person; the details are jointly recalled and an agreed version arrived at through alternating contributions (see Edwards and Middleton 1986). The other is that *listeners are active*, constantly reacting (usually with back-channel responses) to the narrative and asking questions that fill out unspecified detail. The following data sample illustrates this. A and B are telling a series of stories about driving incidents to C.

(5.17) A: I remember that journey, we went from Yarmouth, when we had
          the car⌐
       C: ⌊Yeah.⌐
       A: ⌊and we went into Norwich, and there's a
          ring road round Norwich, and this road to Fareham was off this
          ring road . . . well, we turned right
          if you remember⌐
       B: ⌊Oh I can't remember⌐
       A: ⌊and we went right
          round this ring road, I bet we did twenty miles, and when we
          came back it was the next one on the left to where we'd started.
       C: God (laughs).
       A: I remember that, I thought we were never going to find it.
       C: You went right round the city.
       A: Yes.
       C: Good God, that must have been frustrating.

> A: It was expensive as well (laughs) . . .
> B: But the time I turned into the police station.
> A: Oh . . . dear.
> C: Yeah, what was that?
> B: Dorset Constabulary ⌈ Headquarters.
> A: ⌊ He says you, you
> B: We were going to Lyme Regis.
> A: He gave us the map.
> B: On this tree there was this wooden thing, it had on 'Lyme Regis' and there were these big massive gates, big iron gates
> A: No, it was Iris and I, we said you turn left here, and he turned immediate left, instead of going on to the next road, and it said 'Five miles an hour' and we were creeping along, and there were bobbies looking at us, two of them in a car.
> C: (laughs) Well, well, great, yeah.

(Author's data 1989)

A and B work out a joint version of events, and C makes positive contributions, evaluating the stories, and, in the first of the two, summarising what happened. In conversational data, this sort of joint enterprise with active listeners is very common; stories are not just monologues told to a hushed audience. Another point we have already mentioned briefly is illustrated here: one story sparks off another along similar lines, and in such informal situations, each participant who has a story to tell may demand the floor and tell it.

What difficulties do learners have when telling or listening to stories? For lower-level learners, the usual problems of moment-by-moment lexico-grammatical encoding at clause level tend to interfere with the discourse-level skills, so that we get the bare facts of stories with little evaluation, either from teller or listener. In extract (5.18), a student (A) has had a real-life accident while on a language-school day-trip. The accident was seen as an authentic opportunity to get the student to tell his story to others; a second student (B) was instructed to find out the full story from A:

(5.18)
> B: Hello, Manolo, how are you?
> A: Erm, I'm better, I'm better from my . . . felt in the Lakes.
> B: Why . . . why . . . what did you happen?
> A: Erm, we went to the Lakes for a walk with our teacher of English here and erm, we erm, climb . . . climbed . . . they say climbed, erm, and, erm, when we came back from the mountain I feel . . . felt and broke . . . a little broke of my elbow . . . then I went to the hospital in the night but it take two hours and I must suspect . . . expect . . . erm, for the next day . . . in the morning, and (points to his sling) I have this slip, I think it's a slip, but I don't remember, as well.
> B: The arm, do you . . . is still hurt . . . still, still hurt?
> A: No, no . . . not so much . . . no it's hurting . . . it's not hurting . . .

is, I think it is good because I have my arm very quiet, and it's
good, I don't . . . I sleep well, erm, so well, so, so, and . . . I can
sleep and be
B: Can you have a shower?
A: Yes, yes, every day . . . (etc.)

(ICC data 1988–90)

There is no back-channel from the listener, and she does not react in any
way to the events. She does ask for more details (as she has been instructed
to), and so is active in a small way, but we sense that, if she were speaking
her L1, we might get the equivalent of 'Oh dear, I'm sorry to hear that', or
'That was awful', and so on, as well as constant back-channel responses. At
this level, there is probably little that can be done to help the teller, other
than to point out ways in which he could have made his story more of a
story (perhaps asking him to reproduce, in his own time, a *written* version
of the events which could then be embellished for later oral retelling).

Teachers who want to train learners in narrative skills would do well to
think of listeners as well as tellers, and activity design should take a positive
role for the listener into account. Activities involving joint telling are also
possible, although published language-teaching materials tend to prefer the
single teller. But data is obtainable for those with access to English-
language broadcasting: radio and television chat shows frequently have
guests recounting narratives with an active listener in the form of the
chat-show host, and one recent Australian and British TV success, the
programme *Blind Date*, has a segment each week where a previous week's
guests jointly recount a honeymoon-style trip they have taken in the
intervening period at the programme's expense. Soap operas regularly have
people recounting narratives with reaction and evaluation from other
characters. All these make more authentic contexts than the single narrator
telling a tale to a wall of silence.

Reader activity 6 ⚮

Consider this data extract from the point of view of how the *listener* (B)
behaves. In what way is this particular listener an *active* one? A has been
telling stories about his neighbour:

A: And on Sunday, we were going for a walk and they were ⌈ in
B: ⌊ Mm.
       the distance walking and they stopped and waited for us to
       catch up and introduced us to their daughter.
B: ⌊ Oh lovely.

A: And he's quite a comic ⌜ the fellow ⌜ you know.
B: ⌞ Is he   ⌞ yeah.
A: And their daughter's in Australia, and they've never been to
Australia to see her ⌝
B: ⌞ Oh, haven't they? ⌝
A: ⌞ cos they've got a
dog.
B: Oh, I see.
A: They're tied with the dog, she's a very highly strung dog,
and they don't feel they can ⌜ leave her in kennels.
B: ⌞ leave her with anybody, no.

(Author's data 1989)

In this last reader activity, we note that B *predicts* what A is going to say. Active listeners, like active readers (see Chapter 6, page 169), are constantly predicting what the message will be, based on the evidence of their world knowledge and the type of discourse they are engaged in. Listening activities can test and encourage the development of predictive skills, just as good reading activities often do.

5.8 Other spoken discourse types

We have briefly mentioned how discourse analysts have studied people describing their apartments (section 2.2). Apartment descriptions tend to follow a set pattern where the speaker takes the listener on a 'guided tour' of the rooms starting from the entrance. This real-world, behavioural pattern is reflected in regularly occurring language functions (such as we saw with *this* and *that* references in section 2.2) which can be systematically taught and practised. The same goes for common discourse types such as giving route directions, a favourite activity in the language classroom. Telling someone how to get to one's house, or where to locate things on a map are often the basis of information-gap exercises, and these can be very successful in generating talk. However, as we have argued throughout this book, it is also worth taking a look at what discourse analysts have observed about the organisation of talk in a setting such as direction giving. Psathas and Kozloff (1976) found a typical three-phase structure in their data, consisting of *situation, information and instruction* and an *ending phase*. In the situation phase, the person giving directions must establish (1) the starting point, (2) the goal and (3) the means of transport of the person directed, if these are not already known or obvious. The information phase is where the main route directions are given and the ending phase functions to confirm that the route has been understood and closes the interaction. It is then possible to specify typical linguistic realisations of these phases, some of which will be formulaic, such as *and there you are, got that?, you can't miss it* for the ending phase, and others which will be the familiar boundary markers we have seen dividing transactions elsewhere ('okay, so you're at the Market Place . . . right . . . well . . . if you can see the clock tower, . . . '). Once again, the most satisfactory classroom activities will attempt to emulate these discourse conditions and will encourage an active role for the listener, who will typically require more detail, will check that he/she has understood the directions correctly and will give appropriate back-channel responses. Activities where these features are clearly part of the instructions to participants will probably generate discourse more closely resembling the elements and sequences that discourse analysts have observed in their data.

5.9 Speech and grammar

Brief mention must be made here of the role of grammatical accuracy in unprepared speech. Language teachers tend to work with a set of norms based on the written language, where clause and sentence structure are clearly defined. Spoken data, however, present a different picture, and frequently contain forms that would be considered ungrammatical in writing. Such 'mistakes' usually go quite unnoticed in natural talk, and it is only when we look at transcripts that we realise how common they are. One example is the *wh-* clause structure with embedded reported clauses, as in these two attested native-speaker utterances:

(5.19)   A: And there's a thermostat at the back which I don't know how it works.

(5.20)   A: There's another secretary too who I don't know what she's responsible for.

Native speakers of English are also fond of saying things such as 'the thing *is* is that I don't know her number', 'the problem *is* is . . . ', and we have seen in our data examples how often utterances are grammatically 'incomplete' by written standards, such as 'But that time I turned into the police station' in extract (5.17). Speech abounds in verbless clauses, ellipses that would be frowned upon in 'good' writing (e.g. omitted pronoun subjects), lack of concord and omitted relative particles ('there's a few problems are likely to crop up'), false starts, slips of the tongue and changes of direction midstream in a grammatical structure ('if you like we could there's food in the fridge why don't we could have something if you're hungry'). E. K. Brown (1980) has further examples of such ungrammaticalities in speech.

     Language teachers wishing to encourage natural talk may have to adjust their standards when it comes to correcting learners. For example, the native-speaker *wh-* clause structures exemplified in (5.19) and (5.20) are usually quickly corrected when similar structures appear in the writing of Arab learners of English, and omitted pronoun subjects of verbs are also corrected. In fact, we do not know enough about the acceptable norms of grammar in speech, since, up to now, our grammar books have been largely formulated from introspective and written data. A good grammar of Spoken English, based on natural data, might well contain a few surprises.

Reader activity 7 🗝

Analyse the grammar of these two learners acting out a speaking activity from Collie and Slater (1991). As a teacher, which features do you think need correcting, and which are the sorts of features we might let pass as typical of the kinds of things found even in native-speaker conversational data?

> (The students are exchanging information about skills they once had but have lost for one reason or another over the years.)
>
> A: Any particular musicians than more than another.
> B: And you play piano with the (mimes).
> A: With the papers?
> B: Or as sound?
> A: No, I was not able play by sound, I was, in fact, I had a piano for this but it was more too much technical, too much exercises that was very very hard.
> B: But guitar is more more easy.
> A: Yes, it was more easy for a short time, then I left it.
> B: Prove again with the piano?
> A: Yes.
>
> (Author's data 1989)

5.10   Conclusion

Spoken discourse types can be analysed for their typical patterns and the linguistic realisations that accompany them (e.g. service encounters, business negotiations, telephone calls, chat-show interviews, lectures, trouble-sharing encounters, etc.), and the periodical literature of discourse analysis abounds in detailed studies of a vast range of types. These studies are most often not carried out with any overt pedagogical aim, but are very useful for language teachers and material writers who want to create systematic speaking skills programmes and whose goal is to design activities that will generate output as close as possible to naturally occurring talk. Complete naturalness is probably impossible in the classroom, but the feeling that one is engaging in an authentic activity is important to the learner, as is the feeling that one is being taught authentic and naturally occurring structures and vocabulary to use in simulations of real-life talk. Discourse analysis can supply data where intuition cannot be expected to encompass the rich detail and patterning of natural talk.

This chapter has looked at spoken discourse, from small units to longer stretches, and has tried to relate studies of naturally occurring speech to the goals and methods of language teachers in the classroom. It has brought evidence from data to bear on some of the typical activities that language learners are asked to engage in, and has compared data from both learners and native speakers, using the latter to evaluate the former and to suggest directions for the design of classroom activities. It remains now for us to consider the world of written text, and what discourse analysis can teach us.

Further reading

On conversation in general, several works are worth consulting: Schenkein (1978), Psathas (1979), Craig and Tracy (1983), Taylor and Cameron (1987) and McGregor (1984).

On the elaboration of adjacency pairs, Gibbs and Mueller (1988) is interesting.

On the general question of indirectness and politeness, see Brown and Levinson (1978) and Blum-Kulka (1987), and especially in the cross-linguistic context see Odlin (1989: Ch. 4).

Edmondson *et al.* (1984) and Olesky (1989) contain interesting comparative data on the expression of certain discourse functions (e.g. opening, requesting, giving compliments) in German and English and Polish and English.

Eisenstein and Bodman (1986) look at how native and non-native speakers express thanks.

Back-channel in Japanese conversation is dealt with by Locastro (1987).

Formulaic utterances in general in conversation are illustrated in Coulmas (1979 and 1981).

Melrose (1989) is worth consulting on interpreting functions in exchanges and on situations and roles.

Jokes, stories and anecdotes have been studied in the ethnomethodological tradition, including Sacks (1974), Jefferson (1978), Polanyi (1982 and 1985).

For everyday discussion and argument, see Schiffrin (1985b), and for the analysis of more unordered conversation, see Parker (1984).

Crystal (1981) is good on grammatical and lexical features of natural conversation.

For further work on topic in conversation, see Maynard (1980), Stech (1982), Crow (1983) and Gardner (1987).

How teachers establish topics in the classroom is discussed in Heyman (1986).

Topic markers and discourse marking in general are dealt with in depth in Schiffrin (1987).

Donaldson (1979) discusses the transactional/interactional divide, as well as reciprocity.

The seminal paper on turn-taking is Sacks *et al.* (1974).

Also from that time Starkey (1973) and Duncan and Niederehe (1974) are of interest, but recent rethinking and criticism of turn-taking models has come from Houtkoop and Mazeland (1985) and Power and Dal Martello (1986).

How turns operate where visual cues are absent is dealt with in Butterworth, Hine and Brady (1977) and Beattie (1981).

On telephone calls, see Schegloff (1986).

Toolan (1988) provides a good introduction to narrative, while Hinds (1984) considers Japanese oral narrative.

More on the language of route directions can be found in Psathas (1986).

Bygate (1987) gives good evaluations of published materials for spoken English, while Gardner (1984) discusses the general implications of conversation analysis for language teaching.

Interesting recent works on listening are Richards (1983), G. Brown (1986), and Anderson and Lynch (1988).

6 Written language

'I haven't opened it yet,' said the
White Rabbit; 'but it seems to be
a letter, written by the prisoner
to somebody.'
  'It must have been that,' said
the King, 'unless it was written
to nobody, which isn't usual, you
know.'

**Lewis Carroll: *Alice's Adventures
in Wonderland***

6.1 Introduction

Much of what needs to be said concerning written language has already
been said in previous chapters. Chapter 1 touched on the notions of
coherence, clause relations and textual patterns in written language;
Chapter 2 explored cohesion, theme and rheme and tense and aspect,
taking many of its examples from written texts; and Chapter 3 examined
lexical cohesion and text-organising vocabulary, again exemplifying with a
number of written text extracts. Even Chapter 5, although it was concerned
with spoken language, made points that are relevant to written discourse:
the active listener and the active reader are engaged in very similar processes. Also transferable from the rest of this book are two general principles: that not everything described by discourse analysts is relevant to or
may have any immediate applications in language teaching, and, on the
other hand, that the more we can learn from discourse analysts as to how
different texts are organised and how the process of creating written text is
realised at various levels, from small units to large, the more likely we are to
be able to create authentic materials and activities for the classroom.

6.2 Text types

Unlike our knowledge of speech, our knowledge of written text has been greatly assisted by the existence of huge computerised corpora of written material such as the twenty-million word Birmingham Collection of English Text (the basis of the Collins COBUILD dictionary project), and corpus-building over the years has led to an interest in detailed taxonomies of textual types. However, we still lack hard evidence of just how written text impinges on the day-to-day life of most people. We can obtain statistics for library-borrowing, or for newspaper sales, and get some idea of what most people read of these 'mainstream' text types, but a whole hidden world exists too, of memos, forms, notices, telexes, tickets, letters, hoardings, labels, junk mail, etc., and it is very difficult to guess just what people's daily reading and writing is. Once again, the language teacher is left with a typology based on intuition, or perhaps more often than not, with an imposed syllabus of mainstream texts, as the raw material of teaching.

Reader activity 1 🔑

Look at this list of everyday written texts and decide how often you *read* and *write* such texts, on an *Often/Sometimes/Rarely/Never* scale. Tick the appropriate box and, if possible, compare your results with another person.

	Read				*Write*			
	O	S	R	N	O	S	R	N
Instruction leaflet								
Letter to/from friend								
Public notice								
Product label								
Newspaper obituary								
Poem								
News report								
Academic article								
Small ads								
Postcard to/from friend								
Business letter								

It is certain that most people will *read* more of the text types listed in the reader activity than actually *write* them. Nonetheless, apart from specialist learners, who tend to have precise reading and writing needs, it is still difficult to gauge precisely what types of written text are most useful in language teaching and to find the right balance between reading and writing in most general language courses. For writing purposes, letters of various kinds will always be a useful type to exploit, but, in addition, syllabuses and examinations often demand essays or compositions, whether narrative, descriptive or argumentative, and it is here that teachers find the greatest challenges in devising interesting and authentic activities. We shall therefore consider how learners can be assisted in such writing skills by the insights discourse analysis has provided into text types and the relationships between texts and their contexts.

6.3 Speech and writing

Both spoken and written discourses are dependent on their immediate contexts to a greater or lesser degree. The idea that writing is in some way 'freestanding', whereas speech is more closely tied to its context, has come under attack as an oversimplification by discourse analysts (e.g. Tannen 1982). The transcript of a piece of natural conversation may well contain references impossible to decode without particular knowledge or without visual information. Similarly, spoken 'language in action', where language is used to accompany actions being performed by the speakers, is also typically heavily context-dependent and may show a high frequency of occurrence of deictic words such as *this one, over there, near you* and *bring that here*, which can only be decoded in relation to where the speakers are at the time of speaking. On the other hand, a broadcast lecture on radio may be quite 'freestanding' in that everything is explicit, self-contained and highly structured, which may also be true of an oral anecdote, joke or other kind of narrative.

This same variation in context-dependability is found in written texts. A sign saying 'NO BICYCLES' is highly context-dependent: it may mean 'it is forbidden to ride/park a bicycle here' or perhaps 'all available bicycles already hired/sold', depending on where the notice is located. And while it is true that written texts such as essays, reports, instructions and letters do tend to be more freestanding and to contain fewer deictic expressions, written texts may still encode a high degree of shared knowledge between reader and writer and be just as opaque as conversational transcripts, as in this extract from a personal letter.

(6.1) Dear Simon,
Thanks for your letter and the papers. I too was sorry we didn't get the chance to continue our conversation on the train. My journey wasn't so bad, and I got back about nine.

(Author's data 1989)

We have here references to another text shared by the writer and reader ('your letter', 'I *too* was sorry'), an exophoric reference to '*the* train' (see section 2.2), and the deictic *back*, all of which depend on mutual know-ledge to be fully understood. As eavesdroppers on the text, we can only make intelligent guesses (on mutual knowledge in discourse, see Gibbs 1987). But even transparent, highly explicit texts are written by someone for someone and for something, and their form is determined by these factors. Implicitness and explicitness will depend on what is being communicated to whom, rather than merely on whether the discourse is written or spoken.

Classroom activities which bring out the differences between context-dependent and relatively freestanding discourses can be devised based on a combination of speaking tasks and writing tasks.

In an example of the task-based approach (see also extracts (5.10–12)), a group of German advanced learners of English were instructed to decide on the dispositions of furniture and equipment in a room for a school open day. The first phase of the task was a discussion in the room itself of how best to arrange the furniture; in the second phase, the group had to write a note to the school caretaker explaining their requirements. Thus it was predicted that the spoken phase would be highly context-dependent and the written text detached from its immediate context in time and space. The transcript of the discussion in the first phase contained a number of deictic words and phrases such as 'this corner', 'a little bit to the side', 'there, where the door is', etc. The discussion also contained the turn-taking, exchanges and transaction management that we examined in detail in Chapter 5, as well as reflections on the real-time and planning constraints of speech in progress ('wait a minute', 'now, what's next?'). In short, all sorts of elements occurred that would be out of place in the next (written) phase of the task.

The written phase (the letter to the caretaker) then involved the learners in a number of different discoursal problems typical of (though not unique to) writing: an absent addressee, detachment from the relevant physical environment as a shared context for sender and receiver and the resultant need to be explicit, and the choice of how to 'stage' the text (friendly note? bare list of requirements?). In fact, the two different groups who did the activity produced quite different written output, and the feedback session afterwards with the tutor led to a very interesting discussion on the cultural differences in sending a letter to a school caretaker in Britain and in Germany.

This is the text one group produced:

(6.2)   Group A:
Dear John,
Would you be kind enough to get room no. 4 ready for open day and as games room.
You will need:

2 square and one rectangular table
1 coffee table
14 chairs

5 easy chairs
2 screens
1 dart board
1 monopoly, 1 chess board, 1 set of bridge cards and 1 roulette
Some puzzle and word games and magazines (see librarian)

1. Set up the dart board on the left, on the wall next to door.
2. Arrange 5 easy chairs and 1 coffee table in the left corner near the window.
3. Separate the darts corner and the quiet corner with a screen.
4. Please put a screen on the edge of left window in order to shield off the quiet corner.
5. Have a cup of tea to relax. Thanks a lot for your help!

(ICC data 1988–90)

Reader activity 2

Here is the written text produced by the other group doing the activity. In what ways does it differ from the first group's, and how do the two texts reflect perceptions as to how one writes to a school caretaker?

Group B:
Instructions

1. Put a dart board between the window and the loudspeaker.
2. Parallel to the windows, install a screen to separate the room at distance of the loudspeaker.
3. Put two square tables with four chairs each in front of the screen.
4. Put two coffee tables with two chairs each on the right hand side of the door, between the door and the curtain.
5. In the middle of the room, place another square table with four chairs.

(ICC data 1988–90)

Similar problems arise with writing activities of this kind to those which arise with spoken activities: the learners may misunderstand the task instructions and assume that the caretaker is *expecting* a note about the open day, and therefore not include anything but a list of requirements (as group B's effort seems to do), or else, as mentioned, there may be unseen differences of cultural perception affecting modes of address. What was clear was that the participants did not write in a vacuum and had formed quite clear pictures of whom they should write to and what sort of relationship they had with this person. Thus the activity not only brings out linguistic differences connected with such things as deixis and lexical

F

specificity, but also specific problems that are ever present in writing: who the reader is, what the writer's relationship with the reader is, what the purpose of the text is, and what textual form is appropriate, given that answers to these questions are built into the activity or can reasonably be expected to be shared knowledge. This set of questions encodes in another form of words the *field, tenor* and *mode* constraints of Halliday's model of language in its social context (see Halliday 1978).

Letters are a good example of a discourse type where the receiver is usually a specified individual or group, unlike the classroom or homework essay, which is often written for an unknown audience, but with the overlay of knowing that the teacher/examiner will be the pseudo-reader. Letter-writing activities can therefore raise all the important questions of the relationship between discourse structure and contextual factors, as we have seen. There also appear to be cross-cultural problems concerning letters, especially business letters. Jenkins and Hinds (1987) found significant differences in orientation between American, French and Japanese business letters; the American letters in their data were generally more informal and *reader*-oriented, with the writer strongly projecting the reader's needs and assumed purposes. The French data were *writer*-oriented, with the writer intent upon protecting his/her position and remaining more formal. The Japanese texts oriented towards the mid-ground, the relationship between writer and reader.

So writing is not fundamentally different from speech. While it is true that the writer usually has time to compose and think, and is not going to be interrupted by the reader bidding for a turn or saying 'Sorry, can't stop now, must rush!', all the other important factors constraining what is said and how it is said are present in writing as much as in speech.

6.4   Units in written discourse

In all our discussions on speaking, the sentence was dismissed as being of dubious value as a unit of discourse (especially in Chapter 4). The sentence is more obvious as a grammatical unit in writing, although certainly not in all kinds of writing: signs and notices, small ads, notes, forms, tickets, cheques, all contain frequent examples of 'non-sentences' (lists of single words, verbless clauses, etc.). The internal construction of the sentence has always been the province of grammar, but in Chapter 2, we argued that a number of things in clause and sentence grammar have implications for the discourse as a whole, in particular, word order, cohesion, and tense and aspect. For the purposes of our discussion of these discoursal features, the *sentence* will have no special status other than as a grammatical and orthographic unit which can be exploited where desired for pedagogical illustration, just as the clause can.

It is possible to devise interactive activities which involve decisions on word order, cohesion and sequences of tenses in discourse. The following text-jigsaw has been used successfully with groups at widely different levels to focus on bottom–up choices of these kinds. A text is read in class, and any other desired activities carried out on it. When its content is familiar, it is then presented in jigsaw format, divided up into its individual sentences (or indeed groups of sentences or paragraphs; the decision is purely a practical one). What this means is that one group or individual gets the text with sentences (or paragraphs) 1, 3, 5, 7, 9, etc. and has to recreate sentences 2, 4, 6, 8, etc. in their own words from their familiarity with the content. The other group or individual gets sentences 2, 4, 6, 8, etc. and has to recreate the odd-numbered ones. When all the new sentences are ready, the sentences originally provided are discarded, the two sets of created sentences are put together to see if they make a coherent and cohesive text, and the pair or group together make any changes needed until they are satisfied with the finished product. The activity produces interesting results, as with this group of advanced learners of English:

(6.3)   The original text that was read and then jigsawed was about traffic problems in cities (see extract (3.10)). The resultant text when the two sets of created sentences were dovetailed was:

1. At present, 15% of Englands surface area is covered by some kind of man made material, most of which comes in the shape of long stripes of concrete bond.
2. And yet the government suggests building even more roads in order to cope with the problem of too many vehicles in our country; this can hardly be the answer.
3. While I don't in the least doubt the sincerity of these studies, my own observations lead me to challenge the very principles with which they have been carried out.
4. Day by day I watch the traffic jam on my way to work moving even more slowly than my walking speed.
5. If I was to take this as indicative of a problem with the existing road network, the following could be said.
6. There are four possible ways in which this dilemma might be dealt with: one is to build more roads and thereby destroy our environment, two is to tax cars and petrol heavily, three is to give out licences for those who really need a car, four is to take into consideration the use of motorbikes instead of cars.
7. Conceivably, the first three solutions have been discussed in government circles, but they remain within the simplistic car/road mile computation which don't do the problem any justice. They leave out of sight the proper use of each vehicle. This takes me to the fourth solution, which is in fact the ideal one.

(Author's data 1989)

This activity led to a discussion among the participants. Everyone agreed that 'these studies' (sentence 3) rendered the text incoherent, and alternative superordinates such as 'these policies', 'these views', 'these ideas' were offered to make the text lexically cohesive (see section 3.2). Some in the group were not happy with *conceivably* (sentence 7) and with its front-placing, since (sentence 3) had mentioned road expansion as an idea already put into practice. Alternatives such as 'The first three solutions may well have been discussed', and 'The first three solutions have probably . . .' were proposed. There were also macro-level discussions on features such as the use of first person and what some felt was a clash of register between the 'sarcasm' of sentence 1 and the neutral tone of the rest of the text, but, in the main, the group members were concerned with intersentential links affecting cohesion and word order.

The success of the jigsaw activity was undoubtedly due to the fact that the participants were defending their *own* text, created by themselves, rather than taking a model text to pieces. The decision-making processes were brought to the surface and individuals had to explain and defend their choices, a process more motivating for learners than having to explain the choices of an invisible, unknown author. There has been a tendency in teaching materials to see knowledge of cohesion as something to be tested in relation to textual products, but process approaches can also tackle this area, by getting learners to evaluate their own texts as they are creating them (see Johns 1986 for further discussion of peer evaluations).

Reader activity 3 🗝

Look at these pieces of learner data purely from the point of view of intersentential connexions, that is, ignoring errors which could be said to be principally sentence-internal. Look for problems of cohesion in terms of such things as reference and conjunction and decide what effect such features have on overall comprehensibility and readability.

1. (From an essay on town planning by an Italian town planner doing an English course.)
   Unfortunately, not always the growth of cities go on with an attention research. It's the cause of many problems that people have in living in big cities, and also the destruction of the environment.

2. (From an essay on differences between Italian and British and American teenagers, by an Italian learner.)
   The British, Italian and American teenagers are like, but I think that for the Italian teenagers using to play football more than British and American teenagers.
   So as for the American teenagers using to play rugby more than Italian and British teenagers. For use, British teenagers like to look

videos and listen music. In fact Britain is the country of the best musicians of the world.

3. (From a summary of a text on training astronauts; Italian learner.) The passage speaks about the astronaut's life. There are a lot of problems when one lives in space, and the most important is absence of gravity. It is necessary a long period of training to learn the basic operations which allow the life and the work within the Shuttle. They are trained in simple jobs like as cooking or daily routines and in different operations as emergency procedures, satellite repairs and so on.

(Author's data 1989)

6.5 Clause relations

In section 1.9 we looked at the clause-relational approach to written text, where it was stressed that the units of written discourse, rather than always being co-extensive with sentences (though they sometimes are), were best seen as functional segments (of anything from phrasal to paragraph length) which could be related to one another by a finite set of cognitive relations, such as cause–consequence, instrument–achievement, temporal sequence, and matching relations such as contrasting and equivalence. Individual segments of texts combined to form the logical structure of the whole and to form certain characteristic patterns (such as problem–solution). The sequencing of segments and how the relations between them are signalled were viewed as factors in textual coherence (see Winter 1977; Hoey 1983). In fact, the problems which could be subsumed under the notion of cohesion by conjunction in the last reader activity can also be viewed from a clause-relational standpoint, in that inappropriate use of conjunctions creates difficulties for the reader in relating segments of the text to one another coherently. But we also noted in Chapters 2 and 3 that the borderline between how conjunctions signal clause relations and how certain lexical items do the same is somewhat blurred, and that conjunctions such as *and, so* and *because* have their lexical equivalents in nouns, verbs and adjectives such as *additional, cause* (as noun or verb), *consequent(ce), instrumental, reason,* and so on. Therefore, as well as activities that focus on conjunction and other local cohesive choices, activities aimed at the lexicon of clause-relational signals may also be useful. Segment-chain activities can be used for this purpose. An opening segment (which could be a sentence or more) and a closing segment of a text are given to a group of four or five students, and each individual is given the start of a segment containing a different lexical clause signal. Individuals complete their own segment with as much text as they feel necessary, and then compare their segment with everyone else's in order to assemble the segments into a coherent text. This involves not only being satisfied with the individual segments but deciding on an appropriate sequence for the chain of clause relations that will lead logically to the given closing segment, and making any changes felt necessary to improve coherence. In the following example, groups of advanced German learners were given an opening sentence: 'Young people nowadays are exposed to a lot of violence on television, in films, and so on', and the conclusion: 'This would suggest that some sort of control or censorship may be necessary to solve the problem.' Individual segment-cards had starters such as:

> *The result is . . .*
> *The reason is . . .*
> *The fact is that . . .*
> *This contrasts with . . .*

Typical of the texts produced by the groups was:

(6.4)   Young people nowadays are exposed to a lot of violence on
          television, in films, and so on. The result is that floods of blood
          suffocate the TV news and films all over Europe. This contrasts with
          countries where there is a strict control of TV and films. The reason
          is an uprooted, deculturalized young generation which has ceased to
          stick to the strigent values of their elders. The fact is that the
          situation has got worse and worse recently. This would suggest that
          some sort of control or censorship is necessary.

          (Author's data 1989)

This particular group were unhappy with the relationship between the sentence beginning 'The reason is . . .' and the rest of the text, as they felt that since nothing had been said about young people's *behaviour*, it was pointless to give a reason for it, and a 'deculturalized generation' could hardly be cited as the *reason* for violence on television. The opinion was also voiced that the final text was a little unnatural with so many *front-placed* phrases such as 'the reason is . . .', once again raising new decisions on theme and rheme which had to be taken in relation to the text as a whole. The group finally decided to move the words 'the result is that' from sentence 2 to sentence 4 to replace 'the reason is', and then to reverse the order of sentences 3 and 4.

The aim of the activity was to reproduce some of the processes of choice that are involved in using the lexicon of clause-relational signals, once again as an alternative to only examining textual *products* containing such items. This does not mean that cohesive and clause-relational features cannot also be usefully tackled on readymade texts; alongside the process approach to writing, there is a healthy tradition of problem-solving methods that include exercises in inserting missing linking and signal words in texts. These force the learner to make vocabulary choices that take more than the individual sentence into account (e.g. Coe, Rycroft and Ernest 1983).

Reader activity 4

Look at these pieces of learner data, in which there seem to be problems of how individual sentences relate to one another. Suggest ways in which, either by using conjunctions or lexical signals, the relationships can be made more clear.

1. My field of study concerns architecture. It's not a field of study, I think, it's a huge world going from science to knowledge of materials, to the history and composition of cultures, to knowledge of psychological needs and wishes of men and women in the world.

2. The problems of modern cities are derived from the Industrial Revolution, and also if the cities of my country were not interested from this event it's true that there are relations between every cities.

(Author's data 1989)

6.6   Getting to grips with larger patterns

We have considered larger patterns of discourse organisation at various points in this book. The problem–solution pattern was illustrated in Chapter 1, and again in Chapter 3 in relation to vocabulary signals. Chapter 3 also looked at examples of claim–counterclaim (or hypothetical–real) patterns, and Chapters 2 and 5 referred to narrative patterns.

These are not the only patterns found in texts; another common one is the 'question–answer' pattern, which has some features in common with the problem–solution pattern, but whose primary motivation is the pursuit of a satisfactory answer to a question explicitly posed (usually) at the beginning of the text. For example: ⟫→

(6.5)

London – too expensive?

It's no surprise that London is the most expensive city to stay in, in Britain; we've all heard the horror stories. But just how expensive is it? According to international hotel consultants Horwath & Horwath's recent report, there are now five London hotels charging over £90 a night for a single room.

But even if your hotel choice is a little more modest, you'll still be forking out nearly twice as much for a night's stay in London as elsewhere in Britain. Average room rates last year worked out at around £19 in the provinces compared to £35 in London. ■

(from *Moneycare*, October 1985, p. 4)

In this text, a situation is established which contains an unanswered question. Answers are then offered, along with evidence or authoritative support for them. As with 'possible responses' in the problem–solution pattern, if the answer(s) offered do not answer the original question, then other answers are sought.

Other typical textual patterns include various permutations of the general–specific pattern, where macro-structures such as the following are found:

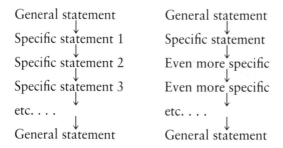

Examples of these patterns can be found in texts such as estate agents' sales literature in Britain, where a general description of the property for sale is followed by detailed descriptions of individual rooms/features, and then, finally a return to a general statement about the whole property again (for further discussion of different patterns, see Hoey 1983).

One point to note about patterns is that they are of no fixed size in terms of number of sentences or paragraphs contained in them. Another point is that any given text may contain more than one of the common patterns, either following one another or embedded within one another. Thus a problem–solution pattern may contain general–specific patterns within individual segments, or a claim–counterclaim pattern when proposed solutions are being evaluated, both of which features are present in this text:

(6.6) # Two-wheel solution

THOUSANDS of acres of our countryside are buried for ever under ribbons of concrete and tarmac every year.

Every few months a Government study or statement from an authoritative body claims that our motorway network is inadequate and must be extended.

Week by week the amount of car traffic on our roads grows, 13 per cent in the last year alone.

Each day as I walk to work, I see the ludicrous spectacle of hundreds of commuters sitting alone in four or five-seater cars and barely moving as fast as I can walk.

Our traffic crisis now presents us with the classic conservation dilemma – too many people making too much demand on inadequate resources.

There are four possible solutions: One,

provide more resources, in this case build more roads and car parks; two, restrict the availability of motorised transport by artificially raising the price of vehicles and fuel: three, license only those with a good reason for needing motorised transport and prohibit un- necessary use; four reduce the average size of motor vehicles, especially those used for commuting purposes.

The ideal vehicle for transporting one person to and from his or her place of work has been in use for as long as the motor car. There is room on our existing roads for present and future needs but not if they are to be clogged up with half-empty cars when the motor cycle would serve the same purpose more than adequately.

Inevitably, objections

will be raised to the promotion of the motor cycle as the saviour of our environment.

It is dangerous: It can be but three-fifths of all serious motor cycling accidents are caused by cars. So, by transferring some drivers from cars to motor cycles, the risk can immediately be reduced.

Department of Transport statistics have shown that a car driver is nine times more likely to take someone else with him in an accident than a motor cyclist, so riding a motor cycle is actually making a contribution to road safety.

Our climate is too cold and wet: Have we British really become so soft that we couldn't face a ride on a chilly morning? A good waterproof jacket costs a lot less than a new bypass.

But I must drive a BMW or Jaguar or I'll have no credibility with my clients, my boss, my shareholders: That is just a matter of fashion which most of the business community follow as slavishly as sheep.

If the right person were to set the lead and exchange his tin box traffic jammer for an environmentally responsible set of two wheels the rest of the business sheep would be falling over themselves to follow suit and some of our traffic problems would be solved at a stroke.

All that is needed is the willingness to sacrifice a little bit of comfort, take a little bit of a risk and dare to be a little different.

On the other hand, what is a few thousand acres of countryside each year and a ten-mile tailback?

(from *Cambridge Weekly News*, 22 September, p. 11)

Here we begin with a general statement and then, in terms of time, a series of evermore specific ones, culminating in a general statement in paragraph 5 of the *problem* that is to form the central focus of the text. The next two paragraphs then put forward possible solutions. The author's preferred solution, the motorcycle, is then evaluated in the rest of the text in a series of claims and counterclaims with justifications for the counterarguments. Only the last sentence breaks the completeness of the patterns by raising a counterargument that the author chooses to leave open, but which brings us right back to the statement of the problem in the very first sentence of his text. So the text is highly patterned, and its author has embedded patterns within the overall structure of the text.

Reader activity 5 🔑

What patterns can you observe in the following extracts from the opening lines of two magazine articles (you have already analysed the second one for modals in section 3.8)? What text pattern would you predict is going to be the dominant one in each of the texts as a whole?

1. Men can mend stereos, drive cars and budget their pay packets efficiently; women are helpless when faced with anything mechanical and are extravagant spenders. Chaps, of course, are cool and rational, while women are swayed by their emotions and are slaves to the lunar cycle. Men are polygamous, women monogamous. Ridiculous stereotypes? Absolutely. So why do quite a lot of men and rather a large number of women still half believe them?

(*Options*, October 1985: 201)

2. # Can citrus peel harm?

Did you know that lemon and orange peel is coated with wax and chemicals?

The skin of almost all citrus fruit sold in the UK is treated with fungicides to stop it going mouldy. And the glossy surface is the result of bathing the fruit in wax.

Could the fungicides used on citrus peel be harmful – particularly since there's some evidence from laboratory tests that, in sufficient quantities, they may produce cancers or mutations in animals?

The Government doesn't feel there is any need to worry because the levels of fungicide permitted are very low. The levels are based on the recommendations of UK and international advisory bodies for the amount that can be consumed daily without any significant effect.

(from *Which?*, January 1984, p. 4)

Finding patterns in texts is a matter of interpretation by the reader, making use of clues and signals provided by the author; it is not a question of finding one single *right* answer, and it will often be possible to analyse a given text in more than one way. But certain patterns do tend to occur frequently in particular settings: the problem–solution pattern is frequent in advertising texts (one way to sell a product is to convince people they have a problem they may not be aware of) and in texts reporting technological advances (which are often seen as solving problems or removing obstacles). Claim–counterclaim texts are frequent in political journalism, as well as in the letters-to-the-editor pages of newspapers and magazines (but see Ghadessy 1983, for a problem–solution orientation to such letters). General–specific patterns can be found in encyclopaedias and other reference texts.

6.7 Patterns and the learner

If we look at learners' attempts to create textual patterns of the kinds we have described above, we find that there are sometimes problems. Just as we noted that learners whose overall competence was poor often got trapped in the difficulties of local encoding at the expense of larger discourse management in spoken discourse, so too can we observe such difficulties affecting learners' written work. If we look again at a text from which we took an extract earlier, this time reproducing the whole text, we can see an attempt at a general–specific pattern which seems to just end in midstream, lacking the typical return to a general statement after the specific examples that is expected in a well-formed text. On the other hand, one could equally say that the text sets out to create a number of descriptive contrasts, but gets 'lost' in a digression about Britain's ascendancy in the world of music:

(6.7) (*general statement*) The British, Italian and American teenagers are like, (*specific: modification of general statement*) but I think that for the Italian teenagers using to play football more than British and American teenagers.
(*specific: parallel modification*) So as for the American teenagers using to play rugby more than Italian and British teenagers. (*new specific*) For use, British teenagers like to look videos and listen music. (*digression?*) In fact Britain is the country of the best musicians of the world. (*end of text*)

(Author's data 1989)

It is extremely doubtful whether the writer (a highly educated, mature person) would write such an unstructured text in his own native language. It is quite clear that the stresses of creating the text (and the frequent

161

crossings-out in the manuscript support this) at the level of local choice of grammar and vocabulary has proved too much, and all sense of overall planning has been abandoned.

At lower levels, clause- and sentence-chaining activities can take the strain off macro-level planning but still produce a learner-generated text for scrutiny in class. As with the clause-relational chaining activity, each learner creates a textual segment relevant to a given topic, but with the segment-starters containing signal words of the (in this case) problem–solution structure. For an all-Italian group of architects and environmental planners on an intensive English course, the topic sentence was: 'Nowadays, more and more people want to use the countryside for leisure purposes.' The starters were:

> *But the problem is . . .*
> *Planners have an important role to play: . . .*
> *One possible solution to the problem is . . .*

These were designed to generate the *problem*, a *response* from planners and a possible *solution*. Thus the next stage of the activity, marshalling the individual segments into a coherent text, is guided by top–down constraints of typical problem–solution sequences. The discussion on sequencing of segments and necessary changes to the text was carried on in the learners' L1 on this occasion. The author of extract (6.7) was a member of the group whose final text is reproduced here:

(6.8)   Nowadays, more and more people want to use the countryside for leisure purposes. But the problem is that the urbanism take over and dominates it. Planners have an important role to play: they have to ensure the community the right distinction between spaces for working time and for leisure purposes, and moreover to locate this last activities in the best convenient situation for most of people. One possible solution to the problem is that people have to know the advantages to live far from traffic and noise, because a calm place where everybody can have a relationship with itself, it is necessary for our soul.

(Author's data 1989)

The author of text (6.7) composed the sentence beginning 'but the problem is . . .', which reflects his lexico-grammatical weaknesses compared with the others in the group, but in terms of the final text, which was used for remedial vocabulary and grammar work, his contribution was as useful as the rest.

Reader activity 6 ⚷

An advanced group of German learners of English produced the following sentences based on the topic card (seen by all members of the group) and segment-starters given (in italics). What, in your opinion, would be the best order for the sentences to make a satisfactory text? How many possible acceptable orders are there? What changes would you like to make to the wording of individual sentences?

Topic: 1. *Football hooliganism is a common phenomenon in a lot of European countries.*
2. *One possible solution* to reduce the worst effects might be, first of all, to stop violent fans from entering the stadium.
3. *The reason* for the fans aggressive behaviour is their social background.
4. *The problem* is how to interfere without cancelling all football matches and without frustrating the real non-violent fans.
5. *The situation* can be described as follows: thousands of people are injured every weekend and a lot of damage is done to the stadiums.

(Author's data 1989)

Another interesting aspect of learners' success or otherwise in macro-level communication in their writing is how they use the kind of discourse-signalling vocabulary discussed in sections 3.5–6. What is sometimes observable in learner data is that, although the overall patterning is present, misuse of signalling words can disorient the reader somewhat. This extract is from a summary of a text on the problems of training astronauts to live in space:

(6.9)   As soon as a man of our century realizes we're going to reach the complete control of communicating and travelling in space, he has to consider the huge number of difficulties that overcome with the developing of space travels.
      Science and technique may develop to hinder a lot of problems, like for example loss of oxygen, intense cold, severe radiation bursts and so on.

(Author's data 1989)

The first infelicity in discourse-signalling vocabulary occurs with 'difficulties that overcome', but here it is not entirely clear whether the problem is lexical; it may be (interference from a cognate form in Italian which hides a false friend) or it could be syntactic, insomuch as many languages use a 'that' construction where English would have an infinitive ('difficulties *to*

163

overcome'), but the vocabulary-choice tends to be dominated by the quite plausible syntax here, and most readers presented with the text suffer disorientation. The second error, 'to *hinder* a lot of problems' is more obviously lexical, and underlines the point made in Chapter 3 about the importance of grouping words together along discourse–functional lines, and suggests a role for the teaching of collocating pairs in the case of such words. A similar collocational problem seems to have occurred in the football hooliganism text in Reader activity 6: one does not normally *interfere* to solve a problem (interference usually suggests making things worse); in English, one *intervenes* to solve problems. Such local errors disorient the reader in the sense that he/she is continuously making predictions about the text as a whole and its likely sequencing and patterning.

6.8   Culture and rhetoric

Our data examples so far show one thing: European learners of English in general are perfectly capable of transferring discourse patterns such as problem–solution patterns from their L1 to an L2 (as witnessed in the chaining activities). Where problems arise, they seem to be relatable to lack of linguistic competence at the lexico-grammatical level and the natural difficulties of coping with global planning when one is under great stress encoding at the sentence level. But what of the writing of learners from cultures quite different from Western ones? Are there established norms of writing in other literate cultures that are different and might therefore be expected to interfere with the macro-level decision-making of the learner writing in English?

   The area of cross-cultural rhetoric studies has spawned a vast literature of its own, and a somewhat confusing one. On the one hand, linguists claim to have evidence of textual patterns in other languages not found in English writing; on the other hand, there is disagreement over whether these patterns are transferred and cause interference when the learner writes in English. A paper by Kaplan (1966), in which he posited a typology for textual progression with different types associated with different cultures, was very influential, but has since been undermined by other studies. Kaplan suggested that English text was characteristically linear and hierarchical, while Semitic (Hebrew and Arabic) text was characterised by parallelism; Oriental text had 'indirection' as a characteristic, and Russian and Romance texts had a preference for digressions. Some evidence seems to support differences in textual structure, such as the acceptability in Japanese texts of what seems to the English eye to be the abrupt insertion of irrelevant matter (see Hinds 1983), or certain features of word order and use of conjunctions that are redolent of Indian languages being carried over into writing in Indian English (Kachru 1987). Similarly, differences in preference of particular theme–rheme sequences (see section 2.3) have been claimed. Even within the same language family differences have been suggested: German academic texts seem to allow a greater amount of parenthetical information and freedom to digress than English writing of the same kind, and there is some evidence that English writers tend to use topic sentences at the beginning of paragraphs where German writers might prefer a bridging sentence between paragraphs.

But by no means everyone agrees that such tendencies are significant, nor that they cause problems for language learners. Typical of the confusion is the case of Arabic and Chinese: Kaplan had spoken of parallelism for Arabic and indirection for Oriental texts, but Bar-Lev (1986) finds more of a tendency to 'fluidity' in Arabic text (i.e. non-hierarchical progression with a preference for connexion with *and*, *but*, and *so*), and claims that parallelism is a property of Chinese and Vietnamese. Aziz (1988), however, finds that Arabic text has a preference for the theme-repetition pattern (the first of the three theme and rheme patterns discussed in section 2.3), making it different from English and indeed suggesting a sort of parallelism. Then again, as regards Chinese, Mohan and Lo (1985) found no marked differences between Chinese texts and English ones. This sort of conflicting evidence does not provide the answers to the sorts of questions language teachers are concerned with. Nor is the picture any clearer with regard to whether there is cross-cultural interference for learners. Language teachers are therefore left with intuition, experience and their own data as the most reliable resources for deciding whether interference is a problem.

What we find frequently in examining Middle Eastern, Oriental and other learner data in English are the same problems noted in European data: that bad discourse organisation often accompanies poor lexico-grammatical competence. Just as we observed an Italian learner failing to produce a satisfactory and complete general–specific pattern in comparing British and Italian teenagers (extract 6.7), so we find similar difficulties with a Japanese low-level learner doing the same task:

(6.10)   British teenagers watching television. Boys and girls many people. My country teenagers very more people watching television, because my country television more select. My country TV have channell no. 1, 3, 4, 6, 8, 10, 12.

British teenagers playing football very famous. But my country teenagers playing baseball very famous.

(Author's data 1989)

Reader activity 7 🖎

Consider this essay on differences between English and Japanese teenagers by a higher-level Japanese learner of English. Does it display better discourse patterning than extract (6.10), and if so, in what way(s)?

> I'd like to compare the habits of teenagers with those of teenagers in my country.
>
> In Britain both boys and girls spent time for watching TV, listening to records and going to disco. That is the same teenagers in my country. Of course there are some leisure for girls and for boys. British girls spent most time for going to the cinema and time with boyfriend. That is a little bit different from teenagers in my country, my sister who is 15 years old, she spent most time for shopping and studying. I think Japan and Britain are different from education system that's why Japanese teenagers spent most time for studying.
>
> British boys spent most time for football because, in this country, football is the most popular sports that's why they spent most time for football. In Japan baseball is the most popular sports so Japanese boys (teenagers) spent most time for baseball.
>
> If the culture is similar Japan and Britain it would be a same result but in fact Japan and Britain are completely different from the culture. For example, food, religion, popular sports and so on. So the result is a bit different.

(Author's data 1989)

The arguments we have been making about the link between lexico-grammatical competence and discourse competence do not mean that particular features in the realisation of discourse patterning cannot be improved or directly taught; the main point is that macro-patterns them-selves do not seem to be lacking once reasonable general competence has been achieved, and that, where the macro-patterns are absent, there seem to be basic clause- and sentence-level problems that demand higher priority in teaching. Nonetheless, we have argued that while lower-order skills are being taught, the higher-order features can be practised through pair and group activities such as chaining and text-jigsaw activities, where the macro-level decisions can be discussed in the learners' L1, or if in L2, then at least divorced from the immediate stresses of encoding the individual clauses and sentences.

The sorts of discourse features that do lend themselves to direct interven-tion are likely to be discourse-signalling vocabulary, appropriate use of conjunctions and other linking words, and perhaps a closer look at refer-ence and ellipsis/substitution. There does seem to be some evidence that learners do not handle anaphoric reference at the text level as efficiently as they might, but again it is not always clear whether this is because some languages tolerate more repetition of the noun head rather than pronomi-nalisation, or that they use ellipsis for subsequent occurrences of the same entity after first mention (as seems to operate in Japanese), or indeed whether local encoding stresses are once more to blame rather than cross-linguistic interference. If we examine two of the sentences from the Japanese learner's text in Reader activity 7, we see an unnatural amount of noun-head repetition:

(6.11)   British boys spent most time for *football* because, in this country, *football* is the most popular sports that's why they spent most time for *football*. In Japan *baseball* is the most popular sports so Japanese boys (teenagers) spent most time for *baseball*.

Something like this might sound more natural:

(6.12)   British boys spend most of their time playing football, because in this country it is the most popular sport, and that is why they spend most of their time playing it.

We might even wish to look at the possibilities for substitution and reduce the last part of the text to 'and that is why this is so'. Such changes to the text do not hide the more obvious lexico-grammatical errors, but they certainly improve the overall feeling of naturalness once the lexico-grammatical errors have also been dealt with. But it is not always easy to separate discourse-level weaknesses from the local lexico-grammatical ones, especially when the latter are thick on the ground in a piece of learner writing.

Reader activity 8 🔑

In what way(s) could this paragraph from a Korean learner's essay be improved in terms of discourse features such as conjunction, anaphoric reference, ellipsis/substitution? You may find it helpful to correct the more obvious mistakes in grammar and vocabulary first, and then to reread the text.

> Korea has developed radically in economy over the past 25 years. All industries have developed and especially mechanical industries have advanced, for example, electric, steel and car industries. As a result development of industries, Korea has become rich country and almost houses have had televisions, videos and cars.
>
> (Author's data 1989)

Paying attention to the grammar-and-discourse features described in Chapter 2 is a partial means of attending to the writer's responsibility towards the reader, in terms of assisting orientation to the writer's argument and giving signals to the reader as to how the segments of the text relate to one another. Process approaches to the teaching of writing tend to include such features anyway, and some materials for the teaching of writing do also take into account the macro-planning of text with regard to patterns such as problem–solution and others we have looked at (e.g. Hamp-Lyons and Heasley 1987).

6.9 Discourse and the reader

We cannot leave this chapter, and indeed, the whole discussion of discourse analysis and language teaching, without considering the influence of discourse analysis on the teaching of reading. What we shall conclude about discourse and reading in fact follows consistently from what we have said in this chapter and in earlier ones: we cannot explain discourse patterning at the macro-level without paying due attention to the role of grammar and lexis; by the same token, we cannot foster good reading without considering global and local reading skills simultaneously.

In recent years, questions of reading pedagogy have centred on whether bottom–up (i.e. decoding of the text step-by-step from small textual elements such as words and phrases) or top–down (using macro-level clues to decode the text) strategies are more important. The debate seems to have settled, quite sensibly, on a compromise between local and global decoding, and there is general agreement that efficient readers use top–down and bottom–up processing simultaneously (e.g. Eskey 1988). This fits with our general view of discourse as being manifested in macro-level patterns to which a constellation of local lexico-grammatical choices contribute. The best reading materials will encourage an engagement with larger textual forms (for example through problem-solving exercises at the whole-text level) but not neglect the role of individual words, phrases and grammatical devices in guiding the reader around the text (e.g. Greenall and Swan 1986, who achieve a balance of both ingredients).

But at both the micro- and macro-level, caution in how to introduce the discourse dimension is called for. In the case of cohesion, for example, the precise relationship between cohesion and coherence is unclear, and focusing on cohesive devices for *reading* purposes may not guarantee any better route towards a coherent interpretation of the text (see Steffensen 1988). At the macro-level, much has been made in recent years of *schema* theory, that is, the role of background knowledge in the reader's ability to make sense of the text. The theory is that new knowledge can only be processed coherently in relation to existing knowledge frameworks, and that the efficient reader activates the necessary frameworks to assist in decoding the text being read. The frameworks are not only knowledge about the world (e.g. about natural phenomena, about typical sequences of real-life events and behaviour), but also about texts, how texts are typically structured and organised, thus enabling us to talk about two kinds of schemata: *content* and *formal*, respectively. The theory in itself seems plausible enough; the more we are locked into the world of the text, the easier it is to absorb new information. It is often held that the teacher's job is to help the reader to activate the appropriate schemata. While we have already tested the value of predicting what textual pattern(s) a given text may be going to realise in Reader activity 5 as an awareness activity for constructing patterns in writing, it is not at all certain whether activating the right formal schema for reading can help much if the right content schema is lacking. If the teacher's job then becomes one of supplying the appropriate content schemata for a possibly vast number of textual encounters, then we are out of the world of discourse as such and firmly in the realm of the teaching of culture, and we are not necessarily teaching the learner any skill that will be subsequently productive.

What we have already said, and what may be repeated now, is that listening and reading have in common a positive and active role for the receiver, and, if any insight is to be taken seriously on board from discourse analysis, it is that good listeners and readers are constantly attending to the segmentation of the discourse, whether by intonational features in speech, or by orthographical features in writing, or by lexico-grammatical signals in both. What is also clear is that good listeners and readers are always predicting what is to come, both in terms of the next few words and in terms of larger patterns such as problem–solution, narrative, and so on. This act of prediction may be in the form of precise prediction of content or a more diffuse prediction of a set of questions that the author is likely to answer. For this reason, interpreting the author's signals at the level of grammar and vocabulary as to what questions he/she is going to address is as useful as predicting, for example, the content of the rest of a given sentence or paragraph. This will mean paying attention to structures such as cleft sentences (see section 2.3), rhetorical questions, front-placing of adverbials and other markers, and any other discourse-level features. The reading text will be seen simultaneously as an artifact arising from a context and a particular set of assumptions of world knowledge, *and* as an unfolding message in which the writer has encoded a lot more than just content, with signposts at various stages to guide the reader around.

Reader activity 9

Try and predict as much as you can about this news text from the first two paragraphs which are given on the following page. What do you think caused the problem of the telephone boxes being out of order? Will the text give us an answer? What other things is it likely to tell us? Will this be a typical problem–solution text?

Public telephones ring again in Newmarket

A NEW era is about to dawn for Newmarket residents who for the past few weeks have been unable to use the public telephone boxes in the town.

Following complaints made over several weeks British Telecom set aside two days last week and several engineers worked to put the faults right.

(from *Cambridge/Newmarket Town Crier*, 1 August 1987, p. 32)

6.10   Conclusion

At this point, we have come to the conclusion not only of this chapter, but of this book. There will no doubt be many other things that will need to be said about discourse analysis and language teaching, for discourse analysis is a fast-moving discipline, and our knowledge of how language occurs in its natural contexts is growing all the time. There is, perhaps, little need to reiterate the conclusions that have constantly reared their heads in the course of this book, but this may be the right moment to restate one fundamental principle: just because linguists can describe a phenomenon convincingly does not mean that it has to become an element of the language-teaching syllabus. The practical pressures of language teaching mean that teachers will always, rightly, want to evaluate carefully any descriptive insights before taking them wholly to heart as teaching points. Discourse analysis is not a method for teaching languages, nor does it claim to be that. But it is my own personal view that discourse analysis has presented us with a fundamentally different way of looking at language compared with sentence-dominated models, one in which the traditional elements of grammar, lexis and phonology still have a fundamental part to play, but one which is bigger and more immediately relevant. What is more, we now know more about what people actually *do* with language when they speak and write, and no longer have to rely on what textbooks largely based on intuition and sometimes, sadly, on Classical-based notions of what 'good' usage is, claim to be the way people speak and write. We know more about the delicate relationship between language forms and particular contexts and users; such knowledge can only be immensely valuable. Teachers will make up their own minds as to whether their methods and techniques need rethinking in the light of what discourse analysts say, but, as with all new trends in linguistic theory and description, it is important that discourse analysis be subjected not only to the scrutiny of applied linguists but also to the testing grounds of practical materials and classroom activities. I hope that this book has done a little of both, and will inspire a good deal more, especially of the latter.

Further reading

On differences between speech and writing, see Chafe (1982), Redeker (1984), Tottie and Bäcklund (1986), Biber (1988) and Halliday (1989).

For more on implicitness/explicitness in speech and writing, see Mazzie (1987).

A very practically oriented approach to speech and writing is found in Freeborn *et al.* (1986).

Good general papers on recent views of writing are to be found in Couture (1986).

Discussion of different approaches to the teaching of writing can be found in Zamel (1983 and 1987), Shih (1986) and Michaels (1987).

On the links between the density of cohesive ties and overall coherence, see Tierney and Mosenthal (1983).

On the status of the paragraph, see Longacre (1979).

For a discourse-segment approach to paragraphs see Stark (1988) and Hofmann (1989).

The arguments for and against cross-cultural differences and interference at the discourse level may be pursued further in Clyne (1981 and 1987a and b), Connor and McCagg (1983), Scarcella (1984), House (1985), Wierzbicka (1985) and Stalker and Stalker (1989).

Rhetoric studies contrasting English with other, specific languages (including Hindi, German, Korean, Mandarin and Japanese) may be found in Kaplan (1983).

Problems associated with top–down and bottom–up strategies in reading are explored in Carrell (1988).

Schema theory is discussed in Rumelhart (1975) and in Carrell and Eisterhold (1983), or the updated version of this paper in Carrell *et al.* (1988), and in Steffensen (1986); whether content or formal schemata affect reading comprehension more is taken up in Carrell (1987).

Hoey and Winter (1986) give further details on the question–answer pattern.

On inference and the language learner, see Carton (1971).

The reciprocal relationship between writer and reader is explored in Nystrand (1986) and in Smith (1986).

Guidance for Reader activities

Chapter 1

Activity 1, page 9

Possible contexts:

1a) A: You caused a bit of a stir.
B: Did I make a fool of myself?
A: No . . . it wasn't that, it's just that you shocked some people.

1b) A: Oh dear! Did I make a fool of myself last night!
B: Why? What did you do?
A: I was invited to Tom's for dinner and before the meal I said I hated curried prawns, and that's what they served for dinner!

2a) A: There's a very good reason why I don't want to marry you.
B: You don't love me?
A: Okay . . . if you want a straight answer . . . yes . . . I'm sorry.

2b) A: You don't love me, my children don't love me, nobody loves me!
B: Oh grow up! Don't be silly!
A: Well, it's true, you said so.

3a) A: What does one normally do with this outside skin?
B: You eat it . . . or some people just throw it away.
A: Mm . . . how interesting.

3b) A: I don't like this porridge.
B: You eat it, and shut up!

4a) A: Switch the light on.
B: (switches it on)
A: Thanks.

4b) A: I wonder how we could see if anything was written on the back . . . through the paper.
B: Switch the light on?
C: Yes, we could do . . . where's the switch?

Activity 2, page 11

It would be strange to *begin* a discourse with 'I mean' in this way; 'I mean' usually occurs as a marker of the speaker making a paraphrase or re-statement of something he/she has already said. 'This new emblem' assumes, in the use of *this*, that the listener knows which emblem is being referred to. We shall look more closely at this sort of assumption made by speakers in section 2.2. It is not clear to us who *him* is, either, though it is quite clear to the speakers. Finally this extract ends with a question; questions normally expect answers.

Activity 3, page 14

1. Other situations: doctor–patient interviews ('okay, let's have a look at you'), church services ('let us pray'), meetings ('right, let's make a start shall we'), checking in at a hotel ('okay, the boy will show you to your room'), hiring a car ('right . . . if you just follow that gentleman, he'll show you where the car is'). There are, of course, many more.

2. In English, probably the most frequent are: *right, right then, okay, so, well, well now, well then, good*. Note that this is quite a restricted set. Are the sets in other languages equally restricted?

3. My pupils have frequently pointed out to me that my own personal favourite is 'o-kee-doe!'

Activity 4, page 17

1. Original order of the transcript:
   1) A: Can I help you?
   2) B: Um have you by any chance got anything on Bath?
   3) A: I'm awfully sorry, we haven't . . . um I don't know where you can try for Bath actually.
   4) B: You haven't no, no.
   5) A: Um I don't really know . . . you could try perhaps Pickfords in Littlewoods, they might be able to help you.
   6) B: No . . . in Littlewoods is it?
   7) A: Yeah they're inside there now.
   8) B: Okay thanks.

Moves (1) and (2) are easy to place: they contain formulaic openings for transactions at shops and service counters ('can I help you?' 'have you by any chance . . . '). The response (3) is equally formulaic in service encoun-ters. (4) is slightly more problematic in that 'no, no' seems a little out of place, but in fact *yes* and *no* are frequently used just as 'fillers' in conversations, without their full meaning of positive and negative polarity. (5) repeats part of (4) ('I don't know'), and (6) has repetition from (5) ('Littlewoods') and the backward referring pronoun *it*. (7) also uses pronominal reference but this time a plural, *they*; *it* and *they* are often used interchangeably by speakers to refer to companies. (8) is then a formulaic closing of a service encounter. Thus the moves easiest to place are the formulaic openings and closings, which all language users recognise instantly.

2.   Examples from other languages: in Hungarian, in a formal situation, a fourth part (equivalent to 'you're welcome'/'not at all') is essential:

A: Elnézést, megmondaná az idöt?   (Excuse me, d'you
                                                            have the time?)
B: Igen . . . fél öt.   (Yes . . . half past
                                                            four.)
A: Köszönöm.   (Thanks.)
B: Kérem.   (You're welcome.)

Informally, the same exchange might have only three parts:

A: Ne haragudj, megmondanád az idöt?
B: Fél öt.
A: Kösz (önöm).

Activity 5, page 23

Here is a suggested analysis:
[ ] = framing moves at the boundaries of transactions;
// = exchange boundary; / = move boundary
Suggested labels for acts are in italics.

     marker   *elicitation*
L: [Well], // that should blow a hole in five pounds, shouldn't it? /

     reply
S1: It's quite cheap actually. /

     comment
L: (laughs) //

                  elicitation
S1: What's the um lecturers' club like, senior, ⌐ senior, you know. /

L: ⌊ Ah it's very

               reply
cosy and sedate and, er, you know, nice little armchairs and curtains . . . there are some interesting characters

who get there. //
       elicitation
S2: Is that the one ~~where they~~ have the toilets marked with er
     gentlemen, no, 'ladies and members'? / ⌐ *reply*
                                     ⌐ Oh, oh ⌐ *comment*
                                          ⌐ Yeah it was
     one of the other lecturers who pointed it out, he ⌐ thought it
     was quite amusing. /   *comment*
L: Yeah, I
     hadn't noticed that, yeah, might well be, yeah. //
             directive
B: Four sixty-seven please. /
     aside
L: Is that all, God, I thought it would cost more than that /
    react   *elicit*
     (pays) . . . thank you . . . // I thought it would cost more
     than that. /
        reply
S1: ⌐ It's quite cheap. /
S2: ⊦ I wouldn't argue with that one. /
S3: ⌊ No, it's quite good. //
     marker   *elicit*
L: [Now] //how are we going to carry all these over? /

The problems here arise from the fact that the lecturer and his pupils have stepped out of role for an informal gathering. Therefore, for one thing, we do not get typical teacher (evaluative) follow-up moves, though speakers still make comments on other speakers' utterances. It is difficult to label the lecturer's 'Oh, oh', since it does not seem to be answering the student's question about the toilets in the lecturers' club. Nonetheless, the questioner comments as though she has had an answer, or perhaps simply to expand her question, and the lecturer just seems to add another comment.

Another difficulty is the lecturer's initial reaction to the price of the drinks; he makes a remark that does not seem to be addressed to anyone in particular, but is rather an 'aside'. After paying, he redirects the same remark to the students, who then reply, three of them speaking at once. The whole transaction, marked off by the two framing moves, functions as a 'socialising' phase while the drinks are being served; the group has to talk about something, since such a long period of silence would not be tolerated.

Activity 6, page 26

Sentence 2: *More continental* is a comparative tie which can only be understood in relation to *traditional* in sentence 1. *You* in the second clause

refers to '*Which?* readers' in the first. *Electric shaver* is repeated.
Sentence 3: *Shaving* is repeated from sentence 1.
Sentence 4: *Women* and *Which? readers* are repetitions from sentences 2 and 3. *Remove body hair* is repeated, and so is *shaver*.

Activity 7, page 30

Text 1: The second sentence is the *reason* for the first.

Text 2: A *cause–consequence* relation exists between the first two segments; with subordination ('which made . . . ') as supporting evidence. The first two segments taken together then become a single, larger segment which stands in a matching relation of *contrast* with the rest of the extract. Note the signal provided by the syntactic parallelism ('In Britain'/'on the Continent').

Activity 8, pages 31–2

Text 1: *Situation* and *problem* are simultaneously identified in the headline. *Problem* is expanded up to 'hazard to health'. *Response* and positive *evaluation* are interwoven in the rest of the text.
General signals:
problem: cause damage/ruin/repugnant/hazard
response: cure/develop
evaluation: guarantee/ensure/for good/tried and tested

Text 2: *Situation* and *problem* are in sentence 1. *Problem* is expanded in sentences 2 and 3. *Response* starts at 'The rudimentary cure', but this response is only partial and not evaluated very positively. The true response comes in the next paragraph ('But we believe . . . ') and the one after that. The last paragraph then gives the positive *evaluation*.
General signals:
problem: badly/suffer/tiring
partial response: rudimentary cure
response: prevention/ways/reducing/explore/techniques
evaluation: rudimentary/result/smooth/effortless

The concocted text was a simplified affair, for the sake of illustration. Real texts are usually more subtly interwoven, like these two. But even here, we can see the elements of our pattern and its signals.

Chapter 2

Activity 1, page 37

Text 1: *It* refers to the situation described in the first sentence.

Text 2: *It* refers to the automatic dog barking unit, and could be substituted by any one of three noun phrases: '(the) automatic dog barking unit', 'Guard Dog', or 'the Boston Bulldog'.

Activity 2, page 39

There is no 'right answer' to this one, but you may find that some examples with *that* will be difficult to fit into the rules we have suggested. Ideally, a massive, computer-based study is needed to clarify this sort of usage.

Activity 3, pages 40–1

The Northern Ireland Secretary: this is rather like *the Queen*, *the Pope*, etc., a reference to a unique figure in an assumed shared world. Similarly, *the jury*, *the judge* and *the Crown*, make references to the English legal system which the writer assumes the readers will be familiar with.

Activity 4, page 42

Cataphoric item: *it* (sentence 1), referring to *the 61st annual feast of the San Gennaro* (sentence 3).

Activity 5, pages 44–5

Ellipses:
Text 1: 'Trips (*are*) taken home'; 'social life (*is*) lived'.

Text 2: 'Yes, don't you (*like watching children*)?'; '(*she*) only looked at the swings'; 'But you wouldn't (*join in*)?'; 'Why *don't* you (*join in*)?'; 'Why don't I (*join in*)?'.

Activity 6, page 46

The writer here obviously wishes to say that he/she will send further information. *Do so* could only be used if *send* or a similar verb had occurred in the previous clause. In fact the previous clause only contains *require*, which makes *do so* inappropriate as a substitute.

Activity 7, pages 48–9

However (line 8): adversative
And (line 11): additive
And (line 18): additive
What's more (line 22): additive
So (line 27): causal

Activity 8, page 50

The extract begins with *and*, which signals the start of a new story in a string of stories that are being told. Speaker A uses *but*, in the same turn, to return the discourse to the main narrative after the 'aside' ('I forget where the village was'). The next *and* is just a linker between the narrative and the reporting of direct speech, a typical function of *and*. *So* is causal (he turned left *because* he was told to).

In A's next turn, she uses *but* to reiterate an earlier statement ('but they all followed behind'). As with Firth's (1988) data, B uses *see* to introduce his justification of events. A then uses *but* again to return the discourse to the next episode of the narrative. Finally, B reiterates his justification with *and you see*.

These examples are typical of how speakers use such small, everyday words to relate chunks of the discourse to one another.

Activity 9, pages 52–3

Examples of variations might be:

1. It's the children Bob takes out every Saturday. (cf. (2.39))
   Every Saturday, Bob takes the children out. (cf. (2.38))
   He takes the children out every Saturday, Bob. (cf. (2.41))
2. What the gardener wants to do this spring is cut down those bushes. (cf. (2.40))
   Those bushes, the gardener wants to cut them down this spring. (cf. (2.37))
   The gardener, he wants to cut down those bushes this spring. (cf. (2.42))

Activity 10, page 57

Text 1: *bill* in the rheme of sentence 1 is taken up as theme (*cost*) in sentence 2. *Study* in the rheme of (2) becomes the theme of (3). The rheme of (3) contains a mention of the collective author of the study, *The Fellowship of Engineering*, which is taken up in the theme of (4) as *the author*. The rheme of (4) names the individual author, Philip Comer, and he becomes the theme (*he*) or (5). We therefore have an overall tendency towards theme–rheme option (a).

Text 2: *The brain*, the theme of sentence 1, is also the theme of sentences 2 and 3. We then have a fronted adjectival phrase ('as soft as a ripe avocado'), but *the brain* is still subject, and therefore part of the theme. Sentence 5 continues with *an adult brain* as theme, as does sentence 6 (*it*). Sentence 7 has *the brain* as theme again, and then the pattern is somewhat broken by the fronted verbal group ('Coming out of . . .'), as the theme shifts to the *brain stem*, which takes over as theme in the last part of the extract. The overall dominant pattern is, therefore, theme–rheme option (b).

Activity 11, page 60

We would have to explain to the student that, conventionally, the clause, 'In this essay I *try* to discuss . . .' would occur in the preface or introduction to the essay, and that present perfect ('I *have tried*') would be used at the end of the essay to look back over the whole essay up to that point. However, '*are* suggested in the last section' is acceptable, since 'last' and the 'conclusion' can be seen as part of the same 'present' segment of the essay.

Chapter 3

Activity 1, page 68

Dozing is reiterated as its superordinate *slept* in sentence 3, and then resurfaces as *dozing* again in sentence 6. Sentence 7 then has a colloquial near-synonym, *kipping*.

Guards is taken up as a synonym, *sentries* in sentence 3 (two occurrences); then as a general superordinate, *soldiers* in (4); then as a hyponym, *airmen* in (6), which is repeated in (8).

There is therefore a considerable amount of lexical variation, even just for these two words. Note, in addition, how *campaigners* (1) becomes *protesters* (2), and resurfaces as *campaigner* in (4); *walk* in (2) is represented by a hyponym, *tip-toed* in (3); *cruise launchers* (2) becomes *cruise convoy* (3), *launchers* in (6), the superordinate *vehicles* in (7), and *convoy* in (8).

Activity 2, pages 70–1

(T = turn)

T1: *knitting . . . knitting*; T5: *knitting . . . knitting*; all repetitions. *Knitting* does not occur after T5.
T1: *garment*; T12: *garments*; T15: *clothes . . . summer dresses . . . shifts*

(persists over fifteen turns, becoming more specific in T15).
T3: *lovely*; T4: *nice* (a short-lived chain)
The most persistent topic is 'clothes'; the sub-topic of 'knitting' gives way
to its co-hyponym 'sewing' in T9, while 'cheapness' emerges as another
sub-topic (T13 and T17).

Activity 3, page 73

Financial here seems to mean 'strictly concerning profit and loss in money
terms'; *economic* seems to concern the broader planning of the economy,
and the role of the railway in the overall budget for transport, services, etc.,
i.e. it is an *asset* (last sentence).

Activity 4, page 77

Text 1: *These questions* refers back to all of sentences 2, 3, and 4.

Text 2: *The issues* refers forward to 'accountability, relationships with
voluntary bodies, what their role is'.

Activity 5, page 78

On page 76 you will find '*this account* (of the work of certain words . . .)',
which refers back to the whole of section 3.5 up to that point. In the next
paragraph '*this* particular lexical *area*' can be read as a reference back to
'the work of certain words in organising discourse'. In the same paragraph,
answers can be seen to refer forward to the descriptions of the contributions
of Winter, Francis and Jordan.
    The paragraph beginning 'Winter's work, and its extension . . . '
(page 78) contains the phrase '*some* interesting *questions*', which refers
forward to the whole of the rest of that paragraph. The next paragraph
then begins with a backward reference (*these questions*) to the same
segment of text.
    It is almost impossible to write academic/argumentative text of this kind
without using such organising words to refer back and forth to different
segments of the text.

Activity 6, pages 81–2

Text 1: Words strongly associated with *problem–solution* patterns:
crisis   coping with   demands   problem   scarcity   provides
developed   answer   solutions   ways   tackling   issues   solution
Claim–counterclaim pattern: adopt the view   argue against
The predominant pattern is *problem–solution*.

Text 2: Words associated with *claim–counterclaim*:
believe strongly in   think (× 2)   hold   on the other hand   places more
faith in   considers   dismisses   believes
The predominant pattern is *claim–counterclaim*. Note the lexical variation
in verbs meaning 'to think/believe something'.

Activity 7, page 86

Modal words: *Can* (headline); *Could; there's some evidence . . . that, may,
can.*

Chapter 4

Activity 1, page 89

Possible realisations in rapid, informal, Standard British English are as
follows:
1. [tenə levm məns əgəʊ]
2. [aɪ aest ɪm wɒʔ went ɒn]
3. [nɒʔ hɜː nɒʔ meərɪ]
4. [kənsɪdrɪm maɪ eɪdʒ aɪ raem maɪlz]
Note particularly how final /n/ sounds anticipate following /m/ sounds and
assimilate to them. Elisions here include dropping the /θ/ sounds of *months*
and the loss of /ə/ between /d/ and /r/ in *considering*. Note also the glottal
stops (ʔ); some speakers consider these to be bad, 'sloppy' speech, but they
are extremely common in the informal, conversational speech of people of
a wide range of social backgrounds.

Activity 2, page 91

Possible readings:
1. What's the matter with Mary?

2. I knew she would come in the end.

3. Put salt on those chips if you want to.

4. He works on a farm, doesn't he?

There are other possible readings (e.g. I knew *she* would come).

Activity 3, page 93

1. Which hat shall Jo wear to the drinks party?
   F   F   R   F F   R R F   F R
   LL L   S   LL L   S S LL   L S

2. I met Bill Smith in town at lunchtime.
   F F F   F   R F   R F   F
   LL L LL   L   S L   S L   S

3. A bottle of mineral water.
   R F RR   F   R   FR
   S L SS   L   S   LA

There are problems here. In (2), in many situations the word *I* would be a reduced sound, almost a schwa, but not quite. Example 3 raises the question of vowels that are elided in rapid speech but which may be present in careful speech (the middle vowel of /mınərəl/. Bolinger's theory does seem to idealise pronunciation and not take context into account.

Activity 4, page 96

1. disused   (2 1)
2. complicated .   (1 2)
3. application   (2 1)
4. dinosaur   (1 2)

Activity 5, page 97

Possible renditions:

1. DOES the SOUP contain MEAT?
2. SOrry to ring you so LATE.
3. WILL you accept a CHEQUE?

Activity 6, page 98

Some apparent misplacings of prominence can be traced to incorrect notions of which syllables are normally stressed in compound words (e.g. 'car PARK' instead of 'CAR park'). Speakers of some languages have a tendency to stress the final word in an utterance, again producing odd perceptions of prominence on occasions where the final word would not be prominent in English (e.g. 'IS mr JONES here? i have a MEssage for HIM').

Activity 7, page 100

Possible tone groups:

1. / i've LOST my **CAR** keys /
2. / SUddenly / a **CAT** jumped out /
3. / it's **MON**days / i hate **MOST** /
4. / **DA**vid / i know QUITE **WELL** / his SISter / i don't know at **ALL** /

Activity 8, page 104

The Hallidayan system does have the advantage that utterances are divided up into small, manageable chunks, and that individual parts of it can be examined separately (e.g. just tone groups or tonics), but it is complicated and forbidding-looking when all the features are indicated simultaneously. Brown's system may be quite good for anyone with a basic knowledge of music (cf. the stave), and long stretches of talk can be visualised at a glance. However, the eye has constantly to jump back and forth between two centres of attention (the text and the notation), which is not so marked with Halliday's system.

Some American phonologists indicate intonation by letting the writing move up and down as the voice would, e.g.:

```
Every                          portant infor
      body        This is im              ma
         listen!                       tion.
```

In the end, different systems will suit different purposes in the classroom, but anything with a strong visual appeal will probably help learners.

Activity 9, pages 107–8

1. / he's a STUpid FOOL! / (e.g. expressing anger/exasperation)

   / he's as TALL as ME! / (e.g. an adult of a child who has grown a lot, expressing surprise)

2. if you Opened your EYES / you'd SEE it! / (exasperation)

   / i'm deLIGHTed to SAY / you've WON it! / (delight/pleasure)

3. / JIM? / i DON't beLIEVE it! / (incredulity)

/ SÓ / he BOUGHT a NÈW one / (narrating, emotionally neutral? Possibly ironic?)

It does seem relatively easy to put almost *any* emotional interpretation on to these tone contours, which suggests that they alone are not connected with specific attitudes.

Activity 10, page 110

1. / IF you see TÌM /CAN you ask him to RÌNG me? /

    (Both fall and fall–rise are possible on 'ring me'; fall–rise will be heard as more 'polite' because it is less closed and final, suggesting less that it is an instruction.)

2. A: / i met JOsie CÒLEman / in TÓWN /

    B: / JOsie CÒLEman? /

    A: / YÈS /
    B's answer with fall–rise indicates that he/she does not consider the information 'closed'; A hears this as a request for confirmation.

3. A: / IS it five o'CLÒCK? /

    B: / FIVE TÒ /

    A: / ÀH! / GÒOD! / JUST in TÌME! /
    A's question is an 'open' meaning (A does not know the time). B's response is definite, closed. A's follow-up is a final, closed statement that requires no further comment from B.

Activity 11, page 112

Likely high- and low-key realisations:

1. A: / i'll ASK CÀRlos / HÉ'S brazilian /
    B: / CÀRlos? he's CHÌlean DIDn't you KNÓW? /

    B's high key expresses something contrasting with expectations.

2. A: / WÈLL / THÀNKS / you've been
    VEry HÈLPful /
    B: / WHÒ? MÉ? / NOT at ÀLL! / it's my JÒB! /

184

A's 'you've been very helpful' is presented as equivalent to 'thanks'; B politely deflects A's gratitude using high key to express a contrast with what A has said.

Activity 12, pages 115–16

The same comments could be made here as were made in Activity 7; a longer stretch of talk like this one could as well be transcribed using Brown's notation. However, if such a transcription were accompanied by a tape-recording in the classroom, its complexities might be lessened somewhat, and, anyway, such a complex transcription would only be suitable once learners had become thoroughly familiar with individual levels of the system beforehand.

Chapter 5

Activity 1, page 120

In British culture, short service encounters (and encounters such as passing security barriers) normally end with server and customer both saying 'thank you', and without either party using phrases such as 'not at all', or 'that's okay'. These are reserved for occasions when genuine favours are done or inconveniences borne (e.g. A: 'Thanks ever so much for looking after Tommy' B: 'Oh, not at all, he was no trouble'). In American English, the follow-up 'you're welcome' is common in service encounters on the part of the server, and is often accompanied by the formulaic salutation 'Have a nice day!' to the customer.

Activity 2, pages 123–4

In general, the adjacency pairs and the exchange structure are realised naturally. What oddities there are seem rather to be lexical and/or grammatical, for example the use of past tense instead of present perfect in 'What happened in this country . . . ?', and the use of 'turned out' by B. A's follow-up ('Oh, I see, that's interesting') is exactly what one would expect, as is his 'doesn't matter' later on. 'Awfully sorry' is perhaps a little unnatural as a second pair-part when apologising for being unable to fulfil a request for information; 'Sorry', or 'I'm sorry' would be more normal in British English (as occurs in B's final turn).

Activity 3, pages 125–6

Taking follow-up moves first, A's 'It's quite interesting' is the only genuine follow-up move of the type common in reciprocal talk; the rest of the time she follows B's replies with new initiations. If we take initiations, A is the one who initiates all the time; she clearly perceives her role as that of interviewer; the only questions B addresses are checks that he has understood A's questions. He does, however, make a long informing move at the beginning when he tells the story behind his name (in the original transcript, A does not ask him to tell the story; he volunteers it spontaneously). In general, then, we might conclude that these two learners perceive their role as interviewer and interviewee, rather than as equal participants in a conversation.

Activity 4, pages 129–30

This is what a 'cleaned up' version might look like:

A: Sit down . . . you're all right then?

B: Yes, okay, Jack. I did a daft thing though, I planned the route out, you know, I had it all written out, and, unlike most people, you see a signpost 'Repley', so I took it and I came over Mistham by the reservoirs, nice it was.

A: Oh, by Mistham, over the top, nice run.

B: Colours are pleasant, aren't they?

C: Yeah.

A: Nice run that.

B: Yeah, we enjoyed it . . . wasn't the way we intended, but as usual it was nice.

A: No, we were just talking about that.

B: Oh, yes, it was all right.

'Cleaning up' the dialogue and making it look like the sort of dialogue one finds in many language textbooks creates problems. Back-channels can be either omitted (as we have done with C's 'Yeah's' while B is telling his story, or else they could be included as separate turns. Another alternative is to include the back-channel in a subsequent turn (as we have done with A's 'No, we were just talking about that'), but then the 'No' seems to be responding to 'It was nice' (which is odd), rather than to 'It wasn't the way we intended', and this might confuse the learners.

Punctuation is also a problem. There are usually several possible punctuations for the same stretch of talk, and decisions will be subjective. However, punctuation does help to clarify the text for the learner, especially in a case such as 'You see a signpost "Repley", so I took it', where the quotation marks tell the learner it is a citation of something.

The text remains reasonably natural. Note the natural grammatical features such as ellipses ('[The] colours are pleasant', '[A] nice run') and note the marked word-order features ('Nice it was', 'Nice run, that'). The exercise does suggest that, with careful editing, natural data can be used for dialogues for classroom use.

Activity 5, pages 134–5

The talk begins with exchanges about the weather at Christmas in Britain. C repeats an earlier remark ('Yes, it was very sunny Christmas Day'), which acts as a summary of the sub-topic; there is then a pause, filled by a series of 'Mm' noises. When B starts the new sub-topic ('When are you heading off again, Bob?'), we might expect a jump to high key. A answers B's question, and then pauses after 'this time' before introducing the new sub-topic of his suitcase. That sub-topic ends, once again, with a couple of 'Mm's from A.

Activity 6, pages 141–2

B is an active listener in that she makes back-channel responses ('Mm', 'Yeah'), she provides an evaluative follow-up ('Oh, lovely'), she uses checking tags ('Is he?', 'Oh, haven't they?'), and she overlaps with an utterance completion in A's last turn, predicting how he will finish.

Activity 7, page 144

Grammatical 'mistakes' occur in the following:

1. 'More than another' (should be 'more than others').
2. 'I was not able play' (should be 'able to play').
3. 'More too much technical' (should be 'too technical').
4. 'Too much exercises' (should be 'too many exercises').
5. 'The guitar is more easy' (should be 'easier').
6. 'Prove again with the piano?' (should be 'to prove [try] again with the piano').

Of these mistakes, (1), (4), and (6) (the omission of 'to') would probably go unnoticed in spontaneous English native-speaker talk, and even (5) might not do more than raise an eyebrow. This is not to say that native English speakers would not reject these as 'bad grammar' on careful reflection.

Chapter 6

Activity 1, page 148

My own personal response would be:

	Read				Write			
	O	S	R	N	O	S	R	N
Instruction leaflet		X						X
Letter to/from friend		X				X		
Public notice	X							X
Product label	X							X
Newspaper obituary			X					X
Poem		X						X
News report	X							X
Academic article	X					X		
Small ads	X						X	
Postcard to/from friend	X				X			
Business letter	X				X			

Thus, even though I read a lot of these types of written text, I never write most of them.

Activity 2, page 151

Group B's text is not a letter as such, but a list of instructions. It is full of imperative verb forms, while Group A's text has softened the first directive to the caretaker by using 'Would you be kind enough to . . . ', and later uses 'please'. Group A have also framed the text as a letter or note, personally addressed, and they end their text with a friendly 'interactional' sentence to relieve the overwhelmingly 'transactional' nature of the rest of the text. In the discussion afterwards, some of the participants argued that it was not necessary to send a friendly letter to the caretaker, since it was his job to provide such services. Others argued that a friendly tone was necessary to establish a cooperative relationship; certainly in a British context the latter would be a wiser course of action.

Activity 3, pages 154–5

Essay 1: The use of *It* in sentence 2 is an example of the confusion of *it*, *this* and *that* as reference items discussed in section 2.2.1. Ideally, the sentence should read: '*This* has been the cause of many problems . . . .' However, comprehensibility and readability are not seriously affected.

Essay 2: 'So as for' at the beginning of sentence 2 is odd. A more acceptable version would be: '*Similarly*, American teenagers play rugby . . . '.

Essay 3: 'They are trained . . . ' in sentence 4 is odd because 'the astronauts' have ceased to be a current focus (see section 2.2.1), other topics having taken over ('problems', 'absence of gravity', 'period of training', etc.). It would be more appropriate, therefore, to re-enter the noun phrase, and say: 'Astronauts are trained in simple jobs . . . ', thus restoring the astronauts to topical focus.

Activity 4, page 157

Essay 1: Sentence 2 seems to contradict sentence 1 as it stands. A more coherent version might be: 'My field of study concerns architecture. *In actual fact*, it is not *merely* a field of study, *but rather* a huge world, going from . . . ', where lexical signals of modification of the previous statement help the reader with the text.

Essay 2: 'And also' causes problems here. An alternative form of linkage could be: 'The problems of modern cities are derived from the Industrial Revolution, and *even though* the cities of my country were not involved in this event, it is *nonetheless* true that there are . . . '.

Activity 5, page 160

Text 1: The first sentences seem to set up a classic claim and counterclaim pattern, with rival opinions being expounded. Signals include *of course*, *stereotypes* and *absolutely*. The final sentence is, however, an explicit question, so we might expect the text to go on to evaluate different answers to the question and to adopt at least one of them, thus creating a larger question–answer pattern for the whole text.

Text 2: This is more obviously a question–answer pattern, with an explicit question posed in the headline. Paragraphs 1 and 2 set the situation, paragraph 3 repeats the question of the headline and suggest that the answer may be 'yes', while paragraph 4 looks at the government's 'no' response to the question. We might expect the text to go on to evaluate the 'yes' and 'no' responses, and, if we are familiar with this particular consumer magazine, we might predict that it is the 'yes' answer which the author will espouse.

Activity 6, page 163

One possible order is: 1, 5, 3, 4, 2. Also possible: 1, 3, 5, 4, 2. Most informants feel that 4 and 2 should always be at the end. Some changes that informants have suggested are:

5. '*The typical situation is that* thousands of people . . .'
'*Week after week*, thousands of people . . .'
4. 'The problem is how to *intervene* without cancelling . . .'

Activity 7, pages 165–6

The essay certainly seems to have more overt discourse organisation. It begins with a preview statement setting out what the text will do, then goes into detailed contrasts, and then ends with a paragraph which generalises on the issue of differences between the two cultures. Extract (6.10) on the other hand, remains on the same level of detail throughout, except for the (somewhat irrelevant) listing of Japanese television channels. The writer of the longer essay also uses overt signalling in phrases such as '*that is the same* teenagers in my country' and '*that is a little bit different from* teenagers in my country'. The only obvious signals of contrast in (6.10) are '*more* people' sentence 3, and '*But* my country' sentence 6.

Activity 8, page 167

If we correct obvious grammar and vocabulary mistakes, we might come up with a version something like the following:

> Korea has developed radically in its economy over the past 25 years. All industries have developed and especially mechanical industries have advanced, for example, the electrical, steel and car industries. As a result of the development of industry, Korea has become a rich country and almost all homes have television, video and a car.

The text is actually now perfectly acceptable, but fine tuning could be applied with regard to reference and ellipsis. The following changes are possible:

> Korea has developed radically in its economy over the past 25 years. All industries have advanced, especially mechanical industries, for example, electrical, steel and cars. As a result of this development, Korea has become a rich country and almost all homes have television, video and a car.

There is no reason why learners' own texts should not be used as the raw data for presenting and practising features such as reference, ellipsis and substitution.

Activity 9, pages 169–70

From real world experience a British person might predict that the phone boxes had been vandalised. If you are lucky enough to live in a country where phone box vandalism is rare, you might predict neglect of technical faults, or perhaps storm damage, or teething troubles with new technology. When we predict, we are constantly trying to relate the new to what we already know and have experienced. We would certainly expect this text to tell us the reason why there was a problem with the phones. We might also expect in a news article like this a statement from a spokesperson for the telephone company, and perhaps some details of the inconveniences caused by the phones being out of order (e.g. an interview with someone affected). We also expect it to be a typical problem–solution text in that the headline suggests that a problem has been solved and that there has been a return to normality.

References

Abercrombie, D. 1964. A phonetician's view of verse structure. *Linguistics*, 6, 5–13.

Allerton, D. J. 1978. The notion of 'givenness' and its relations to presupposition and to theme. *Lingua*, 44, 133–68.

Anderson, A., and T. Lynch. 1988. *Listening*. Oxford: Oxford University Press.

Aston, G. 1988. *Negotiating Service: Studies in the Discourse of Bookshop Encounters*. Bologna: Editrice CLUEB.

Austin, J. L. 1962. *How to Do Things with Words*. Oxford: Oxford University Press.

Aziz, Y. Y. 1988. Theme–rheme organization and paragraph structure in standard Arabic. *Word*, 39(2), 117–28.

Bailey, R. W. 1985. Negotiation and meaning: revisiting the context of situation. In J. D. Benson and W. S. Greaves (Eds.) *Systemic Perspectives on Discourse*, vol. 2. Norwood, New Jersey: Ablex Publishing Corporation.

Bar-Lev, Z. 1986. Discourse theory and 'contrastive rhetoric'. *Discourse Processes*, 9(2), 235–46.

Barnes, B. K. 1985. *The Pragmatics of Left Detachment in Spoken Standard French*. Amsterdam: John Benjamins.

Beattie, G. W. 1981. The regulation of speaker turns in face-to-face conversation: some implications for conversation in sound-only channels. *Semiotica*, 34, 55–70.

Belton, A. 1988. Lexical naturalness in native and non-native discourse. *English Language Research Journal* (ns), 2, 79–105.

Benson, J. D., and W. S. Greaves. 1973. *The Language People Really Use*. Agincourt, Canada: The Book Society of Canada.

Benson, J. D., and W. S. Greaves. 1981. Field of Discourse: theory and application. *Applied Linguistics*, 2(1), 45–55.

Biber, D. 1988. *Variation Across Speech and Writing*. Cambridge: Cambridge University Press.

Blum-Kulka, S. 1987. Indirectness and politeness in requests: same or different? *Journal of Pragmatics*, 11, 131–46.

Bolinger, D. 1986. *Intonation and its Parts: Melody in Spoken English*. London: Edward Arnold.

Borzone de Manrique, A. M., and A. Signorini. 1983. Segmental duration and rhythm in Spanish. *Journal of Phonetics*, 11(2), 117–28.

Boyle, J. 1987. Perspectives on stress and intonation in language learning. *System*, 15(2), 189–95.

Bradford, B. 1988. *Intonation in Context* (Student's and Teacher's Book). Cambridge: Cambridge University Press.

Brazil, D. C. 1985a. *The Communicative Value of Intonation in English*. Birmingham: English Language Research, University of Birmingham.

References

Brazil, D. C. 1985b. Phonology: intonation in discourse. In T. A. Van Dijk (Ed.) *Handbook of Discourse Analysis*, vol. 2. London: Academic Press.

Brazil, D. C., R. M. Coulthard, and C. M. Johns. 1980. *Discourse Intonation and Language Teaching*. London: Longman.

Brown, E. K. 1980. Grammatical incoherence. In H. Dechert and M. Raupach (Eds.) *Temporal Variables in Speech: Studies in Honour of Frieda Goldman-Eisler*. The Hague: Mouton.

Brown, G. 1977. *Listening to Spoken English*. London: Longman.

Brown, G. 1983. Prosodic structure and the given/new distinction. In A. Cutler and D. R. Ladd (Eds.) *Prosody: Models and Methods*. Berlin: Springer–Verlag.

Brown, G. 1986. Investigating listening comprehension in context. *Applied Linguistics*, 7(3), 284–302.

Brown, G., K. L. Currie, and J. Kenworthy. 1980. *Questions of Intonation*. London: Croom Helm.

Brown, G., and G. Yule. 1983. *Discourse Analysis*. Cambridge: Cambridge University Press.

Brown, P., and S. Levinson. 1978. Universals in language use: politeness phenomena. In E. Goody (Ed.) *Questions and Politeness: Strategies in Social Interaction*. Cambridge: Cambridge University Press.

Butterworth, B., R. R. Hine, and K. D. Brady. 1977. Speech interaction in sound-only communication channels. *Semiotica*, 20, 81–99.

Bygate, M. 1987. *Speaking*. Oxford: Oxford University Press.

Carrell, P. L. 1987. Content and formal schemata in ESL reading. *TESOL Quarterly*, 21(3), 461–81.

Carrell, P. L. 1988. Some causes of text-boundedness and schema interference in ESL reading. In P. L. Carrell, J. Devine and D. Eskey (Eds.) *Interactive Approaches to Second Language Reading*. Cambridge: Cambridge University Press.

Carrell, P. L., and J. C. Eisterhold. 1983. Schema theory and ESL reading pedagogy. *TESOL Quarterly*, 17(4), 553–73. Reprinted (with some updating) in P. L. Carrell, J. Devine and D. Eskey (Eds.) *Interactive Approaches to Second Language Reading*. Cambridge: Cambridge University Press.

Carter, R. A., and D. Burton. (Eds.) 1982. *Literary Text and Language Study*. London: Edward Arnold.

Carter, R. A., and M. J. McCarthy. 1988. *Vocabulary and Language Teaching*. London: Longman.

Carton, A. S. 1971. Inferencing: a process in using and learning language. In P. Pimsleur and T. Quinn (Eds.) *Papers from the Second International Congress of Applied Linguists. Cambridge, 1969*. Cambridge: Cambridge University Press.

Chafe, W. 1982. Integration and involvement in speaking, writing, and oral literature. In D. Tannen (Ed.) *Spoken and Written Language: Exploring Orality and Literacy*. Norwood, New Jersey: Ablex Publishing Corporation.

Clyne, M. 1981. Culture and discourse structure. *Journal of Pragmatics*, 5, 61–6.

Clyne, M. 1987a. Discourse structures and discourse expectations: implications for Anglo-German academic communication in English. In L. E. Smith (Ed.) *Discourse Across Cultures: Strategies in World Englishes*. London: Prentice Hall.

Clyne, M. 1987b. Cultural differences in the organisation of academic texts. *Journal of Pragmatics*, 11, 211–47.

COBUILD, 1987. *Collins COBUILD English Language Dictionary*. London: Collins.

Coe, N., R. Rycroft, and P. Ernest. 1983. *Writing Skills: a Problem-Solving Approach*. Cambridge: Cambridge University Press.

Collie, J., and S. Slater. 1991. *Speaking. Book 2*. Cambridge: Cambridge University Press.

Connor, U., and P. McCagg. 1983. Cross-cultural differences and perceived quality in written paraphrases of English expository prose. *Applied Linguistics*, 4, 259–68.

Cook, G. 1989. *Discourse*. Oxford: Oxford University Press.

Cook, V. J. 1979. *Using Intonation*. London: Longman.

Corson, D. 1985. *The Lexical Bar*. Oxford: Pergamon Press.

Coulmas, F. 1979. On the sociolinguistic relevance of routine formulae. *Journal of Pragmatics*, 3(3/4), 239–66.

Coulmas, F. (Ed.) 1981. *Conversational Routine*. The Hague: Mouton.

Coulthard, R. M. 1985. *An Introduction to Discourse Analysis*. London: Longman.

Coulthard, R. M., and M. Ashby. 1975. Talking with the Doctor: 1. *Journal of Communication*, 25(3), 140–7.

Coulthard, R. M., and D. C. Brazil. 1982. The place of intonation in the description of interaction. In D. Tannen (Ed.) *Analysing Discourse: Text and Talk*. Washington D.C.: Georgetown University Press.

Coulthard, R. M., and M. Montgomery. (Eds.) 1981. *Studies in Discourse Analysis*. London: Routledge and Kegan Paul.

Couper-Kuhlen, E. 1986. *An Introduction to English Prosody*. Tübingen: Max Niemeyer Verlag.

Couture, B. (Ed.) 1986. *Functional Approaches to Writing Research Perspectives*. London: Frances Pinter.

Craig, R. T., and K. Tracy. (Eds.) 1983. *Conversational Coherence: Form, Structure and Strategy*. London: Sage Publications.

Creider, C. A. 1979. On the explanation of transformations. In T. Givón (Ed.) *Syntax and Semantics, Volume 12: Discourse and Syntax*. New York: Academic Press.

Crow, B. K. 1983. Topic shifts in couples' conversations. In R. T. Craig, and K. Tracy. (Eds.) 1983. *Conversational Coherence: Form, Structure and Strategy*. London: Sage Publications.

Cruse, D. A. 1975. Hyponymy and lexical hierarchies. *Archivum Linguisticum*, VI, 26–31.

Cruse, D. A. 1977. The pragmatics of lexical specificity. *Journal of Linguistics*, 13, 153–64.

Cruttenden, A. 1981. Falls and rises: meanings and universals. *Journal of Linguistics*, 17, 77–91.

Cruttenden, A. 1986. *Intonation*. Cambridge: Cambridge University Press.

Crystal, D. 1981. *Directions in Applied Linguistics*. London: Academic Press.

Crystal, D., and D. Davy. 1975. *Advanced Conversational English*. London: Longman.

Currie, K. L., and G. Yule. 1982. A return to fundamentals in the teaching of intonation. *International Review of Applied Linguistics*, 20(3), 228–32.

References

Cutler, A., and M. Pearson. 1986. On the analysis of prosodic turn-taking cues. In C. Johns-Lewis (Ed.) *Intonation in Discourse*. London: Croom Helm.

Daneš, F. 1974. Functional sentence perspective and the organisation of the text. In F. Daneš (Ed.) *Papers on Functional Sentence Perspective*. Prague: Academia.

Dauer, R. M. 1983. Stress-timing and syllable-timing reanalyzed. *Journal of Phonetics*, 11, 51–62.

De Beaugrande, R. 1980. *Text, Discourse and Process: Towards a Multidisciplinary Science of Texts*. Norwood, New Jersey: Ablex Publishing Corporation.

De Beaugrande, R., and W. Dressler. 1981. *Introduction to Text Linguistics*. London: Longman.

Donaldson, S. K. 1979. One kind of speech act: how do we know when we're conversing? *Semiotica*, 28, 259–99.

Duncan, S., and G. Niederehe. 1974. On signalling that it's your turn to speak. *Journal of Experimental Social Psychology*, 10(3), 234–47.

Duranti, A., and E. Ochs. 1979. Left dislocation in Italian conversation. In T. Givón (Ed.) *Syntax and Semantics, Volume 12: Discourse and Syntax*. New York: Academic Press.

Edmondson, W., J. House, G. Kasper, and B. Stemmer. 1984. Learning the pragmatics of discourse: a project report. *Applied Linguistics*, 5(2), 113–27.

Edwards, D., and D. Middleton. 1986. Joint remembering: constructing an account of shared experience through conversational discourse. *Discourse Processes*, 9, 423–59.

Ehrlich, V., and C. Koster. 1983. Discourse organisation and sentence form: the structure of room descriptions in Dutch. *Discourse Processes*, 6, 169–95.

Eiler, M. A. 1986. Thematic distribution as a heuristic for written discourse function. In B. Couture (Ed.) *Functional Approaches to Writing Research Perspectives*. London: Frances Pinter.

Eisenstein, M., and J. W. Bodman. 1986. 'I very appreciate': expressions of gratitude by native and non-native speakers of American English. *Applied Linguistics*, 7(2), 167–85.

Ellis, J. 1966. On contextual meaning', in C. E. Bazell, J. C. Catford, M. A. K. Halliday and R. H. Robins (Eds.) *In Memory of J. R. Firth*. London: Longman.

Ellis, J. 1987. The logical and textual functions. In M. A. K. Halliday and R. P. Fawcett (Eds.) *New Developments in Systemic Linguistics*. London: Frances Pinter.

Eskey, D. E. 1988. Holding in the bottom: an interactive approach to the language problems of second language readers. In P. L. Carrell, J. Devine and D. Eskey (Eds.) *Interactive Approaches to Second Language Reading*. Cambridge: Cambridge University Press.

Esling, J. H., and R. F. Wong. 1983. Voice quality settings and the teaching of pronunciation. *TESOL Quarterly*, 17(1), 89–95.

Faber, D. 1986. Teaching the rhythms of English: a new theoretical base. *International Review of Applied Linguistics*, 24, 205–16.

Firbas, J. 1972. On the interplay of prosodic and non-prosodic means of functional sentence perspective. In V. Fried (Ed.) *The Prague School of Linguistics and Language Teaching*. London: Oxford University Press.

Firth, A. 1988. Communicative strategies of Danish learners and English native-speakers. Ms. English Language Research, University of Birmingham.

Fox, A. 1984. *German Intonation: an Outline.* Oxford: Oxford University Press.

Fox, B. 1987. Morpho-syntactic markedness and discourse structure. *Journal of Pragmatics*, 11, 359–75.

Francis, G. 1986. *Anaphoric Nouns.* Birmingham: English Language Research, University of Birmingham.

Francis, G. 1989. Thematic selection and distribution in written discourse. *Word*, 40(1–2), 201–21.

Francis, G., and S. Hunston. 1987. Analysing everyday conversation. In R. M. Coulthard (Ed.) *Discussing Discourse.* Birmingham: English Language Research, University of Birmingham.

Freeborn, D., P. Finch, and D. Langford. 1986. *Varieties of English: an Introduction to the Study of Language.* London: MacMillan.

Fries, C. C. 1964. On the intonation of 'Yes–No' questions in English. In D. Abercrombie, D. B. Fry, P. A. D. MacCarthy, N. C. Scott and J. L. Trim (Eds.) *In Honour of Daniel Jones.* London: Longman.

Fries, P. H. 1983. On the status of theme in English: arguments from discourse. In J. S. Petofi and E. Sozer (Eds.) *Micro and Macro Connexity of Texts.* Hamburg: Helmut Baske.

Fries, P. H. 1986. Lexical patterns in a text and interpretation. In K. R. Jankowsky (Ed.) *Scientific and Humanistic Dimensions of Language.* Amsterdam: John Benjamins.

Fuller, J. W., and J. K. Gundel. 1987. Topic-prominence in interlanguage. *Language Learning*, 37(1), 1–18.

Gairns, R., and S. Redman. 1986. *Working with Words.* Cambridge: Cambridge University Press.

Gardner, R. 1984. Discourse analysis: implications for language teaching, with particular reference to casual conversation. *Language Teaching and Linguistics: Abstracts*, 17(2), 102–17.

Gardner, R. 1987. The identification and role of topic in spoken interaction. *Semiotica*, 65(1/2), 129–41.

Geluykens, R. 1988. On the myth of rising intonation in polar questions. *Journal of Pragmatics*, 12, 467–85.

Ghadessy, M. 1983. Information structure in Letters to the Editor, *International Review of Applied Linguistics*, 21, 46–56.

Gibbs, R. W. 1987. Mutual knowledge and the psychology of conversational inference. *Journal of Pragmatics*, 11, 561–88.

Gibbs, R. W., and R. A. Mueller. 1988. Conversational sequences and preference for indirect speech acts. *Discourse Processes*, 11(1), 101–16.

Givón, T. 1984. *Syntax: a Functional–Typological Introduction*, vol. 1. Amsterdam: John Benjamins.

Goffman, E. 1976. Replies and responses. *Language in Society*, 5, 257–313.

Goffman, E. 1979. *Forms of Talk.* Oxford: Basil Blackwell.

Greenall, S., and M. Swan. 1986. *Effective Reading.* Cambridge: Cambridge University Press.

Greenwood, J. 1981. Pronunciation – perception and production. In G. Abbott and P. Wingard (Eds.) *The Teaching of English as an International Language: a Practical Guide.* Glasgow: Collins.

Grellet, F. 1981. *Developing Reading Skills.* Cambridge: Cambridge University Press.

References

Grice, H. P. 1975. Logic and conversation. In P. Cole and J. Morgan, (Eds.) *Syntax and Semantics, Volume 9: Pragmatics*. New York: Academic Press.

Gumperz, J. J. 1982. *Discourse Strategies*. Cambridge: Cambridge University Press.

Gumperz, J. J., and D. Hymes. 1972. *Directions in Sociolinguistics*. New York: Holt, Rinehart and Winston.

Guy, G., B. Horvath, J. Vonwiller, E. Daisley, and I. Rogers. 1986. An intonational change in progress in Australian English. *Language in Society*, 15(1), 23–52.

Halliday, M. A. K. 1967. *Intonation and Grammar in British English*. The Hague: Mouton.

Halliday, M. A. K. 1973. *Explorations in the Functions of Language*. London: Edward Arnold.

Halliday, M. A. K. 1978. *Language as Social Semiotic*. London: Edward Arnold.

Halliday, M. A. K. 1985. *An Introduction to Functional Grammar*. London: Edward Arnold.

Halliday, M. A. K. 1989. *Spoken and Written Language*. Oxford: Oxford University Press.

Halliday, M. A. K., and R. Hasan. 1976. *Cohesion in English*. London: Longman.

Hamp-Lyons, E., and B. Heasley, 1987. *Study Writing*. Cambridge: Cambridge University Press.

Harris, Z. 1952. Discourse analysis. *Language*, 28, 1–30.

Hasan, R. 1984. Coherence and cohesive harmony. In J. Flood (Ed.) *Understanding Reading Comprehension*. Newark, Delaware: International Reading Association.

Hermerén, L. 1978. *On Modality in English*. Lund: CWK Gleerup.

Hewings, M. 1987. Intonation and feedback in the EFL classroom. In R. M. Coulthard (Ed.) *Discussing Discourse*. Birmingham: English Language Research, University of Birmingham.

Hewings, M., and M. J. McCarthy. 1988. An alternative approach to the analysis of text. *Praxis des Neusprachlichen Unterrichts*, 1, 3–10.

Heyman, R. D. 1986. Formulating topic in the classroom. *Discourse Processes*, 9(1), 37–55.

Hilsdon, J. 1988. Zambian learners' and native speakers' use of conjunctions in English. Ms. English Language Research, University of Birmingham.

Hinds, J. 1979. Organisational patterns in discourse. In T. Givón (Ed.) *Syntax and Semantics, Volume 12: Discourse and Syntax*. New York: Academic Press.

Hinds, J. 1982. *Ellipsis in Japanese*. Carbondale, USA: Linguistic Research Inc.

Hinds, J. 1983. Contrastive rhetoric: Japanese and English. *Text*, 3, 183–95.

Hinds, J. 1984. Topic maintenance in Japanese narratives and Japanese conversational interaction. *Discourse Processes*, 7, 465–82.

Hinds, J. 1986. *Japanese*. London: Croom Helm.

Hoey, M. P. 1983. *On the Surface of Discourse*. London: Allen and Unwin.

Hoey, M. P. (forthcoming). *Patterns of Lexis in Text*. Oxford: Oxford University Press.

Hoey, M. P., and E. O. Winter. 1986. Clause relations and the writer's communicative task. In B. Couture (Ed.) *Functional Approaches to Writing Research Perspectives*. London: Frances Pinter.

Hofmann, T. R. 1989. Paragraphs and Anaphora. *Journal of Pragmatics*, 13, 239–50.

Holmes, J. 1983. Speaking English with the appropriate degree of conviction. In C. Brumfit (Ed.) *Learning and Teaching Languages for Communication: Applied Linguistic Perspectives*. London: CILT.

Holmes, J. 1988. Doubt and certainty in ESL textbooks. *Applied Linguistics*, 9(1), 21–44.

Honikman, B. 1964. Articulatory settings. In D. Abercrombie, D. B. Fry, P. A. D. MacCarthy, N. C. Scott and J. L. Trim (Eds.) *In Honour of Daniel Jones*. London: Longman.

Hopper, P. J. 1979. Aspect and foregrounding in discourse. In T. Givón (Ed.) *Syntax and Semantics, Volume 12: Discourse and Syntax*. New York: Academic Press.

Hopper, P. J. 1982. Aspect between discourse and grammar. In P. J. Hopper (Ed.) *Tense–Aspect: Between Semantics and Pragmatics*. Amsterdam: John Benjamins.

House, J. 1985. Contrastive discourse analysis and universals in language. *Papers and Studies in Contrastive Linguistics*, 20, 5–14.

Houtkoop, H., and H. Mazeland. 1985. Turns and discourse units in everyday conversation. *Journal of Pragmatics*, 9, 595–619.

Hymes, D. 1964. Towards ethnographies of communication. In J. J. Gumperz and D. Hymes (Eds), *The Ethnography of Communication. American Anthropologist*, 66(6), 1–34.

Jefferson, G. 1978. Sequential aspects of storytelling in conversation. In J. Schenkein (Ed.) *Studies in the Organisation of Conversational Interaction*. New York: Academic Press.

Jenkins, S., and J. Hinds. 1987. Business letter writing: English, French and Japanese. *TESOL Quarterly*, 21(2), 327–49.

Johns, A. M. 1986. Coherence and academic writing: some determinants and suggestions for teaching. *TESOL Quarterly*, 20(2), 247–65.

Johns-Lewis, C. 1986. Prosodic differentiation of discourse modes. In C. Johns-Lewis (Ed.) *Intonation in Discourse*. London: Croom Helm.

Jones, L. B., and L. K. Jones. 1985. Discourse functions of five English sentence types. *Word*, 36(1), 1–21.

Jordan, M. P. 1984. *Rhetoric of Everyday English Texts*. London: Allen and Unwin.

Jordan, M. P. 1985. Non-thematic re-entry: an introduction to and an extension of the system of nominal group reference/substitution in everyday English use. In J. D. Benson and W. S. Greaves (Eds.) *Systemic Perspectives on Discourse*, vol. 1. Norwood, New Jersey: Ablex Publishing Corporation.

Jordan, M. P. 1986. Close cohesion with *do so*: a linguistic experiment in language function using a multi-example corpus. In B. Couture (Ed.) *Functional Approaches to Writing Research Perspectives*. London: Frances Pinter.

Kachru, Y. 1987. Cross-cultural texts, discourse strategies and discourse interpretation. In L. E. Smith (Ed.) *Discourse Across Cultures: Strategies in World Englishes*. London: Prentice Hall.

Kaplan, R. B. 1966. Cultural thought patterns in intercultural education. *Language Learning*, 16, 1–20.

Kaplan, R. B. (Ed.) 1983. *Annual Review of Applied Linguistics, 1982*. Rowley, Massachusetts: Newbury House.

References

Kies, D. 1988. Marked themes with and without pronominal reinforcement: their meaning and distribution in discourse. In E. Steiner and R. Veltman (Eds.) *Pragmatics, Discourse and Text: Some Systemically-Inspired Approaches.* London: Frances Pinter.

King, P. 1989. The uncommon core. Some discourse features of student writing. *System,* 17(1), 13–20.

Knowles, G. 1987. *Patterns of Spoken English.* London: Longman.

Labov, W. 1972. *Language in the Inner City.* Oxford: Basil Blackwell.

Ladd, D. R. 1980. *The Structure of Intonational Meaning: Evidence from English.* Bloomington: Indiana University Press.

Leech, G. N. 1983. *Principles of Pragmatics.* London: Longman.

Levinson, S. 1983. *Pragmatics.* Cambridge: Cambridge University Press.

Linde, C. 1979. Focus of attention and the choice of pronouns in discourse. In T. Givón (Ed.) *Syntax and Semantics, Volume 12: Discourse and Syntax.* New York: Academic Press.

Linde, C., and W. Labov. 1975. Spatial networks as a site for the study of language and thought. *Language,* 51, 924–39.

Lindeberg, A-C. 1986. Abstraction levels in student essays. In L. S. Evensen (Ed.) *Nordic Research in Text Linguistics and Discourse Analysis.* Trondheim: Tapir, University of Trondheim, 215–30.

Lindstrom, O. 1978. *Aspects of English Intonation.* Göteborg: Acta Universitatis Gothoburgensis.

Locastro, V. 1987. *Aizuchi:* a Japanese conversational routine. In L. E. Smith (Ed.) *Discourse Across Cultures: Strategies in World Englishes.* London: Prentice Hall.

Longacre, R. 1979. The paragraph as a grammatical unit. In T. Givón (Ed.) *Syntax and Semantics, Volume 12: Discourse and Syntax.* New York: Academic Press.

Maynard, D. W. 1980. Placement of topic changes in conversation. *Semiotica,* 30, 263–90.

Mazzie, C. 1987. An experimental investigation of the determinants of implicitness in spoken and written discourse. *Discourse Processes,* 10(1), 31–42.

McCarthy, M. J. 1987. Interactive lexis: prominence and paradigms. In R. M. Coulthard (Ed.) *Discussing Discourse.* Birmingham: English Language Research, University of Birmingham.

McCarthy, M. J. 1988. Some vocabulary patterns in conversation. In R. A. Carter and M. J. McCarthy *Vocabulary and Language Teaching.* London: Longman.

McCarthy, M. J. 1990. *Vocabulary.* Oxford: Oxford University Press.

McGregor, G. 1984. Conversation and communication. *Language and Communication,* 4(1), 71–83.

Melrose, R. (with S. F. Melrose) 1989. Discourse negotiation of meaning in communicative language teaching. *International Review of Applied Linguistics,* 27(1), 41–52.

Menn, L., and S. Boyce. 1982. Fundamental frequency and discourse structure. *Language and Speech,* 25, 341–83.

Michaels, S. 1987. Text and context: a new approach to the study of classroom writing. *Discourse Processes,* 10(4), 321–46.

Mohan, B., and W. A. Lo. 1985. Academic writing and Chinese students: transfer and developmental factors. *TESOL Quarterly,* 19, 515–34.

Monaghan, J. (Ed.) 1987. *Grammar in the Construction of Texts*. London: Frances Pinter.

Monville-Burston, M. and L. R. Waugh. 1985. Le passé simple dans le discours journalistique. *Lingua*, 67(2–3), 121–70.

Moon, R. 1987. Idioms in text. Ms. English Language Research, University of Birmingham.

Neubauer, F. (Ed.) 1983. *Coherence in Natural Language Texts*. Hamburg: Helmut Buske Verlag.

Noguchi, R. R. 1987. The dynamics of rule conflict in English and Japanese conversation. *IRAL*, 25(1), 15–24.

Nystrand, M. 1986. *The Structure of Written Communication: Studies in Reciprocity between Writers and Readers*. London: Academic Press.

Odlin, T. 1989. *Language Transfer: Cross-Linguistic Influences in Language Learning*. Cambridge: Cambridge University Press.

Olesky, W. (Ed.) 1989. *Contrastive Pragmatics*. Amsterdam: John Benjamins.

Parker, R. 1984. Conversational grouping and fragmentation: a preliminary investigation. *Semiotica*, 50(1/2), 43–68.

Pearson, E. 1986. Agreement/disagreement: an example of results of discourse analysis applied to the oral English classroom. *ITL Review of Applied Linguistics*, 74, 47–61.

Pennington, M. C., and J. C. Richards. 1986. Pronunciation revisited. *TESOL Quarterly*, 20(2), 207–25.

Perkins, M. R. 1983. *Modal Expressions in English*. London: Frances Pinter.

Pike, K. L. 1945. *The Intonation of American English*. Ann Arbor: University of Michigan Press.

Polanyi, L. 1982. Literary complexity in everyday storytelling. In D. Tannen (Ed.) *Spoken and Written Language: Exploring Orality and Literacy*. Norwood, New Jersey: Ablex Publishing Corporation.

Polanyi, L. 1985. Conversational storytelling. In T. van Dijk (Ed.) *Handbook of Discourse Analysis*. vol. 3. London: Academic Press.

Pomerantz, A. 1984. Agreeing and disagreeing with assessments: some features of preferred/dispreferred turn shapes. In J. Atkinson and J. Heritage (Eds.) *Structure of Social Action*. Cambridge: Cambridge University Press.

Power, R. J., and M. F. Martello. 1986. Some criticisms of Sacks, Schegloff and Jefferson on turn-taking. *Semiotica*, 58(1/2), 29–40.

Psathas, G. (Ed.) 1979. *Everyday Language: Studies in Ethnomethodology*. New York: Wiley.

Psathas, G. 1986. The organisation of directions in interaction. *Word*, 37(1–2), 83–91.

Psathas, G., and M. Kozloff. 1976. The structure of directions. *Semiotica*, 17, 111–30.

Quirk, R., S. Greenbaum, G. Leech, and J. Svartvik. 1985. *A Comprehensive Grammar of the English Language*. London: Longman.

Reddick, R. J. 1986. Textlinguistics, text theory, and language users. *Word*, 37(1–2), 31–43.

Redeker, G. 1984. On differences between spoken and written language. *Discourse Processes*, 7, 43–55.

Redman, S., and R. Ellis. 1989 and 1990. *A Way with Words. Books 1 and 2*. Cambridge: Cambridge University Press.

References

Rees, A. B. 1986. The functions of intonation in English and German: a comparative study. In H. Kirkwood (Ed.) *Studies in Intonation*. Coleraine: University of Ulster.

Reichman-Adar, R. 1984. Technical Discourse: the present progressive tense, the deictic 'that' and pronominalisation. *Discourse Processes*, 7, 337–69.

Ricento, T. 1987. Clausal ellipsis in multi-party conversation in English. *Journal of Pragmatics*, 11, 751–75.

Richards, J. 1983. Listening comprehension: approach, design, procedure. *TESOL Quarterly*, 17(2), 219–40.

Richards, J., and R. W. Schmidt. 1983. *Language and Communication*. London: Longman.

Riddle, E. 1986. The meaning and discourse function of the past tense in English. *TESOL Quarterly*, 20(2), 267–86.

Riley, P. (Ed.) 1985. *Discourse and Learning*. London: Longman.

Rivero, M-L. 1980. On left-dislocation and topicalisation in Spanish. *Linguistic Inquiry*, 11(2), 363–93.

Roberts, J. 1983. Teaching with functional materials: the problem of stress and intonation. *English Language Teaching Journal*, 37, 213–20.

Robinson, P. 1988. Components and procedures in vocabulary learning: feature grids, prototypes and a procedural vocabulary. *Interface. Journal of Applied Linguistics*, 2(2), 79–91.

Rumelhart, D. E. 1975. Notes on a schema for stories. In D. G. Bobrow and A. Collins (Eds.) *Representation and Understanding: Studies in Cognitive Science*. New York: Academic Press.

Sacks, H. 1974. An analysis of the course of a joke's telling in conversation. In R. Bauman and J. Sherzer (Eds.) *Explorations in the Ethnography of Speaking*. Cambridge: Cambridge University Press.

Sacks, H., E. A. Schegloff, and G. Jefferson. 1974. A simplest systematics for the organisation of turn-taking for conversation. *Language*, 50(4), 696–735.

Scarcella, R. 1984. How writers orient their readers in expository essays: a comparative study of native and non-native English writers. *TESOL Quarterly*, 18, 671–88.

Scarcella, R., and J. Brunak. 1981. On speaking politely in a second language. *International Journal of the Sociology of Language*, 27, 59–75.

Schaffer, D. 1983. The role of intonation as a cue to turn-taking in conversation. *Journal of Phonetics*, 11, 243–57.

Schaffer, D. 1984. The role of intonation as a cue to topic management in conversation. *Journal of Phonetics*, 12, 327–44.

Schegloff, E. A. 1986. The routine as achievement. *Human Studies*, 9(2/3), 111–51.

Schegloff, E. A., and H. Sacks. 1973. Opening up closings. *Semiotica*, 8(4), 289–327.

Schenkein, J. (Ed.) 1978. *Studies in the Organisation of Conversational Interaction*. London: Academic Press.

Schiffrin, D. 1981. Tense variation in narrative. *Language*, 57(1), 45–62.

Schiffrin, D. 1985a. Multiple constraints on discourse options: a quantitative analysis of causal sequences. *Discourse Processes*, 8(3), 281–303.

Schiffrin, D. 1985b. Everyday argument: the organisation of diversity in talk. In T. van Dijk (Ed.) *Handbook of Discourse Analysis*, vol. 3. London: Academic Press.

Schiffrin, D. 1987. *Discourse Markers*. Cambridge: Cambridge University Press.

Schopf, A. (Ed.) 1989. *Essays on Tensing in English*, vol. II. Tübingen: Max Niemeyer Verlag.

Schubiger, M. 1964. The interplay and co-operation of word-order and intonation in English. In D. Abercrombie, D. B. Fry, P. A. D. MacCarthy, N. C. Scott and J. L. Trim (Eds.) *In Honour of Daniel Jones*. London: Longman.

Scollon, R. 1982. *Analyzing Discourse: Text and Talk*. Washington, D.C.: Georgetown University Press.

Scuffil, M. 1982. *Experiments in Comparative Intonation: a case-study of English and German*. Tübingen: Max Niemeyer Verlag.

Searle, J. R. 1969. *Speech Acts*. Cambridge: Cambridge University Press.

Shih, M. 1986. Content-based approaches to teaching academic writing. *TESOL Quarterly*, 20(4), 617–48.

Sinclair, J. McH., and D. C. Brazil. 1982. *Teacher Talk*. Oxford: Oxford University Press.

Sinclair, J. McH., and R. M. Coulthard. 1975. *Towards an Analysis of Discourse*. Oxford: Oxford University Press.

Smith, E. L. 1986. Achieving impact through the interpersonal component. In B. Couture (Ed.) *Functional Approaches to Writing Research Perspectives*. London: Frances Pinter.

Stalker, J. W., and J. C. Stalker. 1989. The acquisition of rhetorical strategies in introductory paragraphs in written academic English: a comparison of non-native speakers and native speakers. In S. Gass, C. Madden, D. Preston and L. Selinker (Eds.) *Variation in Second Language Acquisition: Discourse and Pragmatics*. Clevedon, Philadelphia: Multilingual Matters.

Stark, H. 1988. What do paragraph markings do? *Discourse Processes*, 11(3), 275–303.

Starkey, D. 1973. Toward a grammar for dyadic conversation. *Semiotica*, 9, 29–46.

Stech, E. L. 1982. The analysis of conversational topic sequence structures. *Semiotica*, 39, 75–91.

Steffensen, M. 1986. Register, cohesion and reading comprehension. *Applied Linguistics*, 7(1), 71–85.

Steffensen, M. 1988. Changes in cohesion in the recall of native and foreign texts. In P. L. Carrell, J. Devine and D. Eskey (Eds.) *Interactive Approaches to Second Language Reading*. Cambridge: Cambridge University Press.

Stenström, A-B. 1984. *Questions and Responses in English Conversation*. Malmö: Gleerup.

Stubbs, M. 1983. *Discourse Analysis*. Oxford: Basil Blackwell.

Stubbs, M. 1986. 'A matter of prolonged fieldwork'; notes towards a modal grammar of English. *Applied Linguistics*, 7(1), 1–25.

Svartvik, J., and R. Quirk. 1980. *A Corpus of English Conversation*. Lund: Liberläromedel.

Swan, M. and C. Walter. 1984. *The Cambridge English Course: Book 1*. Cambridge: Cambridge University Press.

Swan, M., and C. Walter. 1990. *The New Cambridge English Course: Book 2*. Cambridge: Cambridge University Press.

Tannen, D. 1982. Oral and literate strategies in spoken and written discourse. *Language*, 58, 1–20.

References

Tannen, D. (Ed.) 1984. *Coherence in Spoken and Written Discourse*. Norwood, New Jersey: Ablex Publishing Corporation.

Taylor, D. S. 1981. Non-native speakers and the rhythm of English. *International Review of Applied Linguistics*, 19, 1981, 219–25.

Taylor, T. J., and D. Cameron. 1987. *Analysing Conversation: Rules and Units in the Structure of Talk*. Oxford: Pergamon Press.

Thavenius, C. 1983. *Referential Pronouns in English Conversation*. Lund: CWK Gleerup.

Thomas, A. L. 1987. The use and interpretation of verbally determinate verb group ellipsis in English. *International Review of Applied Linguistics*, 25(1), 1–14.

Thompson, I. 1981. *Intonation Practice*. Oxford: Oxford University Press.

Tierney, R. J., and J. H. Mosenthal. 1983. Cohesion and textual coherence. *Research in the Teaching of English*, 17, 215–29.

Toolan, M. J. 1988. *Narrative. A Critical Linguistic Introduction*. London: Routledge.

Tottie, G., and I. Bäcklund (Eds.) 1986. *English in Speech and Writing: a Symposium*. Uppsala: Studia Anglistica Uppsaliensia.

Trosborg, A. 1987. Apology strategies in natives/non-natives. *Journal of Pragmatics*, 11, 147–67.

Van Dijk, T. A. 1972. *Some Aspects of Text Grammars*. The Hague: Mouton.

Van Dijk, T. A. 1980. *Macrostructures: an Interdisciplinary Study of Global Structures in Discourse, Interaction and Cognition*. Hillsdale, New Jersey: Erlbaum.

Van Dijk, T. A. (Ed.) 1985. *Handbook of Discourse Analysis*. 4 vols. London: Academic Press.

Vuchinich, S. 1977. Elements of cohesion between turns in ordinary conversation. *Semiotica*, 20, 229–57.

Wardaugh, R. 1985. *How Conversation Works*. Oxford: Basil Blackwell.

Waugh, L. R., and M. Monville-Burston. 1986. Aspect and discourse function: the French simple past in newspaper usage. *Language*, 62(4), 846–77.

Westney, P. 1986. How to be more or less certain in English: scalarity in epistemic modality. *International Review of Applied Linguistics*, XXIV(4), 311–20.

Widdowson, H. G. 1979. Rules and procedures in discourse analysis. In T. Myers (Ed.) *The Development of Conversation and Discourse*. Edinburgh: Edinburgh University Press.

Widdowson, H. G. 1983. *Learning Purpose and Language Use*. Oxford: Oxford University Press.

Wierzbicka, A. 1985. A semantic metalanguage for a cross-cultural comparison of speech acts and speech genres. *Language in Society*, 14(4), 491–514.

Willems, N. 1982. *English Intonation from a Dutch Point of View*. Dordrecht: Foris.

Winter, E. O. 1977. A clause-relational approach to English texts: a study of some predictive lexical items in written discourse. *Instructional Science*, 6(1), 1–92.

Winter, E. O. 1978. A look at the role of certain words in information structure. In K. P. Jones and V. Horsnell (Eds.) *Informatics*, 3(1), 85–97, London: ASLIB.

Wisniewski, E. J., and G. L. Murphy. 1989. Superordinate and basic category names in discourse: a textual analysis. *Discourse Processes*, 12(2), 245–61.

Wong, R. 1986. Does pronunciation teaching have a place in the communicative classroom? In D. Tannen and J. Alatis (Eds.) *Language and Linguistics: the Interdependence of Theory, Data and Application.* Washington, D.C.: George-town University Press.

Yngve, V. H. 1970. On getting a word in edgewise. In *Papers from the 6th Regional Meeting, Chicago Linguistic Society.* Chicago: Chicago Linguistic Society.

Yule, G. 1980a. The functions of phonological prominence. *Archivum Linguisticum*, XI, 31–46.

Yule, G. 1980b. Speakers' topics and major paratones. *Lingua*, 52, 33–47.

Zamel, V. 1983. Teaching those missing links in writing. *English Language Teaching Journal*, 37(1), 22–9.

Zamel, V. 1987. Recent research on writing pedagogy. *TESOL Quarterly*, 21(4), 697–715.

Zydatiss, W. 1986. Grammatical categories and their text functions – some implications for the content of reference grammars. In G. Leitner (Ed.) *The English Reference Grammar.* Tübingen: Max Niemeyer Verlag.

Index

Index

Index

Index